Cover Art

The cover artwork is an original piece by Dr. (Major) James Watt, retired Salvation Army officer and former Chief Medical Officer at Howard Hospital.

"This sketch was done in ink on location, so the people are as I saw them—with a cart made from the rear axle of a wrecked car, the gate made from a car door, a child with a wire car, men discussing under a tree in the 'Men's Dare,' a mango tree and the Msasa trees in full colour during the 'miracle of Africa,' when new leaves come and fruit ripens before the first rains, the grass remaining dry. The cook hut is identified by the brown, smoke-stained peak of the grass roof. The harvest had been good, corn cobs in a bin, and the granary full. And the hill itself is amazing, with a cave in the back with bushman art in it."

…..James Watt

Cry for Chiweshe

Cry for Chiweshe

A COMMUNITY ABANDONED,
A DOCTOR WRONGED — AND
THE BATTLE FOR JUSTICE

Tina Ivany

Copyright © 2017 **Tina Ivany**
All rights reserved.

ISBN-13: **978-1-7753540-0-0**
ISBN-10: **1775354000**

Dedication

This book is dedicated to the citizens of Chiweshe who raised their voices in a valiant effort to save Howard Hospital and support Dr. Thistle—against a bureaucracy that tried to silence them—and especially the brave nurses and support staff who continued to care for patients through trying times, despite harassment and abuse.

Disclaimer

THE PURPOSE IN WRITING THIS book is not to disparage the entire organization but to encourage honesty, accountability and compassion in leadership, and, ultimately, to see full health services, most especially surgery, restored to Howard Hospital, as well as a formal apology issued to Dr. Paul and Pedrinah Thistle.

The author has endeavoured to ensure that the information contained herein is correct to the best of her ability, but assumes no responsibility for witness statements.

Contents

Dedication · vii
Disclaimer · ix
Foreword · xiii
Author's Foreword · xv
The Players · xvii
Prologue - Marching Orders · · · · · · · · · · · · · · · · xxi

Part I: The Road to Howard · 1
Chapter 1   In the Beginning · 3
Chapter 2   The Story of Howard · · · · · · · · · · · · · · · · · · 15
Chapter 3   Into the Fray · 25
Chapter 4   Club Med No Frills · · · · · · · · · · · · · · · · · · · 28
Chapter 5   Twin Miracles · 38
Chapter 6   Commitment · 47
Chapter 7   Annus Horribilis · 56
Chapter 8   Annus Horribilis Multiplicatus · · · · · · · · · · · 62
Chapter 9   Working at Howard (It Takes a Village) · · · · · 70
Chapter 10 One Step Forward Two Back · · · · · · · · · · · 79

Part II: Saving Howard Hospital · 125
Chapter 11 The Gathering Storm · 127
Chapter 12 Up Against Goliath · 144
Chapter 13 The Brick Wall · 154
Chapter 14 Aftermath - A Humanitarian Crisis · · · · · · · · · · · · 163

Part III: Truth and Consequences · 171
Chapter 15 We Accuse … The Case Against Paul Thistle · · · · · 173
Chapter 16 The Money Trail · 185
Chapter 17 The Strange Marriage of Church and State · · · · · · · 199
Chapter 18 Bending the Rules · 205
Chapter 19 The Truth, the Half-Truth and Anything But…So
             Help Me God · 220
Chapter 20 The Sally Ann – Then and Now · · · · · · · · · · · · · · 244
Chapter 21 A New Beginning · 259
Chapter 22 Consequences · 265

Epilogue – The Accountability Movement – Where
to From Here? · 283
Acknowledgements · 291
References · 293
About the Author · 297

Foreword

Very rarely a true hero emerges. Dr. Paul Thistle is one of the very few true great men of our time. I respect him more than anyone I have ever met.

I have had the privilege to work closely with Dr. Thistle since 1999. I was inspired to volunteer and do whatever I could to help the Howard after witnessing the incredible commitment, professionalism, compassion and devotion with which Paul cared for both his patients and the entire local Zimbabwean community,

I have been practicing medicine for 17 years in Canada and have also worked in the United States, South America and Zambia. In all of that time, I have never seen anyone work as hard as Dr. Thistle. He is the only obstetrician/gynecologist working in rural Zimbabwe and, therefore, is routinely called upon to function as a general surgeon. Several of my surgical colleagues from Canada have worked side by side with him at the Howard, and all are in awe of the technical prowess, efficiency and professionalism with which he gives outstanding care, despite severe challenges. Dr. Thistle is able to do this not only having been blessed with "great hands" and a God-given gift as a surgeon, but also by paying attention to all of the details. No job is beneath him.

Dr. Michael Silverman, August 2012

Author's Foreword

―

Well done is better than well said.....

BENJAMIN FRANKLIN

I'VE ALWAYS BELIEVED THERE ARE two kinds of Christians: those who flaunt the label, but don't wear it well, and those who need no label at all.

The first kind are the ever-ready variety, who love to declare and market their religion as a brand. Every sentence begins with "I'm a Christian." They talk a good game, but are shy on proof. When it comes to putting those words into action, they find excuses, leaving others to do the work.

The second type are easy to spot because there are so few of them. There's an aura about them that shines a light on everything they do and everyone they meet. No moral ambiguity in these people—they know what is right and what is wrong. If there are any grays in the picture they are painted with compassion, and tinted with a touch of wisdom. These are Christ's true soldiers. When it comes time to fight, they stand with the poor, the sick and the disadvantaged.

Dr. Paul Thistle is such a man, a true Christian soldier fighting a war on all fronts—battling illness and disease and an increasingly bloated bureaucracy that has lost its way.

This is his story.

The Players

International Salvation Army Headquarters – London, England:
General Linda Bond – International Leader of the Salvation Army (retired June 2013)
General Andre Cox – Former Chief of Staff - elected International Leader in July 2013
Lt.-Col. Dean Pallant – Director of the International Social Justice Commission and International Accountability Movement Coordinator, International Headquarters
Major (Dr.) Eirwen Pallant – International Health Services Co-ordinator
Major Gillian Brown – Former Associate Director of World Missions Appointed Director of World Missions (retired 2016)
Commissioner Kenneth Hodder – International Secretary for Personnel
Appointed Territorial Commander Kenya West Territory

Territorial Commanders – Zimbabwe:
Commissioner Amos Makina – International Secretary for Africaaa – (retired January 1, 2013)
Commissioner Vinece Chigariro – Former Territorial Commander Zimbabwe
Appointed Territorial Commander Kenya East Territory – October 2012
Appointed Territorial Commander Uganda Territory – 2016
Joice Mujuru – Vice President of Zimbabwe reporting to Robert Mugabe.
Dismissed as Vice President Dec. 8, 2014. Expelled from ZANU-PF Party on April 3, 2015. Formed her own political party, Zimbabwe People First

Territorial Headquarters – Canada and Bermuda Territories – Toronto, Ontario, Canada
Commissioner Brian Peddle – Territorial Commander of Canada & Bermuda Territory - Promoted to Chief of Staff (second highest position in the Salvation Army) Nov, 1, 2015
Colonel Floyd Tidd – Chief Secretary, Canada and Bermuda Territory Promoted to Commissioner - National Commander, Australia
Lt.-Col. Sandra Rice

Interested Parties
Major (Dr.) James Watt – retired Salvation Army Officer and former Chief Medical Director of Howard Hospital
John Sullivan – former officer and United Church minister and son of Salvation Army officers who served in Africa
Allan Bacon – former Director of Overseas Development for The Salvation Army, Canada & Bermuda Territory

Inter-faith Friends of Howard Hospital
A group of concerned doctors and other professionals who worked as volunteers on-site at Howard Hospital and facilitated the procurement and supply of millions of dollars' worth of medical equipment, medicine and funds, including grants from international aid agencies, Canadian registered charities and faith-based groups:
Dr. Michael Silverman – MD, FRCP, FACP, Global Scholar, PAS Centre for International Health, Mount Sinai Hospital, Infectious Disease Specialist and Assistant Professor, Department of Medicine, University of Toronto
Sarah Zelcer – Director of International Projects – Ve'ahavta – The Canadian Jewish Humanitarian and Relief Committee
Brian Nichols – Psychotherapist and member Donwood United Church, Peterborough, Canada
Sarah LeBouthillier – Physiotherapist and volunteer at Howard Hospital
Larry Gillman – President of Beth Israel Synagogue, Peterborough, Canada
Doug McLellan – Photographer and Photo-Journalist, Windsor, Ontario

Prologue - Marching Orders

*What you spend years building may be
destroyed overnight. Build anyway.*

Mother Theresa

On the morning of July 18, 2012, Dr. Paul Thistle grabbed his trusty briefcase, crossed the barren courtyard from his home and entered Howard Hospital to begin another day. It was winter in Zimbabwe. The weather was cool but clear, a welcome change after the stick-to-your-ribs heat of Toronto, from where he had just returned.

Outside, though barely past 7 a.m., the crowd of patients was thicker than usual on news that the good doctor, their revered "Chiremba," had returned from his annual furlough. Paul smiled as he walked again on familiar soil. After his hiatus with family in Canada, it was always good to be home in Zimbabwe, back to the people and the work that he loved. It was not only a new day, but the start of another chapter in his eighteenth year of service to the grateful citizens of Chiweshe.

As was his habit, his morning began with daily prayer, then proceeded to rounds with staff before heading to the Operating Room to start surgery. The rest of the day would be spent in the OR and the outpatient clinic before a brief respite for supper with family. Afterwards, he planned a few hours at the computer catching up with mail and administrative duties—an exhaustive routine by anyone's standards, but just another typical day at Howard.

It turned out to be far from typical. In the middle of surgery, he received a call inviting him and his wife, Pedrinah, to attend a luncheon at the home of the hospital's administrator, Salvation Army Major Bernard Nyahuma. Also present were Territorial Commander Vinece Chigariro, Commissioner Kenneth Hodder, International Secretary for Personnel, and Major Dean Pallant, Under Secretary for Program Resources in charge of co-ordinating international health services. Both Hodder and Pallant had arrived from Salvation Army headquarters in London, ostensibly to look over the new hospital which began construction in the year 2000, but had never been completed due to lack of funding.

Paul approached the gathering with a fair degree of skepticism that anything would be accomplished from another of these mind-numbing meetings. Talk about the new hospital had blown this way before, but little action had come from it. The "new" hospital, a stone's throw from the old hospital, stood on the grounds like a great white elephant—a constant reminder of what could have been. Paul sat through the luncheon with one eye on the clock, ever mindful of his patients who had a greater need of his attention.

When he requested to leave early to get back to his duties at the hospital, he and Pedrinah were pulled aside and the true purpose of the luncheon was revealed. Effective September 1, he was to be reassigned and returned to his home-base in Canada.

The news struck the Thistles like a thunderbolt. None of this made any sense. Paul's head buzzed with questions. What about his patients? What would become of the Tariro Clinic that took care of

HIV and AIDS patients, providing counseling, testing and antiretroviral drug therapy? What about hospital staff? Who would pay them, without the influx of donated funds that covered their salaries? And what of the children in the village, the 1,500 orphans who were attended to and schooled at Howard? Who would cover their school fees without the gift of outside aid?

The answer to all of his questions was the same: "the Salvation Army will look after everything." But given the Army's lack of involvement in the community in previous times of medical and political crisis, Paul was doubtful. Where was the Army in 2008, when thousands of people were dying of cholera; when roving gangs of thugs invaded their villages maiming and killing at random? Blatantly absent from the Army's response was concern for the local people and their health care.

If this group had gathered to discuss plans for the new hospital, obviously their plans didn't include him or Pedrinah, a highly-qualified nurse and midwife who had trained many of the staff. The mandate of this meeting was crystal clear: this was the last supper at Howard and he and Pedrinah were the sacrificial lambs. Before parting, the group's final piece of advice to him was to "forget about his patients and staff at Howard—the Army will take care of it."

As he returned to the hospital, his immediate concern was for his family. His wife and children were born here. His two sons, James and Alexander, had just started back at school. His overtaxed brain ticked off the long list of things to do before his departure. Six weeks wasn't much time after 17 years at the job—17 years of living in rural Zimbabwe, getting to know and love the people, blending in, being accepted and valued as one of their own. Saying good-bye at any time would be difficult, but under these circumstances, it was devastating.

While he could accept the news of his eventual departure, nothing about this speedy transfer was necessary or well-planned. Neither

Commissioner Chigariro nor Hodder had given a reason for his reassignment other than the statement that it was "a routine transfer." But if it was so routine, where was he going and who was coming to replace him? And if this was merely a routine transfer, why the hurry? There was no emergency in Canada requiring his presence; the emergency was right here in Zimbabwe, at Howard Hospital. At the best of times, there were only three doctors—one surgeon (himself) and two general practitioners—to care for Chiweshe's 270,000 citizens. Now, with one of the two GP's on furlough and Paul's speedy transfer, the hospital was down to one doctor and no surgeon. While the Army focused their attention on one person, Dr. Thistle, the meager health system was imploding before them—Nero fiddling while Rome burned.

If the Army was intent on moving him, surely there was a better plan. What about a transition period? Was the new doctor a trained surgeon, an obstetrician/gynecologist like himself? If so, when was he coming?

While Paul received no answers to his many questions, the people of Chiweshe were quick to respond to the shocking news of his imminent departure. The following day, they gathered at the hospital's entrance, demanding answers, prepared to go to battle for the good doctor who was being wrenched from their community. For people with little or no voice, their angry shouts filled the air. This time the good citizens of Chiweshe were determined to be heard—loud and clear.

On news of the demonstration, the two Commissioners, Hodder and Chigariro were forced to return to Howard. A town hall gathering was called, with the community's local leaders, and Hodder and Chigariro, in attendance. After a protracted meeting, it was proposed that Dr. Thistle would stay on one more year in order to prepare the community and staff for a smooth transition in the interim—and all of the stakeholders agreed.

But on August 4, a letter from Commissioner Amos Makina, International Secretary for Africa, was delivered to Paul Thistle at Howard Hospital. Once again this letter made little sense. Its contents offered no further clarification on the Army's decision. Oddly, the letter dated July 25 was a photocopy, not the original, copied to Territorial Commander Chigariro only. There was no mention of the proposed extension to June 2013, no indication of the Thistles' next appointment, and still no indication of who would replace them or when they would arrive.

Chigariro told the Associated Press that on hearing of the decision, she was taken by surprise, insisting that it originated in Canada and that it was a routine transfer. But, in truth, no one is transferred from Zimbabwe without the recommendation of the Territorial Commander. Since she was the Territorial Commander, and despite her bizarre statement, it was obvious that this decision was made in Zimbabwe and was anything but routine.

Paul turned to his dear friend and mentor, Dr. James Watt, for guidance. "Our hearts are weeping for the people of Chiweshe," he told Watt in an e-mail. Knowing that friends and family would have to be notified, he worried about their reaction and the ensuing flood of protest letters. He didn't want the image of the Army diminished or outsiders misinterpreting the decision as originating from the Zimbabwe government, who, he advised, (referring to the Governor's intervention) was making efforts to reach a compromise. Dr. Watt, the former Chief Medical Officer, assured Paul that he was there to support him by any means possible.

On August 6, work at the hospital came to a standstill. Staff and villagers joined hands to protest the decision and Paul was ordered not to report for work. Villagers also barred a truck containing donated medicine and supplies sourced by Paul from entering the hospital. They assumed it had come to remove him.

Unable to attend work, Paul retreated to his office to break the news of his impending transfer. As difficult as it was, he sent a message to the vast network of people on his mailing list—450 friends, family, volunteers and supporters—to inform them that, with deep regret, he would be leaving Howard Hospital effective September 1.

By this time, villagers had become more organized. The community sent a 15-member delegation with a petition to appeal the decision to remove Dr. Thistle from Howard Hospital directly to the Governor and Resident Minister of Mashonaland Central, Advocate Martin Dinha.

Speaking on behalf of the community, Nyachuru headman and chairperson of the community, Mr. Thomas Mudyiwa, told the Zimbabwe Sunday Mail, "We are not happy that they have asked him to go. For this hospital to be this famous, it is because of this doctor. He fundraises for medicines, hospital equipment and funds from his overseas partners. Orphans, widows, the sick, in fact all vulnerable people not only from Chiweshe have benefitted from the presence of Dr. Thistle at this hospital. He has saved thousands of lives and has given hope to those that have given up." The headman said that half of the pupils at Nyachuru Secondary School, which Paul helped to establish, had their fees paid for them through donations sought by Dr. Thistle. "How are these orphans going to make it? He has lots of income-generating projects that he runs with the widows and all the vulnerable people here. What will happen to these people?" the headman pleaded. "We are begging the church to be sensitive and allow him to stay."

Confirming that he had received the petition, the Governor told the Sunday Mail that Salvation Army authorities had asked him to mediate. "I have received text messages from across the country of people pleading for me to mediate on their behalf with the church people to allow Dr. Thistle to stay. Accompanied by the provincial medical director and the provincial security team, I will be travelling to Howard on Wednesday to have a full grasp of what exactly is happening." The Chiweshe community requested that Dr. Thistle's work permit be extended so that he could continue to work, with a decision to be made after the Wednesday meeting. They also requested that Thistle be allowed to treat people since there was no doctor. "He has just started working now and attending to the long queues of patients coming from all over the country," Advocate Dinha reported.

Paul was allowed to resume work on August 9. When a Sunday Mail crew arrived to interview him on August 11, he was too busy to meet with them, as he shuttled between the Operating Theatre, the patient wards and the long queue of outpatients waiting to see him. It wasn't until 8:30 p.m., that he was able to give them a brief statement, confirming only that he had indeed received a letter from the Salvation Army instructing him to leave the hospital and return to Canada by September l, before he left again to attend to patients.

Behind the scenes, in addition to his work, Paul launched a personal appeal to senior officers at the Army's Territorial Headquarters in Canada. In a letter to Colonel Floyd Tidd, he warned that even though the hospital had three doctors on staff, the other two physicians had threatened to resign, despite his efforts to persuade them to stay on. He also appealed on behalf of his children who were suffering from this imposed separation from home, school and family.

To add to the dilemma, phone lines were down, making direct communication with officials in Toronto sketchy at best; but Paul soldiered on, fighting to reverse the decision and be allowed to stay, at least until a replacement was found and trained.

Also complicating matters was the delivery of an ambulance from the Rotary Club in Langley, British Columbia and what to do about it in light of Paul's imminent departure.

On Wednesday August 15, 3,000 community members, including the chiefs of Mashonaland Central, attended a town hall meeting to rally around Dr. Thistle. No one from the Salvation Army attended, nor did the Governor who claimed that he was "not well." The crowd showed their anger by breaking some windows.

Dr. Thistle, who had just sedated a patient and begun to operate, was ordered to stop what he was doing and leave the Operating Room by two Salvation Army officers, Major F. Kapere and Colonel Ncube. Thistle pleaded with them to let him finish the operation, after which he was forced to leave the hospital in the presence of hundreds of people. In an outpouring of affection, villagers lifted Paul onto their shoulders and carried him around the compound. The people had spoken: he was their Chiremba and they wanted him to stay.

The following day, locals numbering in the thousands gathered at Howard Hospital to protest Dr. Thistle's removal. Carrying placards and posters, they marched peacefully outside the hospital grounds, frantic at the loss of Dr. Thistle and furious for being lied to again. Once before, when rumours circulated in April 2012 that the Thistles might be transferred, Territorial Headquarters had assured the community leaders that this was not true. Nurses also went on strike to complain about the loss of their well-loved doctor.

When Salvation Army officials arrived at Howard Hospital to serve a fresh eviction notice to Paul and his family, the situation turned ugly. Local youth threw stones and overturned the vehicle that Army officials arrived in. Police descended on the scene in riot gear, armed with batons, and guard dogs, vaulting tear gas into the crowd in an attempt to disperse them. The group from the Salvation Army was forced to flee the angry locals and seek refuge inside the hospital.

Then police officers moved into the hospital. Armed with a list of hospital personnel drawn up and provided by Salvation Army headquarters, they roamed through the corridors seeking their victims. Twelve members of the community were rounded up and arrested, along with eight nurses who were beaten at their nursing stations before being taken into custody.

Work at the hospital came to a halt as both workers and villagers joined hands in protest. Several patients had to be discharged from the hospital as there was no doctor to attend to them. Emergencies were transferred to Parirenyatwa Hospital in Harare and to Karanda in Mt. Darwin, leaving the hospital dependent on skeleton staff. Other patients fled the hospital, several of whom had compromised lungs. New mothers in the maternity wing picked up their infants and ran to escape clouds of tear gas.

That evening, Paul received a call from Salvation Army local headquarters to return to Harare the following day, Friday, August 17. At that meeting, Paul and Pedrinah were ordered to vacate the hospital grounds within 24 hours and leave the country within 48 hours. According to Commissioner Chigariro, Paul had "made a mess of things." He was responsible for the riots and the people who had caused them and for the international opposition to his transfer from Howard. It was up to him to control the populace and make them understand why he was leaving. He had failed to do so, and as a result, he had incited the violence that led to her car being overturned.

Paul protested that he didn't want to be responsible for the local villagers; that was the headman's job. When he attempted a discussion, asking "How do we reconcile?" she told him, "Don't worry about that." The list of accusations went further. Before the meeting was over, she announced that she had never liked Paul, even as far back as 1998, when she had officiated at his marriage to Pedrinah. Her official send-off was confirmed in a one-page letter riddled with bad grammar and seven misspelled words advising him that he had 48 hours to leave the country. She then handed over four one-way tickets on an Air Emirates flight departing Sunday, August 19.

Shaken to the core, Paul and Pedrinah returned to Howard to pack up the family's belongings and say good-bye to beloved staff and villagers, many of whom were in tears. The boys had just returned from Harare where they attend school and board with Pedrinah's brother through the school week. Fortunately, they had missed the worst of the violence, but, surrounded by riot police and guard dogs, the children were naturally traumatized. The school year had just begun and they were reluctant to leave their friends and the only home they had ever known. Eleven-year-old James, a well-spoken boy, wise beyond his years, asked why the family were not informed ahead of time. If it was a Canadian decision, he reasoned, they could have been told on their recent holiday in Canada. Even an 11-year-old could spot the lack of logic in this order. After 17 years of service, surely the Thistles deserved fairer treatment.

Saturday morning, August 18, Paul sent out another message to his supporters explaining that the issue involved the organization's funds. "The root of the problem has been financial, and control of funds," he wrote. "Within the current Salvation Army system the funds do not arrive, or arrive very late. People are suffering today."

A group of Canadian volunteers—a team of eleven doctors, pharmacists, dentists and other health professionals with Short Term International Medical Missions Abroad (STIMMA) had arrived at Howard just days earlier to help out at the facility. They had planned to stay until August 29, but they arrived to a scene of chaos—rocks being hurled, the air thick with tear gas and terrified children running and yelling "don't go there"—and a hospital and its director under siege.

While hospital staff helped Pedrinah pack up the family's belongings, one of the group interviewed Paul and filmed it with a video camera. In the video, Paul explained, "I had to speak up, because you can't have people suffer because of the inefficiencies of a system that doesn't work." He worried about the impact of how this decision would affect the local people and hospital staff, who are seen crying in the background. "All it takes is a spark to bring a hospital down. As the bible says, 'strike the shepherd, and the sheep will scatter'. I pray for peace, but the reality is that a quarter of a million people will be without health care. What will people do?" Although Paul tried his best to remain calm surrounded by chaos, when it came to the heart of the matter, his forced separation from his patients and friends, it was all too much. The video ended with his choked statement "I love the people of Zimbabwe…" then overcome with emotion, Paul waved off the camera with "no further comment."

The STIMMA volunteers were asked to leave the hospital "for their safety." With no other choice, the Canadian team fled to Harare, where they remained until Monday afternoon, trying to find a flight out of the country.

On Saturday afternoon, August 18, as the moving van pulled away and rumbled down the rutted road, Paul and his family left Howard Hospital for the last time.

Part I
The Road to Howard

CHAPTER 1

In the Beginning

―

It seems impossible until it is done...

NELSON MANDELA

EVERY GOAL BEGINS WITH A dream...

For most people our childhood dreams are long forgotten as we reach adulthood and go about the business of earning a living. All too often life's circumstances take us down a different path. But for some, the dream is the central focus of their lives; the desire to turn that dream into reality is their driving force.

When Paul Thistle was asked about the moment he realized that he wanted to be a missionary doctor, his natural humour came into play. "As a boy growing up in Scarborough, canvassing for The Scarborough Mirror, I would never have forecast the signs. 'Beware of Dog' was the only sign to look out for." His life began in Scarborough, Ontario, a suburb in Toronto's east end. He is the third and youngest child born to James and Melvina Thistle who left their respective small villages in Newfoundland and headed for Toronto to begin their married life.

Paul was a quiet, introspective boy who was camera shy, but early on showed a love for nature that would serve him well in his future travels. He was an exceptional student all through school, who excelled in math and science. When he wasn't in the classroom, he could be found in the library or studying in his room. An entire wall in his parent's home is filled with their son's academic achievement awards, all neatly preserved behind glass and framed. Amongst the awards is first prize for a science project that Paul designed to produce electricity.

Like many other things in his life, he discovered faith on his own. His first exposure to Christianity began at the age of ten when he was invited to attend Sunday school at a neighbourhood evangelical church. Several years later, as a young person still searching for value and purpose in life, he was "prompted by the Holy Spirit to 'check out' the Army." When he walked into the Salvation Army Corps in Scarborough for the first time, he was positively influenced by Sunday school classmates and teachers to invest his future in Jesus Christ.

Paul's determination and commitment to hard work comes naturally from his parents. His sense of humour is also inherited—a gift from his good-natured father, who always has a joke at the ready.

Missionary doctors have a special calling—a voice from God guiding their desire to serve. Paul Thistle's calling came in 1981, the year he turned eighteen, while attending Urbana Inter-Denominational Missions Conference. The call was a need for medical missionaries, especially where the health of mothers and children are concerned and he knew that he wanted to fill that need and make this his life's work.

It helped that he was fond of study and good at math and, as an added incentive, he had the encouragement of a staff of dedicated teachers in a caring community. As he recalls, his days spent at David and Mary Thomson Collegiate in Scarborough were "great formative years, where we could excel beyond our wildest dreams and expectations. The Thomson spirit was such that kids from middle class families in Scarborough could reach for the stars." He had no way of knowing that his "wildest dream" would land him "in the wilds of Zimbabwe."

But although his goal followed a straight path, getting there involved years of study and hard work. As a boy, he delivered the local paper, The Scarborough Mirror. In high school he worked at a dry cleaners and spent summer holidays at Nor-Baker, his father's employer.

After high school graduation, Paul enrolled at the University of Toronto to begin medical studies, enduring long nights of hard work and little sleep that is the bane of every medical student. He completed his internship in a variety of departments and hospitals under the University's umbrella: Toronto General, Wellesley, Mount Sinai, Sunnybrook, North York General, Toronto East General and residency at the Hospital for Sick Children.

He earned his medical degree (M.D.) in 1989, then completed further training in his elected specialty, Obstetrics and Gynecology.

During this time, he made his first foray into overseas medical work as a summer student by choosing to serve as a Salvation Army volunteer. His first experience in the summer of 1985 took him to an Afghan refugee camp in Pakistan during the Afghan-Russian conflict. His duties included photography, medical assistant, and food distribution. This was followed by three summers in 1987, 1988, and 1989 as a medical student/intern volunteer at a rural Salvation Army hospital in East Java, Indonesia.

Paul admits that the route from Toronto to Zimbabwe wasn't planned. After completing his post-graduate studies in obstetrics and gynecology, he offered his services to the Salvation Army. Initially, he was to be sent to Zambia, but his assignment was switched to Zimbabwe before he left. Paul explains it in his trademark humour: "It was my first time in Africa, so I didn't notice the difference. Like a lesson from *Sesame Street*, they all began with the letter Z." He immediately set to work to learn all that he could about the country and its people through a Zimbabwean doctor he met in medical school. Dr. Chizengeya also introduced him to the language of the Shona people and continued to teach him.

Despite his humour, Paul was under no delusions about the task ahead. He was not new to danger. He had witnessed first-hand the horrors of war and famine during his time as a volunteer student in medical school.

For God's surgeons in Africa, to say that life in Africa is a challenge is a gross understatement. If the exhaustion doesn't fell you, there are many diseases that can bring you to your knees. For the poor of Africa, daily life is a struggle just to keep body and soul together. In the list of troubles, Zimbabwe hits the jackpot on all fronts.

In Zimbabwe, people are faced with an endless possibility of ways to shorten their life—war, famine, disease, little or no health care, unemployment and bad governance. Since 1990, many factors have contributed to the downward spiral of the country's economy, resulting in unprecedented human suffering. Less than half the population has proper sanitation. One million people over the age of 15 suffer from HIV or AIDS. One in three children suffers from chronic malnutrition. In Zimbabwe, as Paul would learn, nothing is static. Life and death are at opposite ends of a very short pole. Unless you are among the super-rich or the ruling class who have captured power, collected the spoils and kept them for yourself, the possibility of living to a ripe old age is slim. But it wasn't always so.

To understand Zimbabwe, you have to go back to its roots. The most ancient people were the San, Bushmen who later mixed with other groups and became the Xhosa. The San existed for thousands of years before everyone else, but now exist there only in rare scattered tribes. San paintings, though, are scattered everywhere throughout Zimbabwe.

Still standing are the most prominent remains of a later civilization that began as "Great Zimbabwe", the Shona term for houses of stone. These stone structures were built in stages between 800 and 1500 A. D. and represent the remaining evidence of an ancient capital that thrived on agriculture and commerce. Its massive stone walls, 36 feet high and 20 feet thick in places, undulate across almost 1,800 acres of present-day southeastern Zimbabwe. Within its walls, stands The Great Enclosure, some 820 feet in circumference. This giant structure is the largest edifice in Africa next to the pyramids of Egypt. Today, the ruins are preserved as a UNESCO heritage site that attracts visitors from all over the world.

When archeologists came across the site they were stunned by the ruins' imposing architecture constructed of granite blocks that were honed from an abundant supply of exposed rocks gathered from the surrounding hills, then fitted together stone upon stone, with no mortar in between. At its zenith, Great Zimbabwe housed up to 10,000 inhabitants. As Europe emerged from the Middle Ages, between 1290 and 1450, this kingdom was a major commercial force, trading its gold for silk with China and India, and for pottery from Persia. But eventually the land couldn't support the population and the people were forced to move to greener pastures. From that point on, Zimbabwe endured constant battles for supremacy.

As early as the 17th century, the Portuguese were the first Europeans to establish trade with the region. Fortune hunters and settlers soon followed and thus began the relentless control for power. What was it about this land-locked country to the north of South Africa that has attracted so many to explore and conquer it? European penetration into Zimbabwe began with Christian missionaries. But the emigrants who had the biggest impact were the British settlers who arrived in the late 1800s to a land rich in agriculture and gorgeous scenery. This is the land explored and charted by David Livingstone, the first European to lay eyes on Mosi-oa-Tunya "the smoke that thunders," the Tonga name for the waterfall that he renamed Victoria Falls. Livingstone was captivated by the region's stunning sunsets, and abundant wildlife, "scenes so lovely," he wrote, "they must have been gazed upon by angels in flight."

The Matobo Hills are home to strange rock formations and some of the last of the world's rhinos, including the highly-endangered black rhino. To the west, bordering Botswana, lies Hwange National Park, the largest game reserve in Zimbabwe and home to herds of elephants, antelope, zebras, wildebeest, giraffe and buffalo. To the north is Mana Pools, a wildlife conservation area in a region of the lower Zambezi River where the flooded plain turns into a broad expanse of lakes after each rainy season. As the lakes gradually dry up and recede, the region attracts many large animals in search of water, making it one of Africa's most renowned game-viewing regions and another UNESCO World Heritage Site. With its elephants and colourful birds set among teak, baobab and fig trees, the site has been described as a Garden of Eden. Amongst its legendary hills lay a treasure-trove of minerals and precious ores—everything from gold to platinum, emeralds and diamonds. It is no wonder that everybody wanted a piece of this land—"the breadbasket of Africa"—with the most fertile soil on the continent.

―――

One of those British settlers who ventured forth to Africa was 18-year-old Cecil John Rhodes, who in 1871, joined his brother on a cotton farm in South Africa. With financing from the Rothschild family, the two brothers began acquiring small mining reserves in the Kimberley area. Seventeen years later, together with their partner, Charles Rudd, the brothers founded their own mining company. Later, the Kimberley diamond reserves became known as the De Beers Mining Company, with Cecil Rhodes as its Founding Chairman. With this acquisition, together Rhodes and Rudd controlled ninety percent of the world's diamonds. The high cost of diamonds can be traced back to Rhodes and his partners, who agreed to limit the supply to preserve the jewels' value.

Spurred by the expectation of unlimited wealth to cement his future, Rhodes directed his focus northward to the land south of the Zambezi River. Then it was known as Zambesia, which later became Southern Rhodesia. Today this land has reverted to its original Shona name, Zimbabwe, while the land north of the river became Northern Rhodesia, now known as Zambia.

Rhodes' dream was to create a British Empire. He used his wealth and that of other investors to pursue this goal through the acquisition of mineral concessions obtained from the most powerful indigenous chiefs. By promoting his business interests as though they were part of strategic business initiatives of the British Government, he effectively prevented the Portuguese, Germans and Boers from moving into south-central Africa.

Rhodes' initial attempt to get a mining concession from Lobengula, King of the Ndebele, in the western lowlands of Matabeleland, failed. He then dispatched agents to represent him, who assured the King that no more than ten white men would mine in Matabeleland. But the document, known as the Rudd Concession, which Lobengula signed, failed to disclose this limitation. It also failed to mention that it gave the mining companies total control over their own operations, using them for any purpose they deemed necessary. When Lobengula discovered the true impact of the document, he tried to reverse it, but the

British Government ignored him. Controversy remains as to who was right and who was wrong in the presentation and signing of the treaty. To his dying day, King Lobengula claimed that he was deceived, even pleading his case directly to Queen Victoria, who advised Rhodes and Company to proceed with caution. "It is not wise to put too much power into the hands of the men who come first. A king gives a stranger an ox, not his whole herd." But the warning came too late. Rhodes, who swore that every facet of the document had been properly translated and explained in full, had already deployed 180 settlers to occupy the land. The future of Zimbabwe was a done deal. In 1893, Rhodes' company troops swept into Matabeleland and a short time later Lobengula died in exile from smallpox. Cecil Rhodes, for all intents and purposes, became the new King of Rhodesia.

As a British colony, Rhodesia turned into a massive land grab for white settlers. Thousands of Africans were driven at gunpoint off their land onto reservations, known today as communal lands. With no compensation, the land they had toiled to clear was confiscated and given to Rhodesian soldiers and white settlers—and the circle of control tightened. Following the Land Apportionment Act of 1930 and the Land Tenure Act of 1969, black citizens were prohibited from owning land in white areas, denied the right to vote or run for office, or to hold any prominent position in the army, police or public service. They were excluded from the best schools and residential areas, and barred from other amenities reserved for whites only.

For the white settlers, Rhodesia evolved into a rich agriculture enterprise, exporting wheat, tobacco and corn to the rest of continental Africa and beyond. For the black population, however, Rhodesia had become intolerable. Their beloved land had morphed into a mirror image of South Africa, with similar policies to apartheid.

In 1995, when Paul Thistle accepted a position at the Salvation Army Hospital in rural Zimbabwe, Robert Mugabe had been in power for 15 years. Twenty-nine percent of the population existed below the United Nations Food Poverty Line. To add to their misery, the HIV/AIDS pandemic in sub-Saharan Africa was at its peak. How, then, had this abundant land that was labelled "the breadbasket of Africa" failed to provide for its people?

In 1965, Rhodesian President Ian Smith tore his country away from British rule, which supported black rights, in a unilateral declaration of independence, commonly referred to as the UDI. Smith saw this as his chance to promote his own agenda of the right to independence under black majority rule, but the newly-created state failed to gain international recognition and eventually economic sanctions were imposed.

The black majority also fought back, including Robert Gabriel Mugabe. While working as a teacher in Ghana, Mugabe was influenced by Kwame Nkrumah, who became Ghana's first president following that country's independence two years before. When Mugabe returned to Rhodesia to push for his own country's right to independence under black majority rule, the Smith government objected to Mugabe's strident complaining and sentenced him to prison, where he remained for over 10 years. Behind prison walls, Mugabe relied on secret communications to launch guerilla operations aimed at freeing Southern Rhodesia from British rule. When he was released to attend a conference in Northern Rhodesia, now Zambia, Mugabe escaped. After crossing the border back to Southern Rhodesia, he assembled a troop of Rhodesian guerilla trainees along the way. The battles raged on throughout the 1970s.

By the end of that decade, Zimbabwe's economy was in worse shape than ever. In 1979, after Smith had tried in vain to reach a consensus with Mugabe, the British agreed to monitor the changeover to black majority rule and the UN sanctions were lifted. In 1980, after fifteen years of protracted fighting, British-ruled Rhodesia gained independence and adopted its former name of Zimbabwe. And, as the elected head of the ruling Zimbabwe National Union-Patriotic Front, ZANU-PF, Robert Mugabe became its leader. People responded with liberated joy. Songs were written in his praise: "Mugabe suffered so we could be happy." For the people of Zimbabwe, Robert Mugabe was the hero of the day.

Throughout the 1980s, under Mugabe's rules, the political landscape looked promising. His vision of democracy, social justice, freedom, peace, and respect for human dignity resonated with the people. Although he was born to a poor Catholic family, whose father deserted them when he was a young boy, Mugabe received a good education in Jesuit schools. He then went on to university, eventually earning degrees in Economics and Education. As a former teacher, one of his first priorities as President was to establish free education. As a result of his initiatives and belief in education, Zimbabwe has one of the highest rates of literacy in Africa, with 90% of the population able to read and write.

Travelling to remote regions that had no means of education, he set up schools. And even though black farmers were confined to communal farm lands, this land became the backbone of the country's commerce. In the early 1980s, the communal farm lands produced the world's largest supply of cotton and maize. By 1986, agriculture accounted for 25% of Zimbabwe's economy, with communal farm lands producing 65% of the country's maize, 70% of cotton and 30-35% of beef products.

Watching Mugabe's early speeches, it is easy to see how effective he was in winning people to his side. Good looking, charismatic, well-spoken and well turned out, Mugabe comes across as a charming, erudite English gentlemen. The man is, in fact, a lesson in contradictions—on the one hand loathing the British (he had a particular hatred for the three B's—Blair, Brown, and oddly, enough, George Bush)—but a particular fondness for British singer, Cliff Richards. He was at all times impeccably dressed, also insisting that his fellow parliamentarians follow his dress code.

By 1990, however, the Promised Land had turned to dust. The dream of a better life for the black majority of Zimbabwe's citizens was fast becoming a nightmare. Mugabe had lost his vision. In 1987, his ZANU-PF party swallowed up his chief rival, ZAPU, the Zimbabwe African People's Union, with the use of force by his favourite weapon, his elite Fifth Brigade. He changed the constitution and declared himself Executive President and Head of the Armed Forces. He curried favour with the country's armed forces veterans by granting them a $2,000 per month stipend that had never been budgeted. As well, land redistribution suddenly stopped and the rural majority who had been kicked off their land by the colonialists were quickly forgotten.

It seemed obvious to everyone but Mugabe that his socialist policies could not be maintained. Whereas Ian Smith had used Western Christian ideology against Communism, which he attributed to Zimbabwe's black citizens, Mugabe blamed "white imperialists" for every wrong turn or bad decision. His hatred for the British was so palpable, it coloured his every thought. Now his chief mandate was not what was good for his people, but what was good for maintaining his grip on power, no holds barred.

Some see Mugabe as a two-faced enigma—a master of spin and propaganda—with a public face and a private agenda. Others see a man with a clear-cut vision of his own ambitions, whatever it takes to get there.

Whichever version you choose to believe, there was early evidence of another side to the new leader. In 1981, he launched his Fifth Brigade, an elite Korean-trained unit led by Mugabe's cousin, who answered directly to him. Between 1983 and 1984 they meted out a reign of terror in Matabeleland. More than 20,000 civilians were killed and thousands more tortured.

This, then, was the magnificent and complicated land that Paul Thistle was destined for; and this was the land, that despite its troubles, he would grow to love.

———

Before embarking on his mission to Zimbabwe, Paul Thistle told his mother that although he knew of the dangers of working in Africa, he wasn't afraid. He was well aware of the daunting possibility that he might not return, that he might meet the same fate as other missionary doctors before him and die in Africa, but he was prepared to do the same.

He was going with an open mind. Although he couldn't predict what lay ahead, the one thing he could rely on was his faith. Wherever the road led, he knew that God was with him.

CHAPTER 2

The Story of Howard

A small body of determined spirits fired by an unquenchable faith in their mission can alter the course of history...

MAHATMA GANDHI

CHIWESHE, MAZOWE DISTRICT OF MASHONALAND, ZIMBABWE
HOWARD HOSPITAL SITS AT THE fork of two rivers in the Chiweshe communal land, 80 kilometres north of the Zimbabwe's capital, Harare. From first glance, it is evident that this is no ordinary hospital. Instead of conventional bricks and mortar rising to several levels, its various departments are housed in a cluster of simple buildings, some topped with grass thatched roofs, strung together on a barren patch of earth. Surrounding the hospital are stately acacia trees whose bare trunks rise to leafy tops that resemble umbrellas. Vibrant bursts of bougainvillea provide a welcome boost of colour to the grassless compound. Outside the entrance stands a sign with the hospital's name and, directly above it, the crest of the Salvation Army.

The Salvation Army's links to the country go back to the late 1800s. Since those early days, missions have succeeded in providing health and education for the unfortunate majority of poor countries.

Without them the scourge of disease would continue to flourish unabated, since there is little incentive for the government to provide affordable health care to the nation's poor. The reality for Zimbabwe's twelve million citizens is stark and simple. The poor who can offer little to government coffers, therefore, get nothing in return.

The first Salvationists in Zimbabwe, including the first European women and children in the settlement, set out from Kimberley, South Africa. They rolled into the new town of "Salisbury" in 1891 on a colourful wagon called the Enterprise, after travelling nearly 1,000 kilometres of wilderness in six months, relying on hunting for most of their food. The Salvation Army had "opened fire" in Zimbabwe, prepared to spread the "word" amongst its settlers.

William Booth, the Salvation Army's founder, however, saw the future of the Army among the Africans, not the settlers. Aware that other settlers were being given free land, he persuaded Cecil Rhodes to offer farmland to the Salvation Army. So 3,000 acres just 25 km north of Salisbury, named Pearson Farm, was allocated to the Army, and two of the pioneers who had arrived on the Enterprise were put in charge of starting work among the Shona people.

The Howard, as it is popularly known, began in 1891 when Captain Edward Cass arrived from England to establish the mission at Pearson Farm near Mazowe. Life at Pearson would have discouraged lesser men. The ground had to be cleared and fenced for farming. Lions were a constant threat to livestock, and some nights were spent in a tree guarding the flock. The Shona people were also suspicious of white people.

Five years later, during an uprising against white settlers, the mission was destroyed and Cass was shot and killed. Cass's cook, Bhobho Garande, took Cass's bible and, together with two others, Ben Gwindi and his cousin, Kunzyui Shava, began to spread the Christian message to the local people. These first Christian missionaries were all

Africans, but there were many obstacles in their way. White settlers did not take kindly to evangelistic and educational work among Africans and the rebuilt Pearson mission suffered intense persecution.

In 1920, Captain Kirby was appointed to take charge of cadet training at Pearson Farm. Illness was frequent, and learning the Shona language, vastly different from European tongues, was slow and challenging. Kirby faced constant opposition from surrounding white farmers, who wanted Africans to keep their traditional beliefs and opposed them becoming Christians. Cadets were threatened with arrest if they held open-air services.

An offer of land from Headman Makombochoto to Leonard Kirby, a Canadian missionary, saved the day by providing the foundation for the mission site. In September 1923, a group of 40 students and teachers marched 35 km from Pearson Farms in Mazowe to Nyachuru Village, sleeping under the stars, in order to build the first mud huts and lay down future roads. Little by little the mission that began as a glimmer of hope became a reality. The Kirbys lived with their children in grass huts for the first few months while building their own house. They often took cadets on campaigns into Chiweshe, travelling an entire day by any means possible, by foot, bicycle or donkey cart, just to get there. The Chiweshe people were always kind to the visitors, with offers of food and shelter.

When the Pearson group arrived at Howard, the Kirbys, who had no medical training, nevertheless helped those suffering from malaria, tended to cuts and burns, and applied mustard plasters to pneumonia patients. When malaria struck their son, who thankfully survived, Kirby saw the need for an expanded facility, including a clinic.

Captain Kirby taught the men how to make "Kimberley Bricks" from sun-baked mud—9 by 18 by 6 inches. With visions of a great mission in mind, he drew up plans showing the location of future roads.

A year later 27 brick buildings had been completed and the Nyachuru training home was renamed Howard in honour of the Army's second Chief of Staff.

From 1925 to 1929, Howard Institute was managed by Adjutant Lyman Kimball, an American officer. He added electricity and sank the first bore hole for clean water that had previously been rolled up from the stream in barrels. In September 1928, he added a clinic and dispensary. The new clinic had two wings housing maternity and general beds. This 15-bed hospital, run by nurses, was quickly overwhelmed by the local needs, but it would be another 28 years before anything near adequate facilities were built.

Not only did the Howard become a great mission that offered medicine to the location population, but a source of learning. In its early days, the mission began to train adults as teachers, farmers, builders, nurses and ministers, but quickly extended to children with the construction of Nyachuru elementary next to the mission. Howard now consists of a primary and secondary school, as well as a vocational training school and a school for nurses' training that began in 1939 with two pupils.

In 1943, the Kirbys' son, Captain Leonard Field Kirby married Adjutant Isobel Sloman, who became the nursing sister in charge. When Mrs. Kirby began teaching a three-year program to train nurses and midwives, there was no operating theatre or classroom. Theatre training was conducted at a government hospital and classes were held in the office, or, when the hospital was filled to capacity, moved outside under a tree.

While Mrs. Kirby was expecting her first child, Captain Eileen Stanford was appointed in charge of the hospital. When no doctor was willing to work at Howard, Capt. Stanford embarked on medical training. She later married Major Mackintosh and they were appointed to Kenya. When her husband died, she returned to Howard Hospital as Chief Medical Officer in 1963-64. Tasked with the jobs of both hospital work and training students, she could not cope with the heavy load and was forced to resign from the hospital. She took up a position as Senior Lecturer in Community Medicine at the University of Rhodesia. Later, when a University centre was built at Howard, she returned, accompanied by students who came to learn and help.

Howard Hospital could not have survived or expanded without a succession of dedicated nurses. Sister Salisbury was a tireless worker, up nights delivering babies, teach the students and handling cases meant for a doctor. Starting as a nurse in 1935, she served as Matron for three periods from 1947 to 1969. Her dedication earned Howard a reputation for quality care, bringing more patients to its door.

Major Ben Gwindi's own daughter, Rebecca, served as a nurse at Howard for 45 years. During that time, she married Aaron Mungate and later became Sister in charge of Maternity work. In the mid-1970s, Howard Hospital became the designated District Hospital and referral centre for the Mazowe district of Mashonaland Central Province providing services to a catchment of 270,000 people. By 2012, this full-scale facility included in-patient and out-patient departments, an operating theatre, pharmacy, laboratory, and facilities for x-ray, ultrasound and rehabilitation serving all ages, from newborn to the elderly. A mobile clinic provided outreach services in immunization, pediatric and obstetric as well as family planning to villages within a 100-kilometre radius. A Home Care program served patients with AIDS-related diseases, and a supplemental feeding program was established for children suffering from malnutrition.

―――

Humble Beginnings

Medical work began when Salvation Army Major Bradley administered his scant supply of medicine and prayers to the local people at the height of the 1918 flu pandemic, and continued through the back door of the new mission established in 1923.

No European name is more honored among Shona Salvationists than that of Bradley. When Howard Institute was started, missionaries and Africans alike wanted it named after him, but they were overruled by Salvation Army headquarters. By 1904, Bradley had 15 cadets enrolled. His nickname was "the man who eats sadza with dove" for relishing the traditional African diet made from maze. Though fluent in Shona, no Shona today can remember the content of his sermons, but they do remember what he did. He shook their hands, even though at the time it was frowned upon for a European to shake hands with an African. Bradley would be away from home for weeks at a time, cycling the rough trails, fixing frequent punctures, crossing unpredictable streams. Once, he was cut off from a service he was to perform by a river in flood. He called across the river for the people to come, and the service went ahead—preacher on one side and congregation on the other. He would sleep in the huts of converts, eat whatever was available, pray with the family and carry on to the next village in the morning.

By 1928, the mission operated as a clinic with four wards and the core of the present hospital was added in 1958. From these humble beginnings the Howard continued to expand into a semi-modern facility, despite inadequate support from the government and both the International and local Territorial Headquarters of the Salvation Army.

The Army was not always kind to its doctors either. In the late 1960s Captain (Dr.) Jock Cook came to Howard to serve as its Chief Medical Officer. Before arriving in Zimbabwe, Dr. Cook, a feisty Scot, had already distinguished himself as a member of the Royal Air Force's 617 Squadron—the renowned Dam Busters. During the

Second World War, he flew 39 missions, earning the Distinguished Flying Cross. Dr. Cook was the hospital's first resident surgeon. Prior to that, in the earlier '60s, surgery was performed by government-employed visiting surgeons. Cook immediately set to work expanding the hospital by adding x-ray capabilities, an operating suite, and special isolation for tuberculosis and other infectious diseases. With the new facilities, he was able to perform more complex surgeries than had previously been possible; but in order to keep the hospital running, he was forced to work in private practice on top of his hospital duties.

His successor, Dr. Sven Pedersen, didn't fare much better, succumbing to exhaustion from a year of overwork trying to support the hospital with private practice on the side. With only three days' notice of his appointment, Dr. James Watt was assigned to Howard in 1970, shortly after Dr. Pederson was carried out of the hospital on a stretcher. This was Dr. Watt's first practice after completing extra residencies in surgery and anesthesia. His wife, Bette, was another asset to Howard. She was a teacher, who taught at Howard Secondary School.

Faced with the same impossible workload, Dr. Watt allowed the best of his paramedics and nurses to handle much of the diagnosis and treatment. One became adept at taking X-rays and applying plasters; several became skilled at diagnosis and treatment, including basic dentistry; another became the chief anesthetist, right up to the time of her retirement; still another was skilled at vacuum deliveries, knowing when she needed to consult the doctor. Dr. Watt was then able to pay visits to elderly patients in their homes.

During that time, the hospital was encouraged to increase donations from overseas. Large amounts funneled through International Headquarters for Africa and smaller amounts came directly to the hospital. With the greater influx of funds, gradually Watt was able to relinquish work at the private clinics he had inherited in order to finance the hospital.

As in many African countries, political strife hovered overhead with ominous repercussions for the local population. In 1965, when Rhodesian President Ian Smith tore his country away from British rule in a unilateral declaration of independence, the newly-created state failed to gain international recognition, leading to economic sanctions being imposed.

In 1972, civil unrest broke out, with the black majority fighting oppression from the ruling government of Ian Smith. That same year, Dr. Pat Hill joined the team at Howard Hospital and spoke up against the Rhodesian Government's abuse of the Chiweshe people, saying "Sometimes silence is golden, sometimes it is just plain yellow." The war raged on for seven long years until Robert Mugabe came to power in 1980.

In June 1978, at the height of the revolution in what was then Rhodesia, all women and children assigned to missions across the country were told to leave for the safety of the towns. Gradually, when their families were returned to their countries of origin, the men followed, but Dr. Watt and his hospital staff refused to go. In preparation for impending attacks, they had created several underground safe places, but soon realized they could not guarantee the safety of the student nurses. The last of the expatriate nurses transferred the nursing school to the safety of town. As the last missionary, Dr. Watt remained behind, supported by his loyal hospital staff, despite the dangers.

The Rhodesian Government's Special Branch, an elite anti-terrorist group, had explicitly ordered the hospital not to treat suspected terrorists; the hospital ignored these orders based on the higher authority of internal law and Christian morals. The Special Branch, however, believing the doctor was treating terrorists, made several attempts on his life. One attempt was foiled by the children who often played around his house. In truth, he made no distinction as to who was treated. Anyone arriving in civilian clothes received help. His stance on the war was simple: "as long as there is a sick person, whether it's a gunshot wound, a fracture or any kind of illness, I will go into the villages." This he did faithfully.

The community responded so positively to his demonstration of selflessness that they convinced the freedom fighters to allow the doctor to continue with his work, and the guerillas agreed. Dr. Watt became a local hero and today in Zimbabwe his name is spoken with reverence. But the campaign of terror didn't end there. In August the hospital had a sudden influx of people who had been poisoned by coming in contact with contaminated clothing. Several of them died. Dr. Watt was naturally puzzled by the seriousness of their conditions and shortly afterwards he became ill himself. One of the children spoke up about rumours circulating that he had been poisoned, but Watt was skeptical. When he became too ill to continue full-time at the hospital, he reluctantly made arrangements to stay in town and visit the hospital three days a week. By the end of the war, Dr. Watt was so ill he was forced to lighten his load at Howard Hospital. Following Independence in 1980, he returned to the hospital, with a reduced workload.

In 1981, he took a job as Lecturer of Medicine at the University of Zimbabwe while still living at Howard, but by 1983 his illness had progressed to the point where he was too weak to cope with even limited duties.

In 1984, he requested to be returned to Canada to recover. He spent the next 10 years in Canada at Children's Village in Calgary and helped start a street clinic for the poor. In 1994, somewhat better, he returned to Zimbabwe at Tshelanyemba Hospital in Southern Zimbabwe. In 1995 when he returned to Howard Hospital, the local people gave him the reception of a returning war hero, but the muscle weakness he experienced made even suturing a wound difficult.

It wasn't until 2001, when one of his former students was implicated in the anthrax attacks in the United States, that he twigged to what had been the cause of his symptoms.

With mounting suspicions, Watt decided to phone Howard Hospital to contact Howard Chirikuri, the child who years earlier had mentioned rumours of poisoning. Howard, who was now grown up, revealed that back then he had witnessed two young white men, one in military gear, who had ordered him sternly to silence, then entered the house. On his way out, the man warned, "Do not eat the doctor's food."

"From my symptoms," Dr. Watt says, "they had used thallium, warfarin and possibly the organophosphate paraoxon, the poison used on the community in 1978." Unfortunately, Chirikuri died soon after and Watt was unable to get further answers.

According to the 1996 Truth and Reconciliation report set up to investigate human rights abuses that occurred between 1960 and 1994, chemical and bacteriological weapons had indeed been used in Rhodesia in 1978 as well as the poisoning of anyone, even their own government troops, who might reveal its secret. But neither the U.S. nor Rhodesian governments ever admitted to their use.

In addition to the war, cholera outbreaks, that remained a constant threat, took a severe toll on the operation of the hospital. Chiweshe district suffered the largest outbreak of anthrax ever recorded, but Dr. Watt persevered, continuing to build onto and improve the hospital despite insurmountable odds. By the time the country achieved independence in 1980, the hospital was basically a modern, full-scale 144-bed hospital with the ability to provide expanded services to the community from newborn to elderly, including in-patient and out-patient departments, primary care and advanced surgeries.

It is no wonder, then, that with Dr. Paul Thistle's arrival in 1995, Dr. Watt breathed a welcome sigh of relief, knowing that upon his retirement he was leaving his life's work in good hands.

CHAPTER 3

Into the Fray

---

*I took a walk in the woods and came
out taller than the trees ...*

HENRY DAVID THOREAU

WHEN YOUNG DR. THISTLE ARRIVED at Howard, Dr. James Watt, the hospital's Chief Medical Officer, had never seen anyone like him. He arrived speaking Shona, the local language, and worked tirelessly day and night. According to Watt, Paul Thistle's transition to his new environment was so smooth that he "slipped seamlessly into the community as if he'd been there forever."

Paul loved the work, providing all-too-rare health care to the local communities.

As part of a team of several physicians and a handful of nurses, he provided physical, social and spiritual care to over 270,000 people in the Chiweshe catchment in rural Zimbabwe. He soon adjusted to the constant flood of patients. Three hundred people a day sought assistance on the hospital's doorsteps, and thousands more were served by the community outreach programs.

Paul immediately joined Dr. Watt on his routine visits around the area. Armed with his facility to instantly communicate with the local population, he was quick to find his way and be able to carry Dr. Watt's vision to greater heights than anyone had imagined.

One summer when he came home to Toronto on furlough, he told his mother about a young nurse who worked at the hospital. Her name was Pedrinah Kasanga, a nurse-midwife, born and raised in Zimbabwe, who worked alongside him at the hospital, assisting in surgery and training nurses and midwifes. He was very fond of her, he said, and was going to ask her to marry him. One day he mustered the courage to ask her to accompany him to church. To his delight, she said yes, and when he asked her to marry him, she said yes again.

They were married in Zimbabwe in August 1998 in the nearby Salvation Army church. Their wedding was a grand affair by any standards and the hit of the summer season that year. It's hard to believe that such a beautiful wedding could be planned and conducted with such aplomb in the middle of rural Zimbabwe. There was no wedding planner, no limousines or fireworks or disco dancing, but a whole lot of community spirit and evident joy for this union. With the help of family and friends, the wedding was as splendid as any in the western world, complete with a live band, and special singers, dancing, and even a water fountain. The church was filled to capacity, with the whole community waiting outside to share in the celebration of their beloved young doctor and his bride. Pedrinah was dressed in flowing white satin, as were her bridesmaids and flower girls. All of the dresses, as well as the cakes, were made by a local woman in Harare. The Zimbabweans' love of flowers was evident that day, with beautiful local blooms spread throughout the church.

Paul's proud parents, who had flown to Howard, looked on as their youngest son took Pedrinah to be his wife. His parents were overjoyed that he had found a partner after all his years of study and life as a bachelor. With a loving wife by his side, their fears were lessened, knowing that he wouldn't have to face life in the world alone. On their arrival at Howard, one of the first things his parents noticed in his bachelor's quarters was the lack of food in his cupboards. When his mother suggested that they go into Harare to replenish supplies, Paul preferred to leave it until later when he had more time. Of course, there would never be more time. Even on the day of his wedding there was no time to relax. An hour before the ceremony, he was still working—preparing notes for Dr. Watt to take over his hospital duties so that he and Pedrinah could spend time together as a newly-married couple. But on this day Dr. Watt and his wife had no intention of staying away. Jim and Bette Watt wanted to be there to wish the young couple well and read messages from friends and relatives that had arrived from all corners of the world.

The ceremony was performed by Commissioner Vinece Chigariro, who took hours to get to the point, lacing the ceremony with her own brand of matrimonial advice meted out to everyone in attendance. Although the ceremony had started out in the cooler hours of early morning, by the time the Commissioner got around to the actual nuptials, the heat was rising both inside and outside the church.

After the ceremony, Paul's father rose to thank everyone for the warmth of the Zimbabwean people and the wonderful reception they had received from everyone. In true Zimbabwean tradition, the parents sat with each other's spouses as a sign of welcome into their new families. Another custom that Paul respected was to give Pedrinah's parents the gift of a cow.

A year later, with Paul happily settling into married life, Dr. Watt announced his retirement and Paul became Howard Hospital's new Chief Medical Officer.

CHAPTER 4

Club Med No Frills

Strive not to be a success, but rather to be of value.

ALBERT EINSTEIN

PRACTICING MEDICINE IN THE BUSH requires courage and perseverance, but also vision—a clear view of what you want to achieve and, despite the obstacles, the ability to make it happen. As a married couple, Paul and Pedrinah shared the same vision—commitment to their faith through service to others. Fortunately, for the people of Chiweshe, this formidable medical team working together had all the qualities to be successful, and then some.

In his new position as Chief Medical Officer, Paul discovered that there is nothing sensational about treating the poor in rural Africa—just hard work day and night—and the following day. You quickly learn to do with what you have and to do what you have to do. Although his other official title was Chief of Staff, there were rarely any more than three or four doctors on board at any given time.

Taking his cue from Dr. Watt, Dr. Thistle quickly established a routine. On a typical day he arrived at the hospital at 7:15 a.m. Many patients would already be gathered outside the hospital, waiting patiently on foot or resting on the low stucco walls that serve as benches.

His first job was to check the batteries on the flashlights to ensure that if and when the next power failure occurred, the flashlights would work. If the power failed during surgery, at least he had back-up power to allow the operation to be completed.

Each day with staff began with five minutes of prayer. Next Dr. Thistle reviewed the ward report—"the good, the bad and the ugly" details of what occurred the night before. This was followed by rounds with staff. By 10:30 surgery began. In an ideal situation, with a full complement of three doctors, Thistle was able to attend to surgery, while the other two doctors attended to outpatients. The numbers could vary anywhere from 150 to 200 patients per day. Next came rounds accompanied by staff, and onto a busy Operating Room schedule. After surgery he headed to the Outpatients Clinic, followed by more on-site ward rounds. On a good day, he might break for dinner some 12 hours later to enjoy a brief stint with family. Most nights ended with administrative duties on the computer, but there were few evenings that were not interrupted by a return to the hospital for emergency surgery or some other critical event.

This continued six days a week, year after year, his only break in this punishing schedule a six-week furlough each summer that brought him back to Canada. But no matter how many patients needed his attention, he stayed until the last patient was seen. There is no coming back tomorrow. For some patients, there is no tomorrow—without surgery they will die. He was the only obstetrician/gynecologist in Chiweshe and extra hands were in short supply.

According to the World Health Organization's report released in 2010, there were fewer than two doctors for every 10,000 people in Zimbabwe. In Chiweshe, those numbers are a gross understatement. Howard Hospital's three doctors served a catchment of 270,000 people while medical personnel—physicians, laboratory technicians and nurses—continued to leave the country for greener pastures that offered better working conditions and salaries.

Another part of his job was teaching others how to develop skills. Through his affiliation with the University of Zimbabwe and University of Toronto, he passed his skills on to medical students and other health professionals who came to Howard through on-the-job training. To facilitate this training, an annex of the University adjacent to the Mission allowed medical students to continue their studies on site.

Minor procedures were handled on the spot by doctors, and often by trained paramedics and nurses. More difficult surgical cases were reserved for designated theatre days, Tuesdays and Thursdays. Anesthesia, usually a spinal anesthetic or Ketamine, was provided by one of two specially-trained nurses or by a doctor. But when there were no other pairs of hands to assist him, Dr. Thistle handled it all—surgery, as well as the wards, the outpatient clinic, and any other emergency, medical or otherwise, that cropped up during the day.

At Howard, Dr. Thistle could expect to treat all the usual diseases that a doctor encounters in the developed world, but sub-Saharan Africa brings new challenges to the mix. Cobra and crocodile bites are common here. HIV/AIDS is the prevalent disease that goes hand in hand with various forms of tuberculosis from pulmonary to peritoneal. Skin diseases are just as common. Diabetes, hypertension and sexually-transmitted diseases continue unabated, while polygamous unions, still practiced but discouraged, increase the chances of all sexually-transmitted diseases

Luckily, tropical diseases are not as common. Many, like malaria, are seasonal, creating a problem only during the rainy season, but when they strike those already weakened by other diseases or complications, they can be deadly. Whatever came his way, Paul Thistle would treat them all or invent new ways to deal with them.

As the years of his tenure progressed, and more patients made their way to Howard, the days got busier. Dr. Thistle was now seeing 200-300 patients a day, 75,000-110,000 patients a year. Each year there were 2,000-2,500 babies delivered, many high risk births, with the added complication of mothers infected with HIV and prevention of transmission from mother to child. Many pregnant women arrived early, prior to delivery, as a precaution against problems arising from the difficulties and delays in transportation.

Despite the challenges, Howard was a welcoming place where patients were treated with respect and dignity. Dr. Thistle believes in the holistic approach—treating the whole person, not just the disease—by combining health care with equal doses of compassion and attention to a patient's quality of life.

The road to Howard is a difficult path—for many miles not really a road at all, but a dirt track filled with ruts and potholes deep enough to topple an elephant or swallow a small child when heavy rain pummels the ground. Patients arrive by any means they can—some by oxcart, others by wheelbarrow or other home-made device. Many travel by foot, often walking 18 to 20 miles to get there.

People flocked to Howard because they didn't trust government-run hospitals, which are unreliable and unaffordable; at Howard they knew they would be handled with care and not be charged an arm or leg or sacrifice either in the process. For those seeking treatment at Howard, the hospital offered one-stop shopping. Although equipment was old or second-hand, luckily it was close at hand. Everything a patient required—from seeing a nurse or a doctor to having an X-ray, ultrasound or blood test—could be done in one day.

This one stop shop could easily be labelled the Little Shop of Miracles, because all of this is expected to be accomplished on an operating budget of US$40,000 a year. By comparison, the equivalent needed to fund the same level of service in North America amounts to $100-200 million. This impossible figure of $40,000 might be enough to acquire a 4-wheel drive vehicle with all the trimmings, but it doesn't buy much in the way of healthcare. It could be said that Howard Hospital operated on a wing and a prayer. If not for the influx of donated funds from the various other sources that the hospital depended on to keep it afloat, there would be no shop at all and very few miracles.

Howard Hospital is the hub of the Chiweshe community, but its influence stretches to the world at large. There is a reason why it is close to every one of us. Not only does the hospital care for peasant farmers, but also for their children, some of whom work on commercial farms and mines surrounding Chiweshe. Others, graduating from Howard Institute may well be our workmates in the office or nurses caring for us in Canadian and American hospitals. We could not enjoy our high standard of living without the low-cost labour that they provide. Some of our inexpensive orange juice comes from the great Mazowe Citrus Estates just south of the hospital—Howard cares for their workers. A major crop, both in Chiweshe and in the commercial farms around is soy beans, exported to the west to fatten the cattle and chickens we have on our plates. Another crop, cotton, provides high quality material for our clothes and towels. We have inexpensive stainless steel kitchenware and appliances thanks to the brave miners in the chrome mines just west of the hospital, who also come to Howard for care. The gold in the rings on our fingers may well have come from the Mazowe and Bindura mines to our east. Treating these workers when injured or ill and educating their children is not just a matter of compassion, but of social justice. They are very much part of our lives.

———

The Howard Hospital that Dr. Thistle inherited was in a permanent state of disrepair, with peeling paint on walls, ceilings in danger of collapsing, equipment well past its "best before date", and walls lined with empty shelves. Patient wards were crowded, and, in addition to patients, often filled with family members sleeping on the floor beside their beds. In spite of it all, the Howard was a happy place. As Jennifer Reid, a volunteer from Peterborough, Canada points out "those ramshackle buildings were filled with life and hope and service."

Despite being squeezed from all sides, the hospital carried on as best it could with the aid of sponsorship from outside agencies. A program to provide home-based care to the community was started by the nurses, visiting first on bicycles, then motorcycles and finally extended in range by vehicle with the provision of a mobile clinic sponsored by UNICEF. This later morphed into supervisory visits and education provided by the Stephen Lewis Foundation. An immunization campaign that began as a government initiative in the 1970s and 1980s was sponsored by Rotary International clubs in Canada.

Thistle began a family planning initiative in the 1990s that included a long-acting injectable contraceptive. In 1999, through Paul's efforts, Howard Hospital became the first facility and one of the first in sub-Saharan Africa to offer a program to prevent the transmission of HIV from mother to child. Since its implementation and rapid expansion, the program became enormously successful.

In the early 2000s, with the support of USAID, Dr. Thistle was able to link HIV screening with family planning and screening for cervical cancer.

———

In 2000, a year after his transition to CMO, a glimmer of hope appeared on the horizon when plans for a new hospital began, but it would not be a smooth path. The Commissioner at that time, Amos Makina, objected to any input from the administrators of Howard Hospital or any supervision of the new building. Only at the persuasion of the Army's chief secretary, was Howard's former CMO, Dr. Watt, allowed to see the plans and offer his opinion. At the time, Paul was on furlough in Canada and since Watt had been responsible for previous construction at Howard, he was allowed to see the plans. One million US dollars had been allocated for the hospital's construction, but after examining the blueprints, it was obvious to Watt that the project was grossly underfunded. Several major items were missing: there were no provisions for water or electricity, with special lines for X-ray, no generators in case of power failure—an ongoing occurrence—and inadequate provision for sewage. A minimum of 3.5 million dollars was necessary to complete the project. The architect chosen to build the new hospital apparently had previous experience designing medical facilities in towns, but not for designing hospitals in the bush. So Dr. Watt proceeded to draw up plans for a hospital that could be built for the available funds of $1 million. When his plan was rejected, he went back to the drawing board and created a more workable plan. After consulting with Paul Thistle upon his return, he added more suggestions. Although some were agreed to, the main entrance to the hospital still led nowhere. As Dr. Watt observed, "it was obviously planned to be built, not planned to be used."

When construction began, Commissioner Makina refused to cooperate with the officer who was appointed by International Headquarters in London to supervise the project and oversee the books. Makina denied access to the books as well as the site. Accountability was seen as neo-colonial, the white man's interference. Even when an additional $1 million was added to complete the project, the cost of construction exceeded the budget. When the money ran out again in 2006, construction was halted and the great white elephant sat empty and neglected until the Zimbabwean government declared it unfit for use. The official excuse? Inflation was to blame, despite the fact that the currency was in US dollars and its value had not changed. A more likely scenario was that the US dollars made their way into hands that stood to make a fortune by bringing in and exchanging US currency. The same could be said for construction materials like cement, which have a habit of disappearing onto the black market for immediate cash value.

———

There were changes on the political front as well. In February 2002, following a referendum designed to give him more power, Robert Mugabe lost. Rather than accept defeat, a few weeks later, he began to seize land from white farmers who dared to vote for the opposition party, the MDC, the Movement for Democratic Change. Black politicians, civil servants, business men and women who supported his own ZANU-PF party were given land. The ZANU-PF propaganda machine denigrated anyone who opposed his party. In Harare, the Zimbabwean Daily News presses were destroyed by bombing and the paper was shut down.

Every time there was opposition, Mugabe unleashed the army or police. Prior to the 2002 presidential election, unemployed youth were mobilized to terrorize people into voting for him. People lined up for hours to vote only to find their polling station closed. A woman who supported and campaigned on behalf of MDC was burned with a red hot metal rod and repeatedly raped. Twenty-nine people died during elections. Following this election, the Commonwealth, whose support throughout the years had been on shaky ground, soon called it quits and withdrew for good.

To punish people for rejecting his party in the vote, Mugabe created Murambatsvina or Operation Drive Out Rubbish, a slum demolition scheme, that was supposedly designed to clean up urban areas, but ended up drawing more international condemnation. 700,000 to 800,000 houses were bulldozed and 2.5 million people were displaced. Basic services—electricity, water, gas, sewage—collapsed. Worse, people were beaten or shot, inflation soared, production ceased and money was virtually worthless. Mugabe, who continued to lie and celebrate in style, merely shrugged and printed more money. Now the country that supplied most of the world's maize relied on "Imperialist-nation" handouts to feed its citizens. Those who voted ZANU-PF were rewarded and given food; the rest were forced to rely on the black market. Critics partly blamed food shortages on the land reform program. The government blamed a long-lasting drought, with Mugabe charging Britain and its allies of sabotaging the economy as revenge against his land redistribution scheme.

This was a pattern that would be repeated in future elections. It was also a direct reversal of the policies that had unseated Ian Smith and brought Robert Mugabe to power 20 years ago.

―――

The situation at Howard Hospital was a minor version of the state of things in the country at large. The Zimbabwean dollar continued to slide against the US dollar. In 2001, it was one US Dollar to 300 Zim (Zimbabwean dollar), traded on the black market; officially, it was one to 65, but by 2004, that number equaled one to 7,000. In 2002, The Economist summed up the situation best: Zimbabwean had gone "from breadbasket to basket case."

For the people of Zimbabwe, their only choice was to try to survive under increasingly dire circumstances. For Paul and Pedrinah Thistle, their work continued as their family expanded. In May 2001, they were overjoyed to welcome their first son, James, into the world. In October 2004, there was more good news with the birth of another son, Alexander.

In the summer of that year, the birth of two more babies would bring Howard Hospital to the world's attention and accolades to the doctors who delivered them.

CHAPTER 5

Twin Miracles

---

*Miracles are a retelling in small letters of the very
same story which is written across the whole world
in letters too large for some of us to see…*

C.S. LEWIS

ON THE DAY THAT HER baby boys were released from hospital, Elizabeth Mufuka stood tall and proud beside her twin sons, Tinotenda and Tinashe. Her smile radiated with grateful pride that the twins would grow tall and strong like any other normal boys. But the boys' outlook was not always so positive.

Elizabeth Mufuka is a tall dignified single mother who ekes out a living in Chiweshe as a subsistence farmer. In the summer of 2004, when 40-year-old Elizabeth arrived at Howard Hospital, she was seven months pregnant and had not been seen by any doctor. Upon examination, one of the hospital's midwifes alerted Dr. Thistle to the possibility that she was carrying twins. He conducted a physical examination, then, relying on the hospital's most sophisticated piece of equipment, a vintage ultrasound, he confirmed the diagnosis. The results were startling and a cause for concern: Elizabeth's twins were conjoined.

Conjoined twins are a rarity—fewer than one in every 50,000 to 200,000 pregnancies, and half are stillborn, with one in three surviving for only a few days. There are many variations of fused twins, each with its own anomaly and name. They often share a major organ such as a brain, heart, liver or bowels. Sometimes they share bones, genitalia or entire limbs, but in all cases, they do share our largest organ—skin.

Prior to this mother's arrival, during his ten years in Zimbabwe, Dr. Thistle had encountered only two other sets of conjoined twins, one born prematurely to an HIV-positive mother. Both sets of twins shared major organs including heart and lungs, but died shortly after birth. This was not the kind of information he wanted to share with this mother. In fluent Shona, he told Elizabeth that she was carrying twins who would be delivered by Caesarean section and prepared her for the possibility that they may not survive.

Two weeks after the original ultrasound, Dr. Rachel Spitzer, a 29-year- old resident in Obstetrics and Gynecology at the University of Toronto, arrived at Howard Hospital. This was Dr. Spitzer's second visit, having devoted several days of clinical work at the hospital the year before. Now she returned for a three-month clinical/research residency sponsored by Ve'ahavta, The Canadian Jewish Humanitarian Relief Committee that involved HIV transmission from expectant mothers to their infants. Both doctors shared an easy camaraderie, working side by side while Dr. Spitzer learned about the complexities of dealing with the endemic HIV/AIDS crisis in sub-Saharan Africa. Upon arrival, Dr. Spitzer immediately became involved in the twins' impending birth and was eager to assist in their delivery.

In the early evening of July 20, 2004, Elizabeth arrived for her weekly appointment, feeling uncomfortable, but with no complaints. A quick examination proved the obvious: this mother was clearly in labour. After gathering his staff in the operating room, Dr. Thistle assisted Dr. Spitzer with the C-section and the babies were delivered ten minutes later, their robust screams announcing their arrival to the world. Although the twins' delivery was relatively easy and the babies appeared strong and healthy, the doctors realized that they now had a twin problem on their hands. The babies were also born with cleft lips and palates and without help, their hopes for a normal life were slim. Real questions still loomed. Could the babies be separated, and if so, how? If the twins were to have any chance of survival, a decision had to be made and quickly. It was time for divine intervention and a call to some old friends.

All eyes turned to Toronto, Paul and Rachel's home town.

———

The Hospital for Sick Children sprawls along the east side of University Avenue, a wide flower-laden boulevard in the city's downtown core. To its citizens, the area is Toronto's Hospital Row. Immediately north and wrapping around the corner is Toronto General Hospital. Directly across the street is Mount Sinai Hospital and on its south side stands Princess Margaret Hospital, the world-renowned cancer institute. Across College Street from Toronto General stands Women's College Hospital. Separately and together, these hospitals serve as teaching hospitals in various specialties, with research facilities that have been responsible for many Canadian medical firsts, providing care to half the city's population and extending into the world at large. The wail of sirens as ambulances race toward emergency bay doors is a familiar sound around the clock. Help for any medical problem, from neonatal care to advanced cancer treatment, can be found along this corridor.

Another familiar sound is the whir of helicopters landing on the roof of the Hospital for Sick Children to deliver critical babies or young children from other areas in the province of Ontario. Babies from far-off lands whose own health care systems are barely adequate or non-existent have come to depend on this hospital's world-class health care as their only hope. Since 1966, when the first surgical separation in Canada was attempted, Sick Kids, as it is universally and affectionately known, has been at the forefront of complex medical procedures and advancement in the separation of conjoined twins.

The hospital's most renowned separation in 1984 involved Burmese twins, Lin and Win Htut, who were joined laterally at the pelvis. They were flown in from a Rangoon hospital because local doctors had no idea how to take care of them. Luckily, the twins' dilemma came to the attention of Dr. Robert Filler, who served as the hospital's Surgeon-in-Chief as well as Chief of the General Surgery Department at Sick Kids. Dr. Filler's experience with surgical separation of twins in the United States helped convince the Herbie Fund to provide funding. The Herbie Fund was created in 1979 to address the needs of the world's children by providing life-saving and life-altering surgeries not available to them in their home country. Dr. Filler set about assembling a team of surgeons with advanced knowledge in physiology, anatomy and surgical principles, as well as experience with complex surgeries such as organ transplants.

One of the early team members was Dr. Ron Zuker, a pediatric plastic and reconstructive surgeon and professor. In collaboration with Dr. Filler, they discovered how to cover the large wounds left by separation with the use of tissue expanders, a common technique employed in other plastic surgery, by inserting silicone balloons under the skin close to the future wound area. The balloons are then filled gradually with salt water so that the skin stretches and grows around them.

Within 24 hours of the babies' birth, Doctors Thistle and Spitzer began working the phones, sending out a distress signal to hospitals capable of performing the complex, life-changing surgery. Dr. Jacob Langer, a young pediatric surgeon at Sick Kids was at the top of their list as they pinned their hopes on a positive reply. Langer had assisted in two separation surgeries with Dr. Filler and a third separation as Head of General Surgery, following in Dr. Filler's footsteps. Although other international hospitals responded to Paul and Rachel's inquiries, they had no means of providing charitable support. The Hospital for Sick Children was their best prospect—one of the few hospitals with twin resources—capable of handling the surgery and also providing funding.

Luckily, Dr. Langer's reply was positive: he was interested in the twins' case, but he couldn't do it alone. This type of complex surgery required huge resources and the co-operation of The Herbie Fund. Since its inception, the fund has helped more than 480 children from over 85 countries. The fund's name honours its first miracle, Herbie Quinones, a fragile baby, born in a Brooklyn Hospital in 1978 with a rare birth defect that left his windpipe sandwiched between his heart and his esophagus. Herbie faced death every time he ate, turning blue and losing consciousness some 40 times during his first six months of life. Paul Godfrey, Metro Chairman of Toronto at the time, and his wife, Gina, came to the rescue to establish the fund that raises close to $1 million a year and treats 30 children under the age of 14 annually.

However, in order to convince the director of the hospital's Herbie Fund to come on board, Dr. Langer needed more information.

But 8,000 plus miles away at Howard Hospital, phone service was unreliable or non-existent and sending and receiving e-mails involved an hour's drive to Harare. Even in the capital, Harare, technology was not up to speed—archaic by Western standards.

Dr. Spitzer remained committed and undaunted. In Zimbabwe, as in all under-developed countries, doctors learn to think outside the box and Dr. Spitzer was a quick study. Using the natural elements as her guide, she taped an X-ray to a sun-lit window in Howard Hospital and captured a picture of the image with her digital camera. Then she took to the bumpy roads in a race to Harare and, with a slow internet connection, began the lengthy process of transferring the image, along with other digital photos, to Dr. Langer. Although it took several hours of patience and perseverance, her persistence paid off.

The images confirmed the babies' particular anomaly. They were omphalopagus conjoined twins, i.e. attached abdominally at the liver, but each had their own intestines. More importantly, the X-rays revealed that each baby had all their organs intact, but were unlikely to survive without being separated. The Herbie Fund agreed to cover the cost of the twins' surgery. The $200,000 operation was a go.

―――

By the time the babies were two months old, plans for their separation were in place. The twins would be delivered to Sick Kids for evaluation and surgery. For Paul Thistle, the news was an answer to his prayers. "At Howard Hospital, we no longer believe in miracles," Paul had stated in his annual report the previous year, "we rely on them." For Elizabeth Mufuka and conjoined twins, Tinashe and Tinotenda, it was indeed a God-sent gift—the second trail of hope on their miraculous journey towards a normal life.

By the end of September, Rachel Spitzer's three-month rotation in Zimbabwe came to an end. The twins, who were two months old, were not growing well. Their feeding proved problematic due to their cleft lips and palates, as well as Howard Hospital's limited resources. But once again, Dr. Spitzer was determined to help the babies and as soon as she arrived back in Toronto, she put her resources to work rounding up donations to cover expenses that were not provided by the Herbie Fund. Ve'ahavta, The Canadian Jewish Humanitarian Relief Committee, agreed to cover social support and accommodation for Elizabeth Mufuka and her babies during their recovery. The $5,000 cost of plane tickets was provided by the Salvation Army and the generosity of many individuals, from members of Dr. Spitzer's synagogue to the engineering firm where her father worked.

On December 2, Rachel Spitzer drove to Toronto's Pearson International Airport to pick up Elizabeth and her twins. Accompanying them was Grace, a midwife, who was fluent in English and would act as translator. It was the first time that Elizabeth or Grace had ever seen snow, but that first glimpse from high above Toronto would be only the start of their miraculous journey. Fate had converged to place Dr. Spitzer in the right place at the right time, but for Paul Thistle, who had worked there as a medical student and resident, the response from Sick Kids was "like a homecoming."

Dr. Langer began assembling his team, calling on Dr. Jacob Zuker, a veteran of seven separation surgeries, to assist. The team—25 in total—included two general surgeons, two plastic surgeons, two anesthetists and an assortment of medical residents and eight nurses. Many of the specialists offered their services for free.

Tinotenda and Tinashe, however, were malnourished upon arrival on that cold December day, but by March 2005, thanks to more specialized medical care, they were much stronger and ready for surgery. As the procedure drew closer, more problems surfaced. The tissue expander that covered the shared part of the twins' abdomen and lower chest, and the area of chief concern to Dr. Zuker and his team, had become infected. All the new skin was lost and new techniques were required.

In his years of experience and expertise in repairing abdominal defects in children, Dr. Langer had worked with a variety of materials. He had recently worked with a new support material called Surgisis, a strong and reliable "skin" bioengineered from pig cells that the human body is able to absorb. The patient's own cells grow into the patch. As the patch dissolves, it is replaced by the patient's own scar tissue. Surgisis, Dr. Langer decided, would be used on the smaller twin, Tinotenda, who would be left with the larger wound and need support for his abdomen and chest walls. The team's next challenge was to decide how much anesthetic to give each twin. Because the boys shared a common blood vessel in the liver, shunting more blood and nutrients to Tinashe, it was difficult to determine how much each twin weighed separately and how much anesthetic would end up in the blood supply of the other baby. In the end, the lead anesthetist for the surgery, Dr. Cengiz Karsli, decided to treat the twins as if they were of equal weight. Although their livers joined over a large area, they were actually separate organs, each with its own bile drainage and blood supply.

Finally, on March 7, at 9:33 a.m. the daunting and painstaking task of separating the twins began and a little more than five hours later, Tinotenda and Tinashe were wheeled into the hospital's critical care unit to begin their recovery, lying in separate beds for the first time in their short lives.

A month later, on a sunny afternoon in early April, the babies were released from the hospital and a glowing Elizabeth Mufuka stood proudly displaying her healthy boys to the collected throng of media, eager to catch their first glimpse of them. The babies were strong, they were healthy, and now they were her separate Twin Miracles.

On the last day of May, Tinashe underwent further surgery to repair his cleft lip and palate and on June 8 it was Tinotenda's turn. On July 19, 2005, the twins were the star attraction at a big party in Sick Kids' sunny Atrium along with all the staff who had cared for them, as well as friends from The Herbie Fund, Ve'ahavta and the Salvation Army. It was both a joyous and sad occasion. They had gathered to celebrate the twins' first birthday, but also to say goodbye to the tiny boys who had touched their lives. For the following day, one year after their arrival, the twins would return to the place of their birth, home to Howard Hospital and Zimbabwe.

Today, the boys continue to thrive as separate individuals, going to school, and joining in games with all their friends in the community that surrounds Howard Hospital.

Throughout their lives, Dr. Thistle has maintained a keen interest in the boys' progress. In April 2016, he travelled from Karanda Mission Hospital to see them as part of a documentary filmed by Canadian Television Network's W5 correspondent, Marleen Trotter, who had returned to Zimbabwe to check on their progress after ten years. As the documentary shows, the boys are now healthy 12-year-olds leading "separate, but inseparable" lives, sharing a borrowed bicycle. Their mother Elizabeth and nurse Grace, who accompanied the twin babies to Toronto, remain solid friends, "like sisters." Although they were too young to remember, the boys have never forgotten the doctor who brought them into this world and arranged for their chance to live separate lives, nor the surgeons who made it possible. When Paul Thistle steps out of his vehicle and extends his arms, the boys rush to hug him. Their mother Elizabeth and nurse Grace will never forget their momentous visit to Canada, including the cold and the snow, but most gratefully, the Canadian team who are responsible for the gift of two healthy, happy boys.

CHAPTER 6

Commitment

---

*Be as a tower firmly set; Shakes not its
top for any blast that blows ...*

DANTE

IN 2005, WHEN PAUL AND Pedrinah were invited to become Salvation Army Officers, it was a natural fit, since the work they had been doing was typical of an officer's duty, and then some. For the Thistles, officership was a high mark in their careers, a confirmation of their calling to full-time Christian ministry.

This involved coming to Canada for two to three months to attend Booth University College, and complete training at the Salvation Army's officer-training facility in Winnipeg, Manitoba. After completing training in 2007, they were commissioned as officers, with the rank of Captain.

As a physician, Paul's decision to become an officer had deeper, spiritual meaning: "The challenges and achievements of providing medical and spiritual care to an underprivileged corner of God's kingdom have promoted maturity in my Christian witness. God had called me to commit my life to full time Christian service. The desire to become a Salvation Army officer was an extension... a gradual, natural extension of this calling. I have always believed that a commitment to Christ must be wholehearted. Salvation Army soldiership is a sincere, enthusiastic expression of Christian commitment."

As he explains, his work made his ministry rewarding, "with fulfillment in the little tasks of our mission at Howard: a mother saved in childbirth, a malnourished infant restored to health, an adult living with HIV counseled on healthy living. The axiom I was taught in medical school remains true, 'cure sometimes, comfort always'."

For Pedrinah too, the church had been a part of her upbringing, and becoming an officer had always been a dream.

Now the Thistles would not be just employees, but soldiers in God's Army, committed to a lifetime of service. With their ordination and commission, their path was clear and their future solid. Officership also provided a level of financial stability for their family, but donning the Army's uniform meant so much more. Paul and Pedrinah were now part of an organization that was a perfect fit for their belief in holistic healing—treating the whole person and not just their ailment.

Understanding The Salvation Army

Ask any serviceman, especially those who served in the First and Second World War about the Salvation Army and you'll hear a familiar story: how much he welcomed the helping hand that reached out to him in his darkest hour—a warm blanket and a cup of coffee to shelter him from the cold; a smile and a prayer to boost his spirits when all seemed lost. In every corner of the world, people recognize its uniform and red shield as symbols of help and comfort. Whenever and wherever disaster strikes, you can always count on the good old Sally Ann.

But what exactly is it? A church or a charity? Actually, both. Its soldiers are, in fact, ministers of a church that was forged on the mean streets of London's East End. In 1865, William Booth, a former minister of the Methodist Reform Church, started the East London Christian Mission, based on the principles and teaching of John Wesley. Like Wesley, Booth felt that the traditional church needed to climb down from its Anglican high-horse and rub shoulders with the East Enders who could easily find their way to the neighbourhood pub, but didn't feel as welcome in the local church. As far as Booth was concerned the church was too formal, its music too highbrow and the poor were too intimidated to enter its hallowed hall. The new method "Methodism" catered to the working class, worship was simplified—devoid of fancy vestments—and new hymns were composed.

Booth didn't have to look far for people who needed help. The Whitechapel district was filled with the downtrodden and forgotten—alcoholics, drug addicts and "fallen women." Booth, though, believed that the soul could not be saved if the body was starving, so he gave them liberal doses of the three S's—Soup, Soap and Salvation.

He was also influenced by his wife Catherine, who was a big proponent in equality for women. According to Catherine, only the lack of education and restrictive social customs held them back. William was not so convinced of this equality, but he changed his mind when, a few years into their marriage, he witnessed Catherine stand up and preach. As an inspiring speaker, Catherine helped to promote the idea of women preachers. When William adopted a quasi-military structure for his new church and renamed it The Salvation Army, he assigned women equal responsibility with men in both ministering and welfare work. The new church's soldiers had ranks and a uniform that identifies the wearer as a Salvationist and a Christian—a symbol to those in need.

Not surprisingly, the Church of England did not take kindly to the Booths' new Christian agenda. Booth was called the Anti-Christ, particularly for promoting women to the equal status of men. But the Booths went about their work undeterred. Besides administering to the daily needs of their converts, the couple began a campaign to improve working conditions for women at the Bryant and May factory in the East End. Not only were the women poorly paid, but endangering their health by dipping match-heads into yellow phosphorus supplied by similar manufacturers. Many of the workers suffered from necrosis of the bone caused by the fumes from the yellow phosphorus. The entire side of the face turned green-black, discharging foul-smelling pus that eventually led to death. When William Booth pointed out that the majority of European countries produced matches tipped with harmless red phosphorus, Bryant & May insisted that people would balk at paying extra for these matches which were more expensive to produce.

So in 1891, the Salvation Army decided to open its own match factory using red phosphorus. Employees of the Salvation Army factory were paid twice the amount of their commercial competitors, Bryant and May. Booth conducted organized tours of his model factory for MP's and journalists. He also took them to the homes of the "sweated workers" who were forced to work 11 and 12 hour shifts producing matches for other companies like Bryant and May. The bad publicity that followed forced the company to reconsider their practices and in 1901, Bryant and May's director announced that the company had stopped using yellow phosphorus.

William Booth's good work gradually earned him respect. He was made a freeman of London, granted an honorary degree from Oxford University, and in 1902 invited to attend the coronation of Edward VII.

While William could be seen throughout East London administering to the poor, his wife Catherine garnered financial support for their mission by speaking to wealthier folks who lived in another world on the other side of London.

In 1880, the Army established branches in Australia, Ireland and the U.S., but at home in England, they were not always welcome. Their stance was too rigid, their structure too militaristic and their brass bands too loud. Pub owners, in particular, struck out against the Army, blaming them for losing business. In the United States, however, their response to the Galveston Hurricane in the 1890s and the San Francisco earthquake in 1906 helped to boost their image. Red Kettles began to appear on street corners, soon becoming a tradition heralding in the Christmas Season.

During the 20th Century, their expansion extended to 126 countries, providing services in 175 different languages, with almost two million members worldwide.

The Army's administrative structure is quite complicated, divided into geographical territories, then sub-divided into divisions. Each territory is administered by a Territorial Headquarters (THQ) led by a Territorial Commander who reports to and receives orders from the Salvation Army's International Headquarters in London, England (IHQ) and each division by a Divisional Headquarters (DHQ).

The Army's beliefs are based on eleven doctrines:

1. We believe that the Scriptures of the Old and New Testaments were given by inspiration of God, and that only they constitute the Divine rule of Christian faith and practice.
2. We believe that there is only one God, who is infinitely perfect, the Creator, Preserver, and Governor of all things, and who is the only proper object of religious worship.
3. We believe that there are three persons in the Godhead – the Father, the Son and the Holy Spirit, undivided in essence and co-equal in power and glory.

4. We believe that in the person of Jesus Christ the Divine and human natures are united, so that He is truly and properly God and truly and properly man.
5. We believe that our first parents were created in a state of innocence, but by their disobedience they lost their purity and happiness, and that in consequence of their fall all men have become sinners, totally depraved and as such are justly exposed to the wrath of God.
6. We believe that the Lord Jesus has His suffering and death made an atonement for the whole world so that whosoever will may be saved.
7. We believe that repentance towards God, faith in our Lord Jesus Christ, and regeneration by the Holy Spirit, are necessary to salvation.
8. We believe that we are justified by grace through faith in our Lord Jesus Christ and that he that believeth hath the witness in himself.
9. We believe that continuance in a state of salvation depends upon continued obedient faith in Christ.
10. We believe that it is the privilege of all believers to be wholly sanctified, and that their whole spirit and soul and body may be preserved blameless unto the coming of our Lord Jesus Christ.
11. We believe in the immortality of the soul; in the resurrection of the body; in the general judgment at the end of the world; in the eternal happiness of the righteous; and in the endless punishment of the wicked.

The denomination does not celebrate the Christian sacraments of Baptism and Holy Communion; although its officers conduct marriages, it holds a traditional Protestant belief that marriage was not instituted by Christ and therefore is not a sacrament. It also believes its members should completely refrain from drinking alcohol, smoking, taking illegal drugs and gambling.

The Salvation Army opposes euthanasia, assisted suicide and the death penalty and accepts abortion only in extreme cases such as to save the life of the mother.

Soldiers who join the Army commit to life-long service, adhering to the Covenant, formerly called Articles of War, promising to:

- Be responsive to the Holy Spirit's work and obedient to His leading in my life, growing in grace through worship, prayer, service and the reading of the Bible.
- Make the values of the Kingdom of God and not the values of the world the standard for my life.
- Uphold Christian integrity in every area of my life, allowing nothing in thought. word or deed that is unworthy, unclean, untrue, profane, dishonest or immoral."
- Maintain Christian ideals in all my relationships with others: my family and neighbours, my colleagues and fellow Salvationists, those to whom and for whom I am responsible, and the wider community.
- Uphold the sanctity of marriage and of family life.
- Be a faithful steward of my time and gifts, my money and possessions, my body, my mind and my spirit, knowing that I am accountable to God.
- Abstain from alcoholic drink. tobacco, the non-medical use of addictive drugs, gambling, pornography, the occult, and all else that could enslave the body or spirit.
- Be faithful to the purposes for which God raised up The Salvation Army, sharing the good news of Jesus Christ, endeavouring to win others to Him, and in His name caring for the needy and the disadvantaged.

- Be actively involved, as I am able, in the life, work, worship and witness of the corps, giving as large a proportion of my income as possible to support its ministries and the worldwide work of the Army.
- Be true to the principles and practices of The Salvation Army, loyal to its leaders, and I will show the spirit of Salvationism whether in times of popularity or persecution.

Salvation Army officers are authorized to dedicate children and enroll soldiers; they are authorized to perform marriages; they are authorized to represent the Army before government and sign contracts. An officer's duties are two-fold, split between ministry (corps) work and social services, which could include working in any of the following areas:

Community and Social Services—providing emergency assistance, youth corps, street outreach, homeless or addiction services, Corrections and Justice, Palliative Care, services for the mentally and physically challenged, Young Parent Resource Centres.

Throughout his life, each officer will have worked in most of these capacities. An officer's wife, if he marries, shares the same rank and they work as a team.

Officers commit to a life-long service and, as such, are on call 24 hours a day, 365 days of the year. Their salary is meager. The typical salary for a couple is about $25,000 per year. Split between husband and wife, this amount is just above minimum wage—enough to cover food and clothing,

Officers are supplied with uniforms and all other living requirements are supplied by the Army. This includes a house and furniture and use of a car, including gas and insurance. All household utilities are covered, as well as health insurance, including dental and vision. These are general rules, but may vary according to the territories where the officer is assigned to work.

The Army also operates 27 hospitals in a variety of countries, including three hospitals in Zimbabwe—Bumhudzo Hospital Home for elderly Africans, Howard Hospital in Chiweshe and Tshelanyemba Hospital in the far south-west.

From the first handful of soldiers that rolled into the new town of Salisbury in 1891, the Army grew throughout the 20th century to become an organization recognized and respected throughout the world. And Paul and Pedrinah Thistle had found their rightful place amongst its ranks.

CHAPTER 7

Annus Horribilis

―

I will turn their mourning into gladness; I will give them comfort and joy instead of sorrow ...

JEREMIAH 31:13, NIV

IN 2007, THE YEAR THE Thistles were commissioned, Paul Thistle was able to add a new screening initiative to the hospital's existing programs, with sponsorship from Rotary International. In 2007-8 AIDS and tuberculosis programs, visiting medical practitioner programs and an antiretroviral program for expectant mothers were added to Howard's services.

For the Thistle family, 2008 began with hope and promise, but with the financial collapse that began in the United States and spread to the rest of the world's economies, 2008 turned into a watershed year. In Zimbabwe, the water failed to run and the economy shed all vestiges of common sense or sustainability. The government, with no other solution, continued to print money. Eventually, the rate of inflation reached a stunning 100,000 per cent and the Reserve Bank of Zimbabwe began issuing $25 million and $50 million bank notes—a princely sum that was barely enough to buy three loaves of bread. To add to people's woes, basic commodities and necessities—cooking oil and gas—grew harder to find.

In Zimbabwe, it was election time and tensions were high, with the incumbent ZANU-PF braced against the intrusion of their opponent MDC. In the lead-up to the election, President Mugabe led a campaign of terror against members of the MDC and its supporters. The elections were held in two rounds, on March 29 and June 27, while Zimbabweans waited a month for election results between the first and second votes. Prior to the run-off elections in June, security forces and ZANU-PF militia unleashed a campaign of terror—intimidation, torture and murder against anyone suspected of opposing them. No one, including activists, journalists, polling agents, public servants or civic leaders, was safe. Anything not nailed down was used as a weapon—logs, firewood, metal poles, iron bars and even burning plastic applied to skin.

After two rounds of elections, a run-off was called, but despite Mugabe being declared the winner in the June election, he continued to implement brutal attacks against the political opposition. State-sponsored violence resulted in massive human rights violations, including rape, torture, and forced disappearance. Marauding gangs dressed in camouflage gear, wielding knives and machetes, raided farms and drove owners and workers off the land, forcing them into camps with no facilities and little shelter. And once again, Howard Hospital found itself in the thick of the turmoil, tending to the broken bodies of the victims. Photos of burnt backs and broken limbs taken from hospital beds without permission, then beamed to the world, were shocking. Women and children were dragged from their homes and beaten and raped, often in front of their husbands. Victims were tied to doors or trees and set on fire. Other people were shot where they stood. The list of injuries was horrific. People from Chaona village were beaten until the skin and muscle fell off the bone, then toxic chemicals were poured into the wounds to prevent healing and bring on a slow, painful death. But at Howard Hospital, Dr. Thistle and his staff tended to all who showed up, regardless of where they came from or their political affiliation. They were strictly in the business of healing, not politics, yet politics kept encroaching in their lives.

In addition to everything else and as a result of government neglect, the country's infrastructures had broken down. Landlines were down. Cell phone reception was extremely poor. Though exhausted and overwhelmed with the numbers and extent of the injuries, Dr. Thistle and his team carried on.

The protracted arguments between both political parties over who won the election raged back and forth for over a month, with each side accusing the other of threats and atrocities and requesting recounts. Mugabe railed on, and under mounting pressure from neighbouring leaders, he finally agreed to a coalition with the MDC. Morgan Tsvangiarai assumed the title of prime minister, with control over finances, with Mugabe retaining control of the military. But the coalition remained shaky and South Africa's chief was asked to oversee the combined government.

Following the election, the government decided to abandon its own currency and adopt the U. S. dollar, with limited success in stemming the country's rampant inflation and keeping starvation from the door. At the height of inflation between 2008 and 2009, the government issued a 100 trillion note. Fast forward five years to the summer of 2013 and Zimbabweans faced another election, with Mugabe's image front and centre as always—once again claiming victory and Morgan Tsvangiarai calling it a farce.

This time, though, Mugabe employed a new tactic. Instead of unleashing troops to quell protests and close polling stations, he targeted voter lists.

So Robert Gabriel Mugabe, the man who had the potential to make Zimbabwe the pride of Africa, instead created a land of misery and despair, Today, at age 92, the unseated leader for 36 years clings to power, albeit with a shaky grip and a wobbly gait, but his hair and his heart intact, though as dark as ever.

―――

Human rights activists at home and abroad kept a close watch on the violence, swiftly responding to and condemning the repression of citizens' rights and abuses by the ruling government. In 2007, James McGee was sworn in as the United States Ambassador to Zimbabwe. He is a career diplomat who has served in many countries, including Nigeria, Pakistan, India, the Netherlands and Madagascar. Prior to his diplomatic career, he spent six years in the U.S. Air Force, earning three Distinguished Flying Crosses during his tour of duty in Vietnam. In May, 2008, McGee, accompanied by diplomats from Britain, Japan, the Netherlands, the European Union and neighbouring Tanzania, visited Howard Hospital. They were on a factfinding mission to corroborate reports of violence carried out on local citizens.

The hospital administrator was reluctant to allow visitation, but several members of the group talked to patients while Dr. Thistle briefed the Ambassador and his charges. In the previous week, he told them, Howard Hospital had treated 22 victims of violence, including four women. The injuries followed a typical pattern of beating: deep bruises on the buttocks of several men and broken feet. One patient, in obvious pain told them he was a teacher who had served as a polling supervisor. He and about 30 others had been rounded up and severely beaten on the buttocks and feet. Sadly, five of them had died as a result of their injuries. Another victim succumbed at Howard from internal hemorrhaging. Deep cuts in one patient's wrist were caused by struggling against handcuffs.

Before leaving, the Ambassador and the group took pictures of the patients' injuries. Along the road, as they made their way back to Harare, their 13-vehicle convoy was intercepted by police, who questioned the Ambassador about pictures he had taken. After being detained for over an hour, the police allowed them to continue on their way, presumably with photos intact.

McGee immediately fired off a letter to the state-run Herald newspaper, accompanied by a picture of a man with severe wounds to his buttocks, stating that there was undeniable evidence that Mugabe's ZANU-PF party was behind the systematic campaign of violence "intended to intimidate opposition supporters before a run-off presidential election." As a supporter of human rights, McGee said in his letter that he felt compelled to speak out against "the atrocities being committed across Zimbabwe" and he vowed to press for the prosecution of the perpetrators of the violence.

A furious Mugabe shot back, threatening to throw the Ambassador out of Zimbabwe.

The Herald published the letter alongside an unsigned editorial rebuking his views. The paper blasted McGee, accusing him of "very scandalous acts" and of breaching diplomatic procedure by speaking out on the violence that has plagued Zimbabwe since its March 29 elections.

On May 15, McGee filed his report by cable from Harare to the U.S. Secretary of State. In his report, he describes Howard Hospital as "relatively large for Zimbabwe and well-stocked with medicine." The account of his fact-finding mission lays out in detail the results of the team's findings on visits to two medical facilities—Howard Hospital and the Avenues Clinic in Harare—as well as a torture camp, purported to be used by a killer squad loyal to Mugabe.

More than ever, Paul and Pedrinah looked forward to their annual summer trip to Canada for a brief respite from the turmoil. A surprise notice from the Royal College of Physicians and Surgeons of Canada brought other good news. Paul was being honoured by the college for his humanitarian service, the first of its kind conferred on one of its members.

The award is named in honour of Dr. Lucile Teasdale and Dr. Piero Corti, married physicians who served in the poverty-stricken Gulu region of Uganda for 35 years. Their 35 years in Uganda providing medical care throughout a protracted 25 years of civil war, saved thousands of lives. And their teachings and perseverance transformed a small missionary dispensary into a modern teaching hospital and medical centre. St. Mary's-Lacor Hospital is almost entirely staffed by health care professionals from Uganda.

The purpose of the Teasdale-Corti Humanitarian Award is to acknowledge and celebrate Canadian physicians who go beyond the accepted norms of routine practice, even to the inclusion of personal risk. According to Canadian Medicine News, "the recipient exemplifies altruism and integrity, courage and perseverance in the alleviation of human suffering."

Dr. Rachel Spitzer, the University of Toronto resident who was instrumental in the campaign to separate the conjoined twins born at Howard Hospital in 2004, is one of the people who nominated Paul Thistle for the award. For Rachel, there was no one more deserving of the award. "Paul is an extraordinary individual," she says. "He is honestly and truly a good humanitarian."

CHAPTER 8

Annus Horriblis Multiplicatus

―

Love knows no limit to its endurance, no end to its trust, no fading of its hope; it can outlast anything. Love still stands when all else has fallen ...

BLAISE PASCAL

FOR PAUL THISTLE, HIS HUMANITARIAN award couldn't have come at a more appropriate time. While his skills were being recognized in Canada, back in Zimbabwe they were being severely tested with the outbreak of cholera in August. This, combined with President Mugabe's disastrous mismanagement of the country's economy, plunged Zimbabwe into a virtual shutdown of all services.

Cholera is not uncommon in Zimbabwe. The annual rainy season, from November to March, brings its usual share of cases, but what was unusual about this year was that the disease began and spread during the dry season in August. Cholera, a bacterial infection of the small bowel, causes severe diarrhea and dehydration, but nobody has to die from it. Cholera is treatable with fluids and rehydration therapy, ideally with the use of a pre-packaged mix of a sugar-salt solution to replace fluid and restore and maintain electrolyte balance. If the water supply is kept safe and users are able to handle the sanitary disposal of human waste, the usual outbreaks are manageable. But since cholera is spread by passage through the intestinal track, failure to maintain water and sanitation systems increases the risk dramatically. Throw in a population whose immune systems are compromised with HIV or TB, not to mention widespread nutrition deficiency coupled with malnutrition, and you have the perfect prescription for disaster.

Despite warnings as far back as 2004, the government failed to act. When the disease first surfaced, they dragged their heels for months, letting the disease fester and spread to neighboring countries.

The outbreak, as reported in the New York Times, was yet more evidence that Zimbabwe's most fundamental public services—including water and sanitation, public schools and hospitals—were shutting down, much like the organs of a severely dehydrated cholera victim. One family alone lost five of their children who had been playing in sewers contaminated with human excrement. Their deaths were followed by their aunt and grandmother who had looked after them.

Another child, a five-year-old, was taken to a clinic south of Harare by her two aunts. Nurses there had trouble inserting an intravenous fluid line because the little girl's veins had collapsed with so much loss of fluid. She was given rehydration fluids instead, but was never seen by a doctor. All through the day, the child suffered from thirst and a stomach ache. When night fell, nurses advised her aunts to take her to the city's hospital because they could do nothing more for her.

The hospital was 2-1/2 miles away and there was no ambulance. So, one of her aunts bundled the child onto her back and walked the 2-1/2 miles through the dark moonless night. Taking a short cut through a maize field, she had to leap across another putrid sewage spill. By the time they arrived, her aunt's clothes were soaked with the child's watery diarrhea, and hours later the little girl died.

Hospital staff were also at risk. According to the New York Times, reporting on the epidemic, one nurse said she was afraid of treating cholera patients, reporting that her clinic had no running water, no chemicals to clean toilets and no gloves to wear other than the few provided by the Red Cross.

When local physicians and other healthcare professionals took to the streets of Harare to protest poor working conditions and wages, and marched in peace to the Ministry of Health building, they were attacked. Fifty police spilled out from armoured personnel carriers to stop them, beating them with wooden batons. According to a medical student interview, the doctors, readily identified in white coats were, "treated like dogs."

The nation's schools, once the source of African pride, also shut down when teachers' salaries were reduced to a trickle, not even enough to cover the cost of the bus ride to school. The hospitals were in worse shape, when the two government-run hospitals in Harare ceased to function. Doctors, whose salaries had been reduced to a trickle, walked off the job.

As the dead continued to pile high in the morgue in Harare, only the coffin makers were doing well in the failing economy, with one manufacturer stating that he used to sell one child-sized coffin per week. Now that number had climbed to 15.

Water cut-off is a common occurrence and often prolonged, but by early December the taps had run dry. People in Harare's densely-populated suburbs were left with no drinking water or the means to keep clean and wash their food. The city's main water system is supplied by Lake Chivero. The river that feeds into the lake glowed a ghastly phosphorescent green from plant life thriving on sewage and human waste.

When teachers joined other unpaid professionals by not showing up for work, schools were shut down. On the rutted streets, crowds of children joined out-of-work adults amongst the rotting piles of garbage that formed a thick brown sludge that bubbled up from burst sewer lines. It was chaos in the streets as inflation hit the quintillion mark—i.e. the number 8 followed by 18 zeroes.

Even Mugabe's once-loyal soldiers, the muscle behind the throne, joined the throng of civilians in protest. Troops were enraged that they could no longer withdraw their meager salaries to buy food or send their children to school. Meanwhile, the children of top government employees with political connections to President Mugabe were in private schools while theirs played in the filthy streets.

As days turned to weeks and weeks turned into months, the disease continue to spread, spilling over into neighbouring countries. Given the chance by other countries' own physicians to control the disease, Harare City Council declined their offer, announcing that they had the situation under control. And despite calls from the international community for Mugabe to step down, he continued to deny the severity of the situation. In typical fashion, one day after the World Health Organization warned that the outbreak was grave and carried "serious regional implications," Mugabe announced that the epidemic had come to an end. His Minister of Information and Publicity downplayed the seriousness of the epidemic by telling the government-controlled media that it had "given the country's enemies a chance to exert more pressure on the President to leave office."

In the months of June through August 2008, the government banned all charitable organizations from distributing food or from operating in Zimbabwe's rural areas, denying its citizens even the most basic needs for survival. In the following months between September and November, wards in public hospitals gradually shut down. November 17, 2008 proved to be the worst day when the premier teaching and referral hospital, Parirenyatwa, closed, followed by

Harare Central. The Medical School at the University of Zimbabwe was also closed indefinitely.

By December, the country had hit rock bottom and the rest of the world was reeling in recession. At year's end, there were no functioning critical care beds in the public healthcare section. Human rights organizations called for intervention, this time with UN backing. In early December 2008, the Elders, a group of seasoned human rights advocates—former Secretary General Kofi Annan, human rights activist and wife of Nelson Mandela, Graca Machel, and former U.S. President Jimmy Carter—organized a fact-finding mission to Zimbabwe to commission a report that was to be presented to the UN Security Council. In a move to prevent the investigation, Zimbabwean authorities denied the group's visas, but there were other watchdogs ready to take up the cause.

Physicians for Human Rights is an independent, non-profit organization which has been active in tracking and documenting health rights violations in 22 countries, including Afghanistan, the former Yugoslavia, Kosovo and Rwanda. This organization managed to enter the country, clearly stating the purpose of their visit, but once again their efforts were thwarted. Following their investigation, the Mugabe government falsely reported their arrest. For seven days, December 13-20, 2008, they sent a team to investigate the man-made disaster taking place in Zimbabwe. The team, comprised of four human rights investigators, two physicians with expertise in public health and epidemiology, travelled to four provinces—Harare, and Mashonaland Central, West, and East—and conducted interviews with 92 participants from a broad field of healthcare workers, medical students, teachers, water and sanitation engineers, farmers and school teachers.

When the team arrived at Howard Hospital, they found the wards filled to capacity and then some, with corridors lined with patients and patients sleeping on mats between beds. Asked if this was normal, Dr. Thistle explained that the numbers were actually down from the previous week. The overflow from Harare had lessened because patients who couldn't afford the transportation had no means of getting there. Patients who don't have access to 500 US dollars in cash, the fee for admittance to private clinics, simply stay home or die. And for staff, when the cost of getting to work exceeds your salary, there is no sense in showing up for work.

During their investigation the team discovered that throughout Zimbabwe, maternal health mortality figures had increased at an alarming rate in the previous decade, mainly due to HIV/AIDS, but also to a decline in availability and quality of maternal health serves. The situation had worsened dramatically in the previous month with the withdrawal of maternity services in the public health sector, particularly in urban areas. Large and increasing numbers of pregnant women were forced to deliver at home or travel outside urban areas to receive care at private or mission facilities. Many arrived too late to deliver, with the fetus already dead in the womb. Others were at risk of death from the five most common obstetric complications: bleeding, infection, complications of abortion, high blood pressure associated with pregnancy and prolonged or obstructed labour.

One patient, a 30-year-old primary school teacher, who had travelled from Harare to Howard Hospital, was interviewed on December 16. She told the interviewer that she had been on leave from her position since August because the pay was so poor. She was scheduled to deliver her second child at a government-run maternity hospital by Cesarean section on November 24, but when she arrived on that day, she was told that the operation was cancelled because there were no nurses, doctors or anesthesiologists at work. She was referred to a private obstetrician who demanded a $200 registration fee, plus $500 for delivery, plus the cost of accommodation, use of the OR supplies and medicines. When she arrived at Howard Hospital, a series of emergencies delayed her operation until December 11, when she was already in labour, but there were no complications and the woman delivered a healthy baby.

Government neglect had not only strained maternal health resources to the limit, but the abrogation of health care services further compromised patients suffering from tuberculosis and HIV/AIDS.

The public-sector TB program in Zimbabwe had been in sharp decline since 2006, but by 2008, the national laboratory for testing was reduced to one technician and the data collection system had ceased in 2006 as well. The absence of testing and interruptions in treatment increased the chances of contracting the most severe and drug-resistant form of the disease, particularly amongst those affected with HIV/AIDS. As the team discovered, this could lead to a lasting public health catastrophe greater than the spread of cholera.

2008 would be a year that many people in Zimbabwe would like to forget. That year of man-made disasters, Paul Thistle had earned his awards and more.

2009

Human rights watchdogs identified the crisis as "the ruling ZANU-PF leadership's diversion of resources away from basic public health towards sustaining its illegitimate rule, personal enrichment and oppressing its MDC opponents."

With 126 mission hospitals and clinics scattered throughout Zimbabwe's 10 provinces, these privately-run facilities account for 68% of healthcare delivery in rural areas, and nowhere was the collapse of the country's healthcare system more acute than in critical care. With the closing of the two main hospitals in Harare, critical care and everything else fell into the hands of mission hospitals.

Howard Hospital's annual operating grant from the Ministry of Health in Zimbabwe would normally represent the equivalent of US$40,000 for medical and surgical services. But in 2009, it was reduced to $2,000—to care for 155,000 patient visits. As Paul noted, "a lollipop per child in the doctor's room would consume our budget."

Trying to communicate with the rest of civilization was also frustrating. Howard Hospital had no conventional telephone service since the middle of 2008 when the heavy rains unleashed the poles and sent them hurtling down the rivers of water. The copper wires also went missing and there were no repairmen to fix the problem. For many months, the only reliable way of sending a message from Howard to the outside world was a precarious 85 km trip to Harare to connect to dial-up e-mail. The one spark of good news was the restoration of Internet and cell phone service which replaced the need for copper wires.

Summer brought further honours to Paul Thistle. On July 2, while on furlough in Canada, he was invited to the University of Windsor where he accepted the honorary degree of Doctor of Laws, honoris causa. In addressing the graduating class, he encouraged the students to serve their communities wherever they may be. Through their efforts, he said, the world would become a better place in the future. In his words, "we must always remain focused on our purpose, not our problems." That year, he also received the Paul Harris Fellow Award from Rotary International.

CHAPTER 9

Working at Howard (It Takes a Village)

Vision without action is but a daydream….

PAUL THISTLE IN SPEECH TO ROTARIANS

LONG BEFORE DR. THISTLE RECEIVED honorary recognition for his humanitarian contributions, volunteers and staff were already familiar with his exceptional skills.

His "great hands" were at work every hour of the day, six days a week plus Sundays when trips to the emergency room were common. Throughout the years, Paul was grateful for the steady influx of volunteers who came to Howard to learn from his skills and share in his compassion.

Marnie Mitchell, a regional pharmacist with Health Canada in the First Nations and Inuit Health Branch worked with Paul to secure funding for Tariro HIV Clinic and took part in the HIV research program on site. Working at Howard, she says, changed her life—witnessing how a dedicated few could have an enormous impact on the life of many. In a letter to the Salvation Army, she states, "we donate significant funds to Howard because we trust that the money in Paul and Pedrinah's hands will be put to good use."

Dr. Vanessa Litman, who volunteered at Howard from December 2008 to March 2010, stated that she had yet to meet another doctor who is as comfortable practicing general medicine as Dr. Thistle. As she observed, his skill set is truly amazing—general surgery, ultrasonography, pediatrics, adult medicine and infectious diseases, in addition to his specialty, obstetrics and gynecology.

In 2010, Dr. David Shaye, a Facial Plastic and Reconstructive Surgery fellow, spent one month in surgical training at Howard. He was impressed with its true community—with the goal of self-improvement through education, health care and faith. In his words, the nursery school, elementary school and teaching hospital formed a vibrant community that may have lacked resources, but was rich in heart. Howard Hospital, he said, was a shining star in this world.

Dr. Tushar Mehta travelled to Howard in 2007 with two other medical students from St. Joseph's Health Centre in Toronto. Previous to volunteering at Howard, he had also worked in India and other parts of Africa; but, he vowed, "Howard was the best run hospital in any developing country that he had come across."

Dr. Lori Lichtom, a clinical psychologist from Ann Arbor, Michigan and a long supporter of Howard Hospital's various programs worried about the orphans and child-run families left behind when their parents died of AIDS. Howard was able to support children going to school for $5 per term.

A steady group of volunteers from Peterborough—Jennifer Reid, her husband, Larry Gillman, and Brian Nichols had travelled to Howard since 2001. Jennifer Reid is a midwife and Brian Nichols is a psychotherapist. Throughout the years, Howard's patients benefitted from their "hands on" approach—Reid delivering babies and Nichols' ability to bring relief from pain by sitting with patients, filling the wards with joyful music, and providing Thai massage. With the ravages of HIV/AIDS, and the fear and stigma associated with it, many patients live without the human touch. Relatives and friends desert them, so no one comes to visit. Volunteers, then, serve a vital role in providing fundamental human contact. Larry Gillman organized yearly benefits to attract donors. Between the free labour they provided and the dollars they brought in, volunteers were an essential element to the hospital's survival.

Sarah and Chris LeBouthillier are, in their own words, spouses, best friends, adventurers, health care professionals and thrill seekers.

Sarah is a physiotherapist at a rehab hospital in Toronto, working with individuals who have suffered traumatic brain injuries at work or in motor vehicle collisions. Chris was a Physician Assistant student at McMaster University who decided to take a leap of faith and complete his final clinical placements at Howard Hospital in Zimbabwe. In the summer of 2011, the LeBouthilliers travelled to Howard Hospital to further their training and spend time in other parts of Africa. This was Sarah's third visit to Howard Hospital and Chris's first. She had come to support a new initiative to train rehabilitation aides. Chris, who had completed placements in emergency medicine, internal medicine, surgery, psychiatry, family medicine and Ob-Gyn, was excited to use some of these skills in a completely new environment. They spent five weeks at Howard Hospital from July 28 to August 24, 2011.

Their five weeks at Howard were full of surprises and memories that will last a lifetime. Though accommodation at Howard is very basic, it was plenty enough for their needs. With most work days extending to eleven hours, they didn't spent much time in their 250 sq. ft. bachelor apartment, but they didn't complain. Even in their tiny abode, where the power goes out several times a day, where you have to walk two kilometres to get water when the taps run dry, where you have to boil water or bring it in from a working tap to draw a bath, without TV or radio or a reliable internet connection, they knew they were still living a cushy life.

Unlike the locals, they had the luxury of indoor plumbing, a sink with running water and a flush toilet, something even middle-class Zimbabweans don't have. They didn't have to walk two to seven kilometres to school or stay overnight to study because there are no lights or electricity at home. They didn't have to grow their own vegetables or struggle when the rains don't come or because the 20 dollars a month they are paid isn't enough to feed their family. There was, however, an animal in their ceiling. Sometimes they'd hear it fighting with another animal up there. "It was either a rat or a cat," Chris says, "but neither of us was going up there to confirm which it was."

In fact, the whole place was teeming with animals of one type or another. Goats and chickens that belong to people are let loose to feed. Outside the derelict new hospital cows grazed on the grass, keeping it short. Even the operating room was not immune. Although the theatre was clean and sterilized, rats scrambled freely over the feet of the staff and climbed onto shelves. The staff were used to it, but visitors were startled. At Howard, though, everything had a solution. Bring in a cat, and the problem was solved. This is what Dr. Thistle referred to as the hospital's CAT scan—"a feline that prowls the wards and scans everybody." The other solution? Wear boots and you hardly notice what's beneath you.

Mice, in fact, are a Shona delicacy. Corn grows tall in the surrounding fields and on any bit of arable land available, because the government allows it to be planted on any government-owned property for free. Amazingly, no one steals another's food or animals. Although people here are, for the most part, desperately poor, they are happy and polite. That is the Shona way.

Other food grows in abundance—onions, cabbage, tomatoes, potatoes, bananas and oranges, most of them picked the same day they're bought. For the most part the couple were able to fill their stomachs with the amazing local produce, eggs, bread and meat from the surrounding area. As they can attest, the peanut butter, a lot of it homemade by locals, is so fresh its container is still warm from the roasted peanuts. What's more, the food is reasonable. Bananas cost 16 for $1.00. In November and December, when mangoes are in season, $1 buys you 20. With a little help from hospital staff or other volunteers, Chris became adept at slaughtering chickens the same day they are eaten for dinner. In Sarah's words: "It takes the 100-mile diet to a whole new level when the majority of your food is less than 50 kilometres away."

It's a king's feast compared to the local diet called Sazda, a mixture made from corn flour that resembles mashed potatoes, but thicker. It has little taste, but takes on the flavor of whatever it's served with. Locals eat it every day for lunch and dinner; sometimes once a day if that's all there is.

In their five weeks at Howard, Sarah and Chris's duties covered the hospital's full range of services, leaving them exhausted at the end of their 11 and 12 hour days, but with plenty of memories to take back home. Luckily, they each kept a diary and shared notes at the end of each long day.

The Howard is divided into several different departments and services and each one tells its own story.

The Children's Ward

There are no bracelets here, not even plastic ones. Instead of wearing identification on their wrist, children have theirs taped on their forehead.

The Therapeutic Feeding Ward feeds malnourished children suffering from HIV, tuberculosis, thrush. This is where mothers bring their children to receive supplemental nutrition and feeding. As Chris learned, many of the children who arrive at the hospital are 2-3 years old, but look like small babies. Fortunately, with the help of the therapeutic feeding program, most will recover and many will thrive.

Cosmos is a 7-month old boy, weighing 10 pounds and unable to hold his head up or sit up on his own. Little could be done for him until his weight increases. Tino is two years old, but barely the size of a one-year-old and hasn't learned to walk. Sarah has taught his grandmother how to use a pediatric walker and now he's running around with a smile on his face.

Shelton is 11 years old and afflicted with cerebral palsy. In Canada, Sarah's homeland, Shelton would be zooming around in a power wheelchair, receiving Botox injections to decrease the rigidity that prevents him from sitting on his own without help. He'd be attending school, receiving daily therapy and socializing with other kids with disabilities.

Shelton is the son of one of the rehabilitation aides, Caroline. They live in a hut with no electricity or running water, but Sarah finds him enjoying the sun on the veranda outside his home on a road that is inaccessible by car. Caroline is a single mother passionate about giving her son the best life possible, which is one of the reasons she wanted to become a rehabilitation aide

The Rehab Aides

There are 13 of them. Part of Sarah's job is seeing how the rehabilitation program is working. Aides work on a part-time basis, six hours per day. Their job is to rotate between the community, following up on patients and carrying out exercise programs in patient's homes. They bike up to 20 kilometres to get to outlying patients, travelling in the heat of the day to reach the hardest corners of the area, spending six hours a day to care for their patients. The road is hard—unpaved and filled with potholes. What's worse, Sarah's bike has no brakes. Her first patient is five kilometres away and a 500 metre walk. He is a 17-year-old paraplegic named Innocent, who is cared for by his grandmother. The aides' job is to educate her about pressure sores; then the aides carry out his exercise program. Innocent is isolated from friends and unable to attend school. But he has a great spirit and managed to climb up a steep rocky slope after his injury.

There are many other inspiring patients whom the aides are able to help. A 40-year-old woman with advanced hip arthritis and one leg longer than the other and in obvious pain, who limps to relieve the pain, is fitted for a forearm crutch. After molding a heel lift out of Plaster of Paris to insert in her shoe, the woman's gait is much smoother and more stable.

In another instance, a 70-year-old woman comes in with a walking stick that keeps slipping on the floors. Feeling weak and unstable, the woman is unaware that anyone over 65 in Zimbabwe gets free medicine and equipment. After she's given a rollator walker, a huge smile comes to her face. The walker is beautiful and she wishes that she could take it home. When Sarah tells the woman she can keep it, she shakes Sarah's hand, thanking her over and over again.

While Sarah struggles over the rough terrain by bicycle, Chris is busy in the outpatient department with Dr. Thistle. As Chris discovers, Thistle is the only person in the hospital capable of operating an ultrasound comfortably, and he is teaching Chris how to use it.

He's already completed many obstetrical, abdominal and prostate ultrasounds and is anxious to learn more if only the power would stay on. With the power going out 4 or 5 times a day, usually for 10 to 15 minutes each time, some women are having to wait up to 4 hours for the procedure.

It's not long before Chris gets his chance working alongside the Howard's three surgeons in the OR. As every volunteer has learned, the one thing you can count on at Howard is a steady stream of patients. Just when you think it can't get any busier, when your back is about to break, when your eyes are about to close, and your legs are giving out, there's always an emergency to keep you going.

During one hectic Sunday alone, there were 12 babies born, so Chris is learning to do ultrasounds with increased efficiency. One night, at 11 p.m. they are called to the OR to perform a Caesarean section when a woman's uterus ruptures internally, calling for immediate delivery of the baby so they can do the repair. In the end, mother and baby are well and happy.

One of the complicating factors for doctors in Zimbabwe is polygamy, which is relatively common. In a civil ceremony, men pledge to not take on any more wives than they have. In a traditional wedding, men can have as many wives as they want.

For pregnant women with sexually-transmitted diseases, the protocol is to treat her and her partner and educate them about protective behaviours. One woman asks "what do we do about the other woman in the relationship?' When she is told that the other "wife" would have to be treated too, the couple decide to remove her from the relationship.

Mondays are typically very busy in the outpatients department. Now that Dr. Thistle is back from furlough, the aisles are clogged with people who have waited for his return. At 5 p.m. there is still no relief. Some will wait until 8 p.m. to see a doctor.

With no access to blood sugar monitors, diabetes advances quickly here. Many people ignore their health problems for a long time, but there are several factors involved. It could be financial or cultural or just having so many other things to contend with. But by the time they are seen, their choices are dire—submit to amputation or die from infection. Death is no stranger to any age here. A 26-year-old man with suspected meningitis is found dead when nurses try to wake him.

The surgeons do what they can. Today, Chris helps out with a bone resection of a diabetic foot. Another patient requires amputation of the leg below the knee. Gangrenous fingers too often have to be amputated. Just like the steady flow of patients, the lessons never stop. You do what you can and keep on going.

For these Good Samaritans who gave of their time and energy to Howard, it was time well spent that will stay with them forever.

CHAPTER 10

One Step Forward Two Back

―

"Fall seven times, get up eight."

JAPANESE PROVERB

2010
By 2010, PAUL WAS MARKING his fifteenth year at Howard Hospital. Hundreds of thousands of patients had passed through its weathered doors. With a decade and a half of instruction for medical, nursing and midwifery students, the vicissitudes of administration, research and community projects out in the villages behind him, he could reflect on Howard's accomplishments. He was especially proud of the decline in HIV prevalence provided by the Tariro clinic—from 27.5% in 1999 to 11.1% a decade later in 2009—lower than the national figures of 13.9%.

The new year began with rays of optimism peeking through the dark clouds of the country's political and economic crisis. And despite the dysfunction of the new coalition government, its citizens were cautiously content. Having food returned to store shelves and hard currency in their pockets as well as solid jobs and a regular income, made a real difference to their lives.

On the downside, the semi-privatization of education and health care services meant that they paid for their most basic needs. A child's school fees could exceed an entire family's income.

As institutions adopted a cost-recovery plan, health care remained unaffordable for the majority of people. Health insurance for people who, if lucky enough to be employed, might earn a dollar a day in wages, remained unaffordable.

Paul faced a host of persistent challenges, both inside and outside the hospital. The problem at Howard and thousands of other health centres across Africa is not just a shortage of technology and therapeutics, but brain drain and brain fatigue, not to mention wear and tear on body and soul. Some 90% of medical students leave Zimbabwe after graduation and the doctors who remain migrate to practice in urban centres for a better lifestyle. In a province of 1.5 million people, he remained the only obstetrician-gynecologist.

In rural Chiweshe, Howard Hospital was bursting at the seams. Paul reasoned that the hospital could employ more professionals if they could offer basic accommodation and incentives. His hope was to start a new four-unit housing block soon. And there were other challenges that he could do nothing about. Howard Hospital's persistent power outages meant performing surgery under the most stressful conditions.

One day, with electricity blinking, Paul and his team proceeded with a hysterectomy for a 30-pound ovarian tumor, an emergency caesarean for a ruptured uterus, and a laparotomy for an infant's twisted bowel. Two of his most pressing challenges remained human resources and crowded space. There were never more than two or three full-time doctors at Howard and only forty nurses to cover the complete general medical and surgical services, in addition to outreach within the community. As a result, it was necessary to task shift duties to nurses' aides, Red Cross volunteers and others in order to manage the pharmacy, X-ray, operating theatre, laboratory and home-based care.

In spite of the challenges, Thistle felt they had much to be thankful for. They had managed to replace the two Zimbabwean doctors and the handful of nurses lost in the previous year and were busy teaching the new recruits some of the advanced life-preserving skills that were needed in the bush.

Volunteers continued to make the trek to Howard. The guest accommodation was filled to the brim and supporters continued to provide much-needed resources with containers of medicine, surgical supplies and food.

The Thistle children were healthy and doing well in school. James was learning to play the guitar, while Alexander cared for his class's pet hamster. Pedrinah continued to juggle responsibilities as mother, nurse educator, counsellor and, as Paul says, "just about everything else." She volunteered to lead a support group of professionals living with HIV/AIDS. Despite the drive to educate people about the disease, the stigma of being affected with the virus and discrimination persisted, especially among teachers and nurses within their community. Pedrinah wanted to address this much-neglected area of ministry.

In the face of the obvious difficulties and unforeseen challenges, Paul's commitment remained strong. The only way to survive the rigours of long hours, mental and physical fatigue and keep plodding year after year was to put one foot in front of the other—step by step. As Paul discovered, the key element to survival was vision, a need to see beyond the problems of today to the possibilities of tomorrow. "By the grace of the Lord," he vowed, "we will keep the doors of Howard Hospital open—or at least the ones that are still on hinges. Living in a world of privatized medicine in Zimbabwe, we are obliged to remember that a sick person is not just a paying customer but a human spirit with a will to live and a sense of dignity and personality."

2011

Those small steps led to bigger initiatives and in 2011, Paul was able to establish several new community programs such as cervical cancer screening, sponsored by Rotary, a physiotherapy aide project, and a support project for young mothers living with HIV/AIDS and their infants.

Nevertheless, the hospital's resources were severely stretched. Outpatient services had risen to treating 110,000 people. The number of operations had tripled to 4,000 a year in the previous decade due to the demand for affordable surgical care in Zimbabwe. Once again, through the generosity and care of outside donors, Howard found a way to provide that care and more.

In early February of that year, three volunteers from Peterborough made the trip to Howard. One of them, Brian Nichols, was an annual visitor who arrived with carpenter Jeff Mathers who had come to work on much-needed repairs around the hospital. Sadly, the lack of building materials dashed his hopes of completing the more ambitious tasks he had in mind. Accompanying the group this time was reporter Galen Eagle from the Peterborough Examiner, who was there to do a story on Paul and life at Howard Hospital. In part of his 8-page feature entitled ""Surviving in Zimbabwe" Eagle covers a typical day in the life of a missionary doctor.

As the reporter quickly learned, following Dr. Thistle required an early rise and a quick step. In the space of a few hours, Thistle covered a lot of ground: visiting children, checking on new mothers in the Maternity ward, attending to 80 patients in the women's and men's wards before heading into the operating theatre at 11:30 a.m. In between he was expected to fit in a meeting with administrators, and all this before noon. In the brief time he has with a patient, he has learned to listen well. He must assess, reassure, counsel and decide on a course of action. As he told the reporter, "If I spend five minutes on each patient in the wards, I'd be here for more than three hours. I don't have time for that. I have a golf game this afternoon and a squash match." This is Paul's sense of humour, which is never far from the surface even as he keeps up an exhausting pace.

Eagle talked with patients he encountered who were thankful for Thistle's care: Roselyn Ndawona, a 22-year-old mother with a 5-year-old son who had a large burn on his back from a cooking oil accident; a 51-year-old man who was being treated for a chronic illness in Harare, but made the trip from Harare to see Dr. Thistle because, as he told the reporter, Dr. Thistle cares. "Here is better than Harare. Dr. Thistle, he talks to the people. He loves the people. He doesn't throw people out."

In the operating theatre, Eagle watched as Paul attended to a young girl with a broken arm. She is put to sleep with Ketamine, a hallucinogen widely-used in mission hospitals because it's easy to administer, is fast-acting and easier to monitor post-surgery. While a nurse pulls on the girl's shoulder, Paul pulls on the broken arm, setting it back in place. Although his specialty is obstetrics and gynecology, a far cry from orthopedics, Thistle has become equally adept at setting bones. When he is in orthopedic mode, his staff refer to him as "Captain Crunch."

It's close to 5 p.m. before Paul exits the operating room and heads for his office. There's another line of 25 patients waiting to see him, including expectant mothers waiting for ultrasounds. Due to staff restraints, he is the only person qualified to perform this basic procedure. He has no idea what time he will finish. He will stay until the last patient is seen. Treating the sick is not a start and stop-type job. You can't put down your scalpel, go for a coffee and come back and close up a wound when you're finished. And if something goes wrong, there are very few options; but the solution is left up to you.

Tonight is a special night. Pedrinah is organizing a feast for all of the hospital's visitors. Included are the Thistles' four guests from

Peterborough as well as volunteer medical personnel. Finally, at the end of another long day, Thistle walks across the compound to join his wife and their guests.

As Galen Eagle reported, this is just another day in the life of a missionary doctor. Not only are conditions rough, supplies and support meagre, they also have to find ways to work around political and economic restrictions or outside of contentious rules. Each day brings joy and sorrow, not necessarily in equal amounts. The losses are hard to bear—mothers dying in childbirth, babies lost to malnutrition, men and women succumbing to disease long before their time—but there is little time to mourn. Tomorrow is another day, with another line of patients, with another set of new challenges, but Dr. Thistle will do it all again and return to his family each night.

In spite of the rigours of the day he remains positive with his sense of humour intact. As he tells Galen Eagle: "If you didn't laugh, you would cry and you can't spend your entire years of service weeping. You deal with all the horror, but you have to work that out and see if you can improve your service. But when it fails, you have to be able to pick up the pieces and move on to treat the next person and the next. By the Grace of God, the majority of people who come to Howard walk out alive on their own two feet."

———

In April 2011, Betty Nyakwima, one of Howard's HIV counsellors, was struggling with a heart problem that required surgery not available in Zimbabwe. Paul arranged for the surgery to be done at Sunnybrook Medical Centre in Toronto, but before Betty could make the cross-world trip to Toronto, the money for her flight and accommodation had to be found. Paul put out an appeal to friends in Canada, who responded with enthusiasm, holding benefit concerts and collecting personal donations from interested parties. The $30,000 raised were beyond expectations. Due to the generous support of donors, Betty was able to fly to Toronto where she received a double heart valve transplant. Following months of recovery in Canada, she was able to return to Zimbabwe and resume her counseling work once again. As Paul said, "When small stones move, avalanches happen."

On annual furloughs to Canada, in between fundraising, Paul reconnected with family and friends. That year he was able to visit Betty Nyakwima who was still recovering in Toronto before her return to Zimbabwe in June.

While in Canada, the Thistles' home base is Paul's parents' home in Scarborough, Ontario. The family's country property in rural Ontario just north of Peterborough, is where they can truly relax and spend time fishing and swimming. The boys are in their element here, especially spending time fishing with their grandfather or trolling the lake in the boat. The boys love playing cricket and soccer at summer sports camps or, for something completely different, lacing up a pair of skates for a whirl around the ice rink. The cottage also allows Paul to reconnect with his friends and supporters in the Peterborough area, just visiting, or attending fundraisers that the group has organized while Paul is in Canada. But, as always, his few respites were brief. Their furlough was also focused towards the future of Howard and how to keep it going. This meant summer breaks filled with an ever-expanding round of conferences and councils, speaking engagements to introduce the work of Howard to new congregations and concerned individuals. But that's not all. In order to pay for trips and schooling and just keeping the family afloat, Paul fills in for vacationing physicians at hospitals in Scarborough and Whitby, Ontario.

Back at Howard Hospital, the focus continued to be on people, not programs or protests. In order to survive and be able to continue treating people, God's surgeons in Africa need boundless energy and forward thinking. They need to be able to think on their feet, adapt to local conditions and customs, the lack of equipment and supplies and learn how to survive in a state of permanent exhaustion.

For Paul, his foundation was his faith and an ability to look to the future, not the past. A steady influx of volunteers was a tremendous help, providing a break from the throngs of outpatients and string of surgeries. There was even time to learn new techniques thanks to a visiting urologist in August.

Pedrinah, in addition to her duties as mother, midwifery instructor and mentor, continued her studies towards a master of nursing science.

Even small progress was reason for hope. There was hope for the completion of the new hospital. There was progress in the development of a new effective follow-up program for HIV-positive mothers who delivered their babies at Howard, as well as their infants and their families. In September, the hospital's Eyes for Zimbabwe camp performed a record 168 cataract operations in three days.

But for every success there are the inevitable failures of the system. Dadirai, a 37-year-old mother of four whose husband ran away when she tested positive for HIV, was admitted to Howard four months pregnant. She was also emaciated from tuberculosis, pneumonia, gastroenteritis and anemia. A normal person's blood cell count would be above 700, but Dadirai's immune system was so depleted, her count was down to 40.

Paul and Pedrinah didn't believe this mother would survive her pregnancy, but with the help of TB and antiretroviral treatment, combined with nutritional psychosocial and spiritual support, she pulled through. She gave birth to a healthy girl whom she named "Ropafadzo," which means "Blessing" in Shona. Sadly, blessings are not enough. Howard's community volunteers reported that Dadirai had a sudden onset of flu symptoms three months after delivery; and because there was no affordable ambulance in the village, or a telephone to dial '911,' she died a day later. Thankfully, the little blessing "Ropafadzo" was HIV negative and thriving.

By November of 2011, even with the adoption of the U.S. dollar and South African Rand, the Zimbabwean economy was still in deep decline. People who had earned an average of $760 US per annum in the 1990s earned less than half by 2007. Government spending on public health care also declined, from $34 to $7 per person per annum compared to $1,800 in Canada.

2012

2012 began much like any other year, with a fresh influx of volunteers to Howard Hospital.

Early on, ominous signals were on the horizon when a large Canadian government grant intended for HIV/AIDS treatment was rejected because the local leadership refused to comply with the regulations pertaining to its use. The hospital administrator, on instructions from Salvation Army leaders in Harare, wanted complete control over how the funds were spent, but this was against the rules and regulations set down by the Canadian government in the awarding of grants, so the money was refused. For Paul and his medical colleagues who had fought so hard to win the award, this was the final straw in a long line of disagreements over funding to keep things running at Howard. The loss of $250,000 to a hospital in North America would be significant enough, but to the HIV/AIDS sufferers it was designed to help, the loss was shattering.

In April 2012, rumours began to surface that Dr. Thistle was being transferred. When villagers objected by holding demonstrations outside the hospital, the local Army officials assured the community, through their headman, that the rumour was not true.

A glimmer of hope persisted for the completion of the new hospital. A $3 million donation from the U.S. in 2011 brought renewed optimism that the hospital would finally be completed, but again there were problems. The engineers and contractors hired to work on the completion hyper-inflated the bill to $9 million. The team who arrived from Salvation Army headquarters in August intended to search for a new firm after the previous one was fired.

In early June, Paul, Pedrinah and their sons left for their annual furlough and continued to do as they had always done: meeting with donors and supporters, and raising awareness of the needs of the people of Zimbabwe cared for by Howard Hospital. Paul was able to assure his supporters that most of his visions for improving health care for the people of Chiweshe had been accomplished. They were not merely dreams, but reality on many fronts. Preventative measures to reduce the spread of HIV were working. The prevalence of HIV had dropped from 29 percent in 1999 down to 5.7 percent by April 2012. The Tariro (the Shona word for Hope) Clinic was up and running at full capacity with 3,000 people on treatment and another 4,000 decentralized to Howard's district clinics. As a result, AIDS, the dreaded word associated with shame and suffering, had now become a chronic disease that was manageable, much like diabetes or hypertension.

Still, HIV, pregnancy and poverty continued to be a triple threat. Unity, a 30-year-old mother of three from a village 15 miles away, arrived at Howard HIV positive. She had no antenatal care and, therefore, no access to life-saving antiretroviral drugs. On admittance to Howard, she was in a coma following fits at home that had occurred for several days. She suffered from eclampsia, a common condition seen among mothers in rural Africa, but there was no affordable means of transport to get her to the hospital sooner. Her twins had already died in the womb. To make matters worse, it was the middle of the night and the hospital had no oxygen. And there was no money in the bank to purchase oxygen. Unity died a few hours after arrival.

This, Paul says, "is the straw that breaks the camel's back, but when your back is broken from a night of broken rest, you still have to get up for work the next morning because there are 100 more waiting in the queue. And when your get up and go just got up and left, what motivates you to continue on is professionalism, a sense of duty, compassion, and that glimmer of vision."

But, again, others were there to pick up the broken pieces of this rural hospital and put it back together again. The generosity of groups like the Rotarians in Ontario and British Columbia provided grants to support laboratory services, the provision of antiretroviral drugs to treat pregnant women, and general medical and surgical supplies to Howard and its neighbouring clinics. Bicycles were provided for home-based care volunteers. Diesel fuel to fire up the generator and a four wheel drive vehicle was provided for Howard's community care program and an ambulance for village patients in distress. Paul's Peterborough supporters responded enthusiastically with a huge fundraiser in June to raise money for the completion of accommodation for volunteer professional staff.

On Friday, July 13, the Thistles left Toronto bound for Zimbabwe. They arrived home two days later with renewed enthusiasm, unaware that an ill wind was about to blow their way. Nor that its impact would change their lives forever.

Great Zimbabwe – The Great Enclosure

The Enclosure – Great Zimbabwe

'The Smoke that Thunders' - Victoria Falls, Zimbabwe

The Old Howard Hospital – Front Entrance

Dr. Paul Thistle

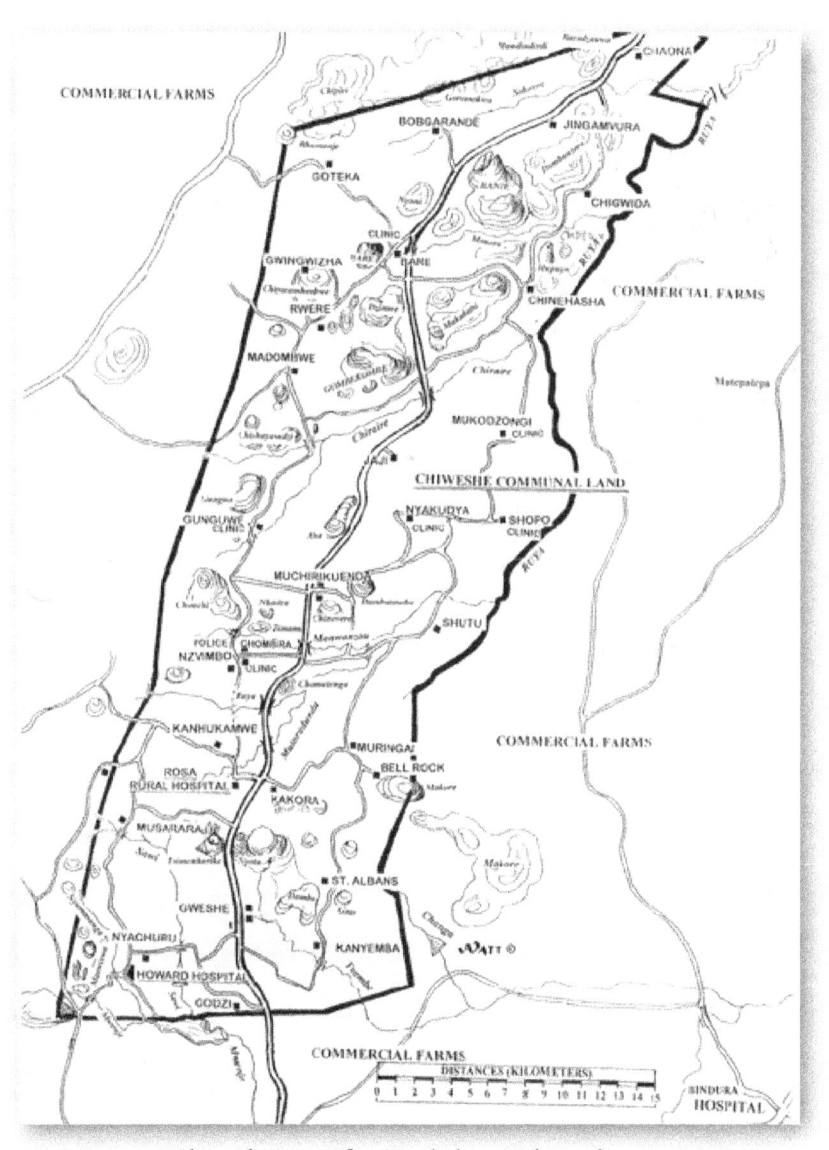

Chiweshe map after Zimbabwe Independence

Mufuka conjoined twins waiting for surgery – March 2005

Déjà vu – Tinotenda and Tinashe Mufuka – Age 11

Hockey – Zimbabwe style – Paul and son James

Cry for Chiweshe

Chiweshe protest against Dr. Thistle's Marching Order

Chiweshe Villagers Supporting Dr. Thistle

The Three Amigos – From Left - Shirley Watkinson,
Dr. Lorraine Irvine and Jan Corley

Dr. (Grandma) Lorraine visiting school children

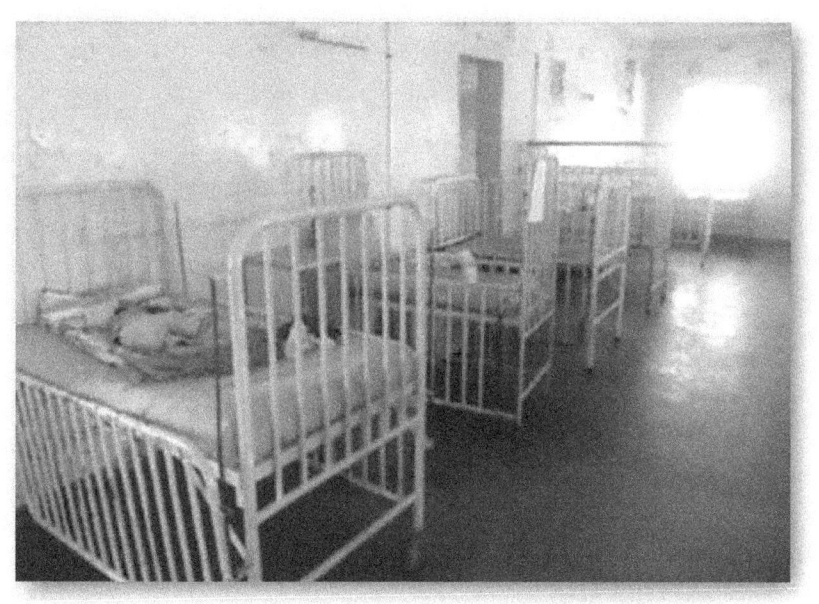

Photo taken October 2013 – Children's Ward – Howard Hospital

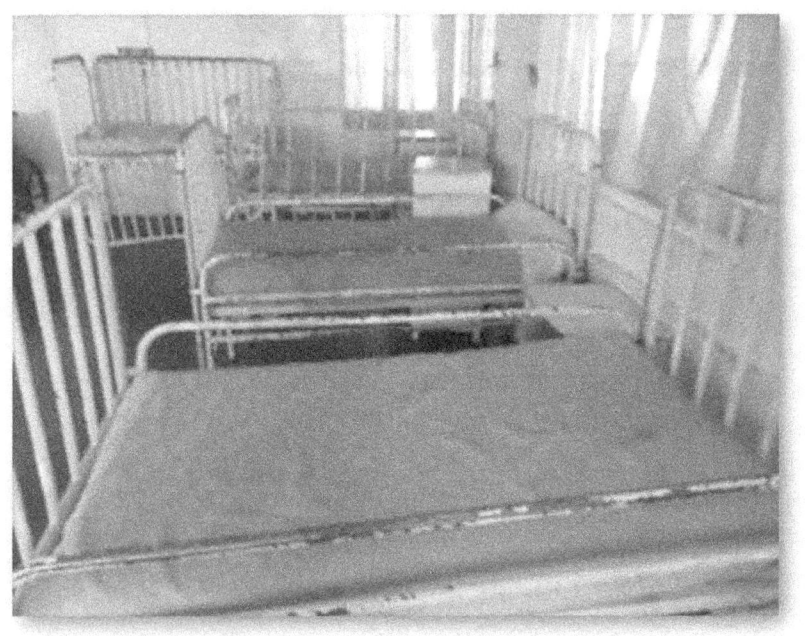

October 2013 – Children's Ward – Howard Hospital

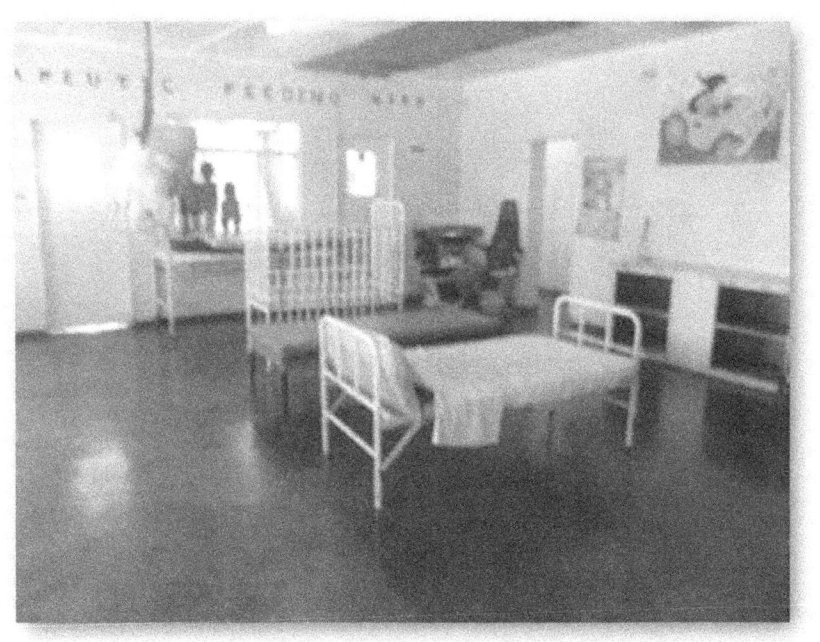

October 2013 – Children's Ward – Howard Hospital

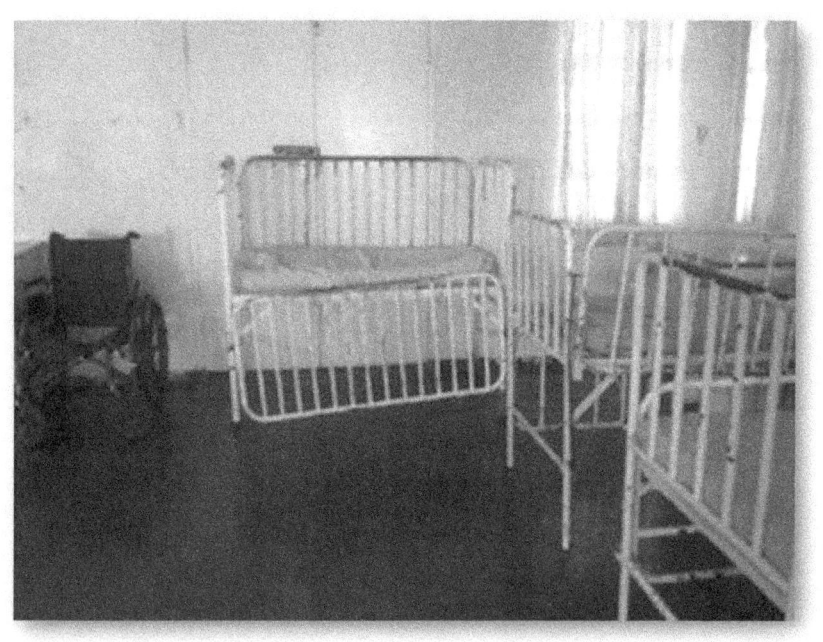

Tina Ivany

October 2013 – Children's Ward – Howard Hospital

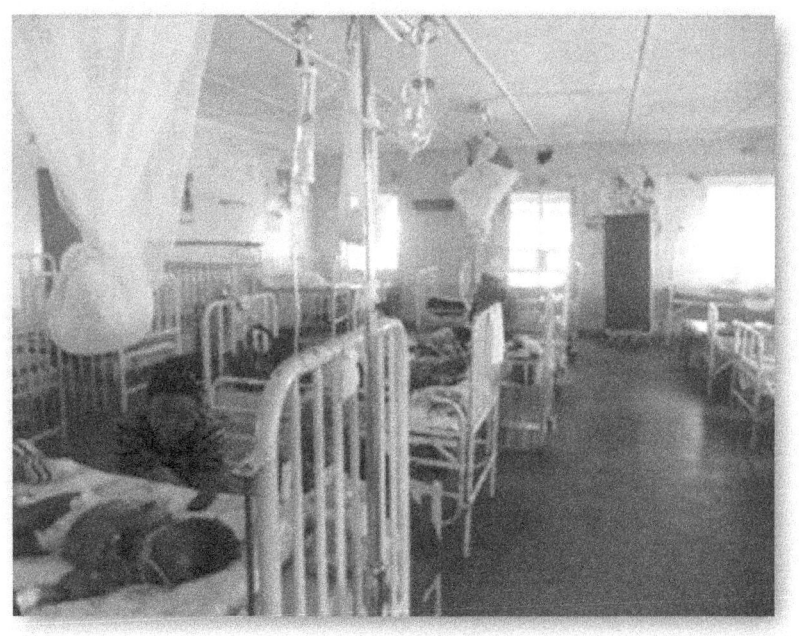

October 2013 – Children's Ward – Howard Hospital

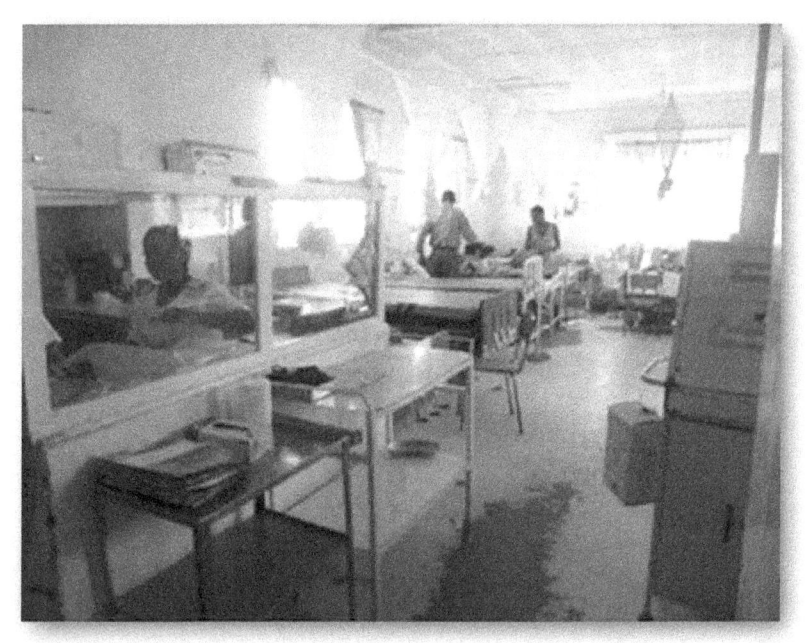

October 2013 – Male Ward – Howard Hospital

October 2013 – Outpatients Department – Howard Hospital

Karanda Mission Hospital

Outpatients Department – Karanda Mission Hospital

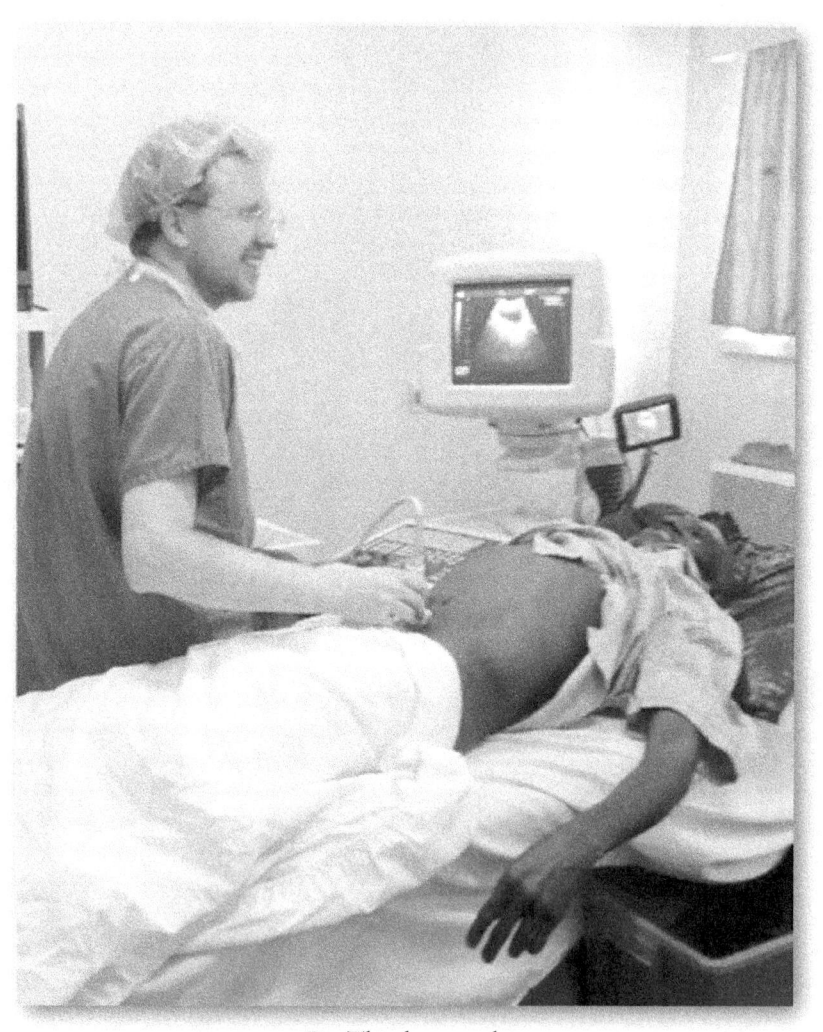

Dr. Thistle at work

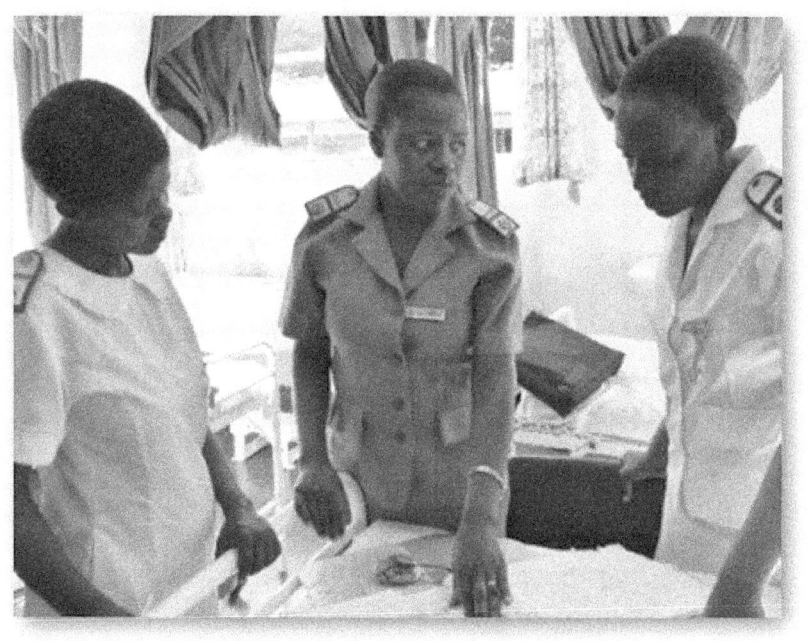

Pedrinah Thistle teaching midwives

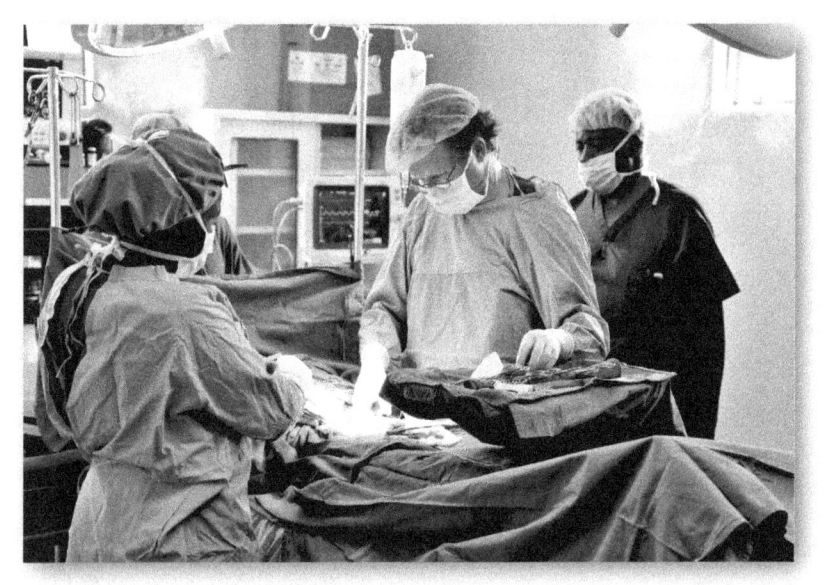

The Theatre of Operations – Karanda

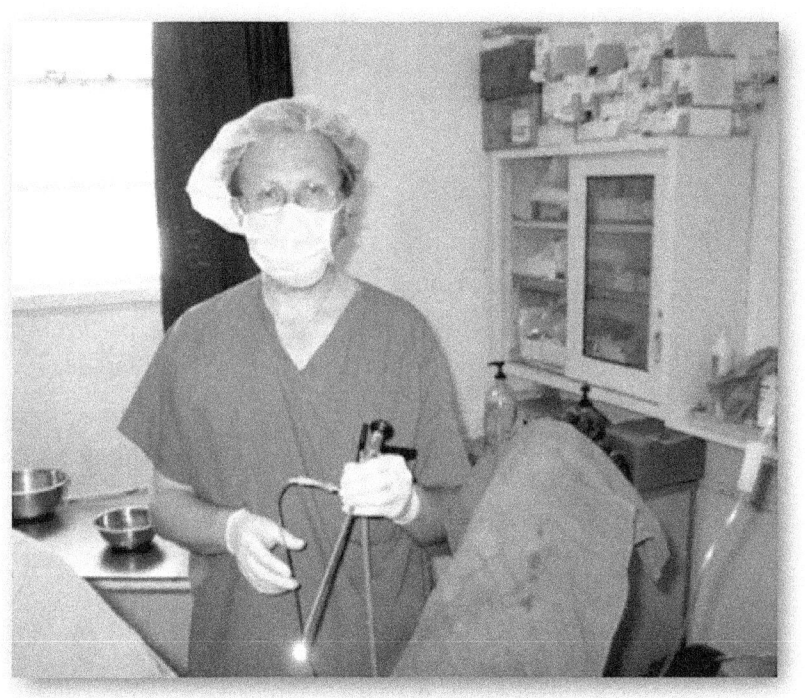

Dr. Thistle and The Guilding Light

The washed out road to Karanda

Sunday School at Karanda

Party for Karanda orphans

Salvation Army Headquarters, London, England

New Howard Hospital opening, November 2014

New Howard Hospital opening ceremony, November 2014

Tina Ivany

New Howard Hospital front entrance

The Thistle Family May 2015 – Paul, Pedrinah,
James, Alexander and Andrew Jacob

Part II
Saving Howard Hospital

CHAPTER 11

The Gathering Storm

―

It is my purpose, as one who lived and acted in these days, first to show how easily the tragedy of the Second World War could have been prevented; how the malice of the wicked was reinforced by the weakness of the virtuous ...

WINSTON CHURCHILL

AUGUST 18, 2012
AFTER BEING FORCED TO LEAVE Howard Hospital, Paul and Pedrinah and their boys made their way to the home of Pedrinah's brother, Gutu, and his family, in Harare. This arrangement allowed the boys to return to school and for their parents to collect their bearings. The Thistles appealed to anyone who would listen to remain in Zimbabwe, while supporters and donors in Canada began to mobilize their own small army.

One of Paul Thistle's staunchest supporters is Dr. Michael Silverman, a specialist in Internal Medicine and Infectious Diseases, Assistant Professor at the University of Toronto's Faculty of Medicine, as well as a Global Scholar in International and Public Health. He began working with Paul Thistle in 1999 and helped him establish the anti-retroviral drug program for expectant mothers infected with HIV.

As soon as he heard of the Thistles' dilemma, Dr. Silverman swung into action by teaming up with others supporters of Howard Hospital: Sarah Zelcer, Director of International Projects of Ve'ahavta, The Canadian Jewish Humanitarian Relief Committee, and a group from Peterborough who volunteered at Howard Hospital and held annual fundraisers to benefit the hospital. They formed a group called the Inter-faith Friends of Howard Hospital (IFFHH) and began to make plans for a concerted campaign to save the hospital they had long supported and restore proper healthcare to the people of Chiweshe.

In Calgary, Canada, Dr. James Watt was also busy contending with a flood of e-mails from fellow physicians and other members of the Salvation Army seeking clarity and explanations about the contentious situation at Howard. Staff at the hospital had been silenced: ordered not to speak out under threat of dismissal. But Dr. Watt would not be silenced and waged his own campaign, hammering away at Salvation Army Canadian Headquarters to provide answers to the disturbing questions that swarmed around the Howard debacle. He also maintained regular contact with Zimbabwe to gather first-hand reports and regular updates of what was really going on.

Letters of appeal were sent to the head of the Salvation Army, General Linda Bond, and even to President Mugabe from numerous other organizations and foundations involved in humanitarian relief. These included the World Health Organization, the Stephen Lewis Foundation, Ve'ahavta, and the Head of the United Church in Canada. However, none of the letters addressed to the General in London were ever responded to directly, but handed over to other people. A gag order was placed on all officers world-wide not to discuss Howard Hospital or mention the name of Dr. Paul Thistle on on-line social or media sites. E-mail and on-line messages sent to

Salvation Army Headquarters in London were automatically directed to the Army's Canadian website, headquartered in Toronto.

The most distressing concern for both Paul and his medical colleagues was the deteriorating situation at Howard and the fate of the people of Chiweshe who had been so callously abandoned by the Army. As a physician, reports from relatives of patients whose mother or sister had died for lack of access to medical care were devastating.

Another worry was the treatment of the eight nurses still in detention and awaiting trial.

Meanwhile, the Thistles remained in the capital away from the media spotlight and removed from the people and community they loved. Although The Salvation Army had provided them with accommodation at a hotel in Harare, Paul and Pedrinah preferred to be with family. They felt safer staying with Pedrinah's brother where the children were surrounded by aunts and cousins and school friends, while their parents decided what to do.

But for the Thistles, the safety of Harare turned out to be an illusion. When Paul and Pedrinah refused to board the scheduled flight on August 19, the harassment began in earnest. At Pedrinah's brother's house, the phone rang every hour, with Salvation Army officials demanding to know when they were leaving. The family believed they were protected because the Army had no knowledge of where they were staying; but when a second set of tickets was hand-delivered to the home in Harare, they knew better. Of significance was the fact that the first two sets of tickets were issued under the instructions of IHQ to THQ Zimbabwe. The covering letter included with the first set of tickets ordering deportation within 48 hours was not copied to International Headquarters in London and the second set of tickets had no covering letter.

Even more disturbing than the incessant phone calls, were calls from relatives of the nurses held in jail, who appealed to Paul to stay in the country, for fear that if he left, their plight would be forgotten. According to one of the nurse's relatives who had been allowed access to visit them, they had been "physically and emotionally tortured"—beaten and denied food for three days.

For this reason, and still clinging to hope that common sense and compassion would resolve the crisis at Howard, the Thistles decided to stay in Zimbabwe to support the nurses and await the outcome of their trial.

———

Another of Pedrinah's brothers, Ngoni, who lives in London, sent a series of e-mails to General Bond, describing the anguish the family was going through: phone calls day and night in an attempt to pressure the Thistles to leave immediately; and members of the Salvation Army visiting ZANU-PF members within the community, spreading rumors that Dr. Thistle was a member of the opposition MDC party. This was dangerous talk, considering that in Zimbabwe such an allegation is akin to a death sentence.

When the opposition MDC party was asked to check their membership rolls, they confirmed there was no Dr. Thistle on record, nor any indication that he carried a party card.

Ngoni stated that the whole family felt uneasy with the Army's push to hustle the Thistles out of the country and tickets delivered out of the blue. Ngoni ended his letter by asking the General not to forward any messages that he sent on to the Secretary for Africa in London, which would only lead to "more prosecution and danger for his family back in Zimbabwe."

His appeal for the General to intervene directly was once again ignored. Instead, a reply came from Commissioner Cochrane, International Secretary to the Chief of Staff, but it was the same old

Army spin: this was a normal transfer. Cochrane offered no comment on the urgency to leave the country, nor any concern for the people left without medical aid. Ngoni then appealed to Colonel Floyd Tidd in a phone call to Toronto, but he got no further. Canadian THQ, he was told, had no control over ticket purchases; decisions were made by IHQ.

―――

For her part, Vinece Chigariro told the Associated Press that Thistle had challenged church leaders and that he was being reassigned "for the good of the church." Then she threatened the Thistles with excommunication if they did not leave the country immediately. "If he refuses to go back, he ceases to be a Salvation Army officer. If he ceases to be a Salvation Army officer, we cannot do anything. It will be up to the government whether they want him or they don't want him here," she told The Herald newspaper in Zimbabwe. This was a veiled threat referring to her association with Zimbabwe's Vice-President, Joice Mujuru, an active member in the Salvation Army, and Chigariro's close friend. It should also be noted that the Herald is the Zimbabwean government's official mouthpiece, used by the President and his cohorts to spread propaganda about his achievements and those of his ruling party, ZANU-PF, so the Commissioner was in her comfort zone, free to spread venom wherever it would land.

Dr. Thistle, Chigariro stated, had signed a covenant with the church as a Salvation Army officer, meaning that he was, in her words, "supposed to obey their commands. If the leadership says you are moving you don't argue…you go," she added, insisting that "the situation had nothing to do with his objections over the alleged theft of funds from the Church and his dismissal order was handed down by the Salvation Army's International Headquarters in London."

Meanwhile, The International Headquarters maintained in an e-mailed statement that the decision to transfer the doctor "has been made as part of The Salvation Army's internal processes involving appointments of Salvation Army officers around the world. In line with The Salvation Army's procedures, leaders at its International Headquarters have approved this decision. The Salvation Army is not aware of any danger to Captain Thistle or his family," the statement said, adding that "robust systems of internal and external audits are in place. Any reported concerns about accounting procedures are given the strictest attention. Captain Paul Thistle made no such report to International Headquarters."

In Canada, when the Army's spokesman, Andrew Burditt, was questioned by reporters about whether or not there was any truth to the reports of fiscal mismanagement at Howard, he would only say that although they were aware of the allegations, they were unable to comment on them. The organization's "main priority," he said, was the Thistles' safe return to Canada.

———

But no matter how much spin the Army put on the story, the local people were just as adamant about not being fooled. They had been down this road before, lied to by both church and state. As Paul told the STIMMA volunteer who filmed him before he left Howard Hospital, "the people aren't stupid. They have cell phones and access to the media. I don't want to tarnish the name of the Salvation Army worldwide, but we have a crisis in the church leadership in Zimbabwe."

A resident in Chiweshe told SW Radio Africa that the community had been left devastated by the decision to expel the doctor, explaining that he was a key part of their lives. "The hospital is now barely operating and we know even with another appointment we won't get the same service. People are angry."

With few options open to him, Paul appealed to Territorial Headquarters (THQ) in Toronto for guidance on the way forward. Now that they had been dismissed by Zimbabwe Territorial Command, he asked whose command they were under—IHQ London or Canada? Since his sons were enrolled in school for the next term, he requested that their transfer date be postponed to the original September 1st deadline in order to keep the boys in school as long as possible. He emphasized that his children, who had been traumatized by their forced departure and the violence that ensued, were having a hard time adjusting to the upheaval.

Paul's pleas were once again ignored. On August 30, a third set of airline tickets arrived. Accompanying the tickets was a letter from International Headquarters Africa Zone dated August 30, stating, "The issues concerning the nurses awaiting trial—and also the proposed General's delegation to Zimbabwe—are out of your hands. You need to let go of these now and trust that the Lord will handle these matters. Your responsibility is to leave Zimbabwe on Saturday." Clearly, the order to obey was the only consideration; Dr. Thistle and his family and the people of Chiweshe were to be sacrificed in favour of protocol. Thistle's only duty was to get out of Dodge—and be quick about it.

But Paul was determined not to abandon the nurses, as he had been ordered to abandon his patients at Howard Hospital. He and Pedrinah vowed to stay to support them and await their trial date. Paul and Pedrinah visited the nurses, arranged for legal counsel and covered the lawyer's fees out of their own pocket. No one from the Salvation Army offered any support or came to visit the nurses in jail.

While the scene in Zimbabwe was fraught with chaos and tension, the community outside the country was also reeling from the shock of the Thistle family's accelerated removal and impending departure. As expected, Paul's supporters around the world gathered their thoughts and put them to paper in a storm of protests that hit the internet and the international press. The official Salvation Army website was soon buzzing with more activity in one week than they see in a year. Hundreds of letters from within Canada and beyond were sent to the head of the Salvation Army, General Linda Bond, pleading with her to intervene and reverse the decision. Everyone from medical professionals and volunteers from various countries to friends and family rallied to Paul's side, expressing disbelief and dismay. Anyone who knew the Thistles' work at Howard knew this had to be some huge mistake.

On August 12, Brian Nichols, a psychotherapist from Peterborough, Ontario e-mailed Zimbabwe THQ to report that his fundraising group had donated $20,000 delivered to Dr. Thistle before he left for Zimbabwe a month prior. Nichols advised that the money sent with Dr. Thistle was not to be used if he was being evicted from the hospital and the group of volunteer medical professionals that Nichols belonged to were no longer welcome. He explained that the Canadian government does not allow charitable donations to go to projects outside Canada without direct involvement by the donors. Once again, all of Nichols' attempts to communicate directly with the hospital, The Salvation Army in Zimbabwe and in Canada were ignored. E-mails sent to the Army's headquarters in London were automatically re-directed to the Canadian territory's website.

The following day, gag orders were e-mailed to all officers from Commissioner Floyd Tidd at Canadian territorial headquarters: "We would at the same time ask officers to cease Facebook or any other social media tools to reference the Thistles or Howard Hospital. This is creating significant issues for the leadership in Zimbabwe." This was an obvious reference to Commissioner Chigariro and a clear indication of the Army's priorities.

On August 8, the Medical and Dental Practitioners Council of Zimbabwe wrote to the Zimbabwean Association of Church-related Hospitals to remind them of the rules in place.

> *"Please note that in terms of Council Policy a practitioner is not allowed to leave an institution without alternative plans in place. As the Clinical Director, he is required to give at least 3 months' notice before leaving the institution. This period will enable the Board of Directors which should include a Medical Director (who is a registered medical practitioner) to look for a replacement who will continue to run the institution.*
>
> *The purpose of this Policy is to ensure that at no time will a health institution be permitted to operate without a registered Clinical Director who is responsible for the clinical governance issues of the institution. This includes the care of patients.*
>
> *In this respect may Council be advised of the plans that you have for the continued operation of the Institution."*

Letters from both the Ministry of Health and the Zimbabwe Association of Church-related Hospitals were sent to Commissioner Chigariro explaining how mission hospitals are run—that donors work directly with the hospital. She brushed off both directives, stating that "the Salvation Army doesn't work that way."

As she later told the Associated Press, "Dr. Thistle was being reassigned for the 'good of the church,' adding that ordained Salvation Army officers 'sign a covenant with God and make an undertaking to be loyal to the church leadership. Any transfer that is done is not questionable and should be saluted and respected'."

The Covenant referred to by the Commissioner pledges officers *"to maintain the doctrines and principles of The Salvation Army, and, by God's grace to prove myself a worthy officer."* The last line reads*: "Done in the strength of my Lord and Savior, and in the presence of the Territorial Commander, training college officers and fellow cadets (the wording to be adapted to local circumstances)."* Nowhere does it state that its leaders have the right to "ex-communicate" a fellow officer or order someone out of the country. Quite the opposite is true: Salvation Army officers also pledge to refrain from any involvement in political matters.

In fact, the Mugabe government, represented by the Governor, confirmed that Paul and his family were welcome in Zimbabwe, but since this was an international Salvation Army matter, he couldn't intervene—thus supporting the government's mandate that there was a clear separation of church and state.

Chigariro then began to spread rumors that Paul was staying in the Canadian Embassy because he had something to hide. "People take refuge inside their embassy because they've done something," she said. When questioned in Ottawa, the Zimbabwean Ambassador to Canada thought that Paul had left the country on Sunday, August 19. Other rumours also surfaced, including one that involved a US$20,000 reward to harm the Thistles and their children that, thankfully, never came to pass.

Paul's supporters, although confused about unfolding events in Zimbabwe, were solidly behind him, their commitment expressed in passionate e-mails.

On August 15, retired Salvation Army Major, Dr. Jim Watt, wrote to General Bond warning that Dr. Thistle's abrupt removal from Howard Hospital would result in deaths of patients and suggested that they be transferred to Karanda, another mission hospital north of Harare. Once again, the General ignored this advice and took no action.

Medical colleagues from around the world rallied to Paul's side—from the President of the College of Family Physicians of Canada to Harvard Medical School; from volunteers in Canada and the United States to Germany, Norway and South Africa—praising Paul's dedication and expertise in the practice of medicine, as well as his devotion and compassion for his patients and their welfare. Fellow physicians familiar with Dr. Thistle and his work, echoed his own shock that a church recognized universally for its humanitarian service would be privy to the humanitarian crisis taking place in Chiweshe.

They joined the barrage of messages, calling for the General to "do something"—correct the untenable situation with the Army in Zimbabwe and conduct a disciplinary review of Commissioner Chigariro.

Dr. Liesly Lee, an Associate Professor of Medicine at Sunnybrook Health Sciences Centre in Toronto had worked throughout Africa for the past 20 years. According to Dr. Lee, he established a formal elective arrangement between the Neurology Division at the University of Toronto and Dr. Thistle at Howard Hospital to allow further training for Canadian physicians in Zimbabwe "because Dr. Thistle was reliable and responsible—an individual who could be trusted to deal with the obvious hurdles in trying to bridge the gap between First World medicine and the developing world. That program would not develop because Thistle's role was not replaceable in that setting. The hospital was able to function, he stated, because of this one individual. Others were primarily supporting staff, able to uphold what Paul had been doing."

Other supporters sent pleas on behalf of Pedrinah. One nurse who had taught her called her one of the best students she had ever had the privilege to teach. Jennifer Reid, the midwife from

Peterborough, Ontario who had volunteered at Howard, questioned how the Army could let her go. Pedrinah herself wondered how things could have gone so wrong: how she had gone from delivering babies one day to having to gather up her life in 24 hours. More importantly, how the hospital could possibly survive with both its surgical and midwifery program in jeopardy? As Jennifer Reid noted in her letter to General Bond, the situation was compounded by the imminent retirement of Major Joan Gibson, an accomplished and progressive educator and the hospital's senior midwifery tutor. Upon Major Gibson's retirement, Pedrinah had been slated to take over, but what would happen now? Unfortunately, for the Thistles, there were more questions than answers, and no time to contemplate the outcome.

Paul's Christian colleagues advised him to resist and not give in to demands to abandon 270,000 people without alternate access to the same level of healthcare that Howard Hospital provided.

In letters and internet appeals directed to the Salvation Army, supporters and patients were unanimous in their admiration for the Thistles as a team. "You could not have selected a better ambassador for your beloved mission hospital," wrote Dr. Kavitha Passaperuma, Medical Oncologist at Mackenzie Health, in Richmond Hill, Ontario. "He is not merely their doctor, she not merely their nurse—Paul and Pedrinah were their neighbours, their friends, their support and their guidance—morally, ethically and spiritually. Their loss extends far beyond simply losing a doctor."

As a physician, Paul Thistle's Hippocratic Oath came before any promises made to the Army and every fibre in his being fought against the senseless order to abandon his patients. What was more important—obeying the demands of a vengeful superior or trying to restore healthcare to people in dire need? Did the Army's hierarchy come before his obligation to his patients?

The answer was a mere prayer away. He would fight for the people of Chiweshe, just as he had fought to keep the hospital afloat. As for his Army affiliation, on Wednesday, August 24, Paul's "case" was officially handed over to International Headquarters in London.

Paul continued to correspond with the Army in Canada. E-mails flew back and forth while attempts to speak by phone were thwarted by bad connections. In their replies, Army officials in Toronto appeared more concerned about lack of communication and media coverage than anything else.

For their part, local Salvation Army authorities continued reports to the press that the Thistles had taken up residence inside the Canadian embassy in Harare. "That's where he and his family have been living since they left Chiweshe last month," they told a local radio outlet.

In a letter dated August 30, Paul sent a message to THQ Toronto to explain that his children were not coping very well with the news. Guidance counsellors and teachers at their school in Harare recommended that the boys stay in school as long as possible. Paul suggested that he and Pedrinah could travel ahead and call for their children when re-settled. He also appealed on behalf of the eight nurses who had been arrested, beaten and deprived of food for four days, with no support or pastoral care from anyone from the Army. Their trial was pending, set for September 4. He expressed his belief that the nurses would be exonerated and released, but he wanted to wait for the formal outcome.

In Harare, at Pedrinah's brother's house, the family continued to receive numerous calls from relatives of the nurses pleading for Paul to remain in Zimbabwe, fearing that his leaving would put them in further danger with the government. Once Dr. Thistle left, they believed, the media focus would shift and they would be forgotten and left to rot in jail. Just as important, an investigative team from the Salvation Army was due to arrive the following week and Paul felt that no investigation would be complete without the Thistles' input. Given all that, Paul asked for an extension on his departure until the end of September.

He received a reply from Lt.-Col. Margaret M. Wickings, Under Secretary for Central and West Africa at International Headquarters in London. The message was curt and final: no extension, no explanation. Its focus was clearly on removing him from the scene. The reason stated for the family's urgent departure was for their "safety and well-being," but, as Paul assured her in his reply, they were in no immediate danger. They had followed orders to vacate the hospital when ordered to do so, since the hospital was no longer a "safe place for patients, staff and family with riot police tear gas and dogs on the premise."

Paul also notified Wickings that the first two sets of tickets were issued under instruction of International Headquarters, the covering letter had not been copied to anyone in London and the second set was dispatched without a covering letter.

Once again, Paul repeated his desire for an extension to Colonel Floyd Tidd at Army headquarters in Toronto. The fate of the nurses arrested at Howard was still on hold. A lawyer in Harare had taken their case on the same day that the Thistles arrived in Harare. Paul had arranged it and paid their fee. At their court appearance on September 4, the nurses' lawyers asked that they be allowed to return to work until their case was finalized. The request was granted and the nurses were back at work the following day. The 12 villagers were also released, with the provision that the group of 20 arrested at Howard back in August would return to court on September 24.

Tidd replied on September 7, 2012, that as the Thistles had failed to leave Zimbabwe by September 1, following the issue of a third set of airplane tickets, they were no longer officers on international service, but now under the command of Canada and Bermuda territory. Tidd further stated that since the Thistles were currently without an appointment (due to their failure to return to Canada), they were now "absent without leave." (This was referred to as an "extended furlough" in subsequent correspondence.) Once again, Paul was asked to state his intentions about returning to Canada, as it was the Canadian territory's responsibility to arrange for transportation.

On September 12, Paul received a letter from retired Salvation Army Commissioner John Swinfen, who grew up in Rhodesia and was familiar with Howard Hospital from a young age. Later, he returned as an officer to work in the educational programs there. Swinfen wrote advising that he was "part of a team that the General had put together to help resolve the current situation at Howard and issues related to it."

According to the retired Commissioner, the General had asked him to approach Paul and act as a go-between. The General, he said, highly respected all of the good that Paul had brought to Howard and Chiweshe. She valued his skills, his capacity and dedication; this despite the fact that she had done her best to avoid him at every turn and by appointing others to represent her.

Although not surprised to receive another intervention from yet another of the General's ambassadors, Thistle took this opportunity to lay bare his case. In his written reply, he reminded Swinfen that twice agreements made between the community leaders and the Army's territorial cabinet had been broken: the first in April 2012, when rumors circulated that the Thistles might be transferred and the community was assured that the family was merely going on furlough in June; the second following a meeting on July 19. In the presence of the International Secretary for Personnel, it was recommended that the Thistles' appointment be extended until June 2013, with the need for a comprehensive transition plan in the interim. Part of the reasoning was the need to prepare the hearts and minds of the community during the transition. This was an inference to one of Territorial Commissioner Chigariro's accusations that it was Paul's responsibility to prepare the community for his transfer.

He also stated that the letter confirming his transfer was not an original, but a photocopy. The only person copied was TC Chigariro and it failed to mention the proposed extension to June 2013, nor any indication of the Thistles' next appointment.

Although Chigariro insisted that the decision took her by surprise, that it originated in Canada and was a routine transfer, the community did not buy into this argument and were particularly upset over the lack of consultation they had been promised. Paul recounted the local Territorial Command's attempts to discredit him—spreading rumors that he was hiding in the Canadian Embassy, being accused of inciting violence and labelled a member of the MDC. As Paul stated, these were lies that he considered totally unethical and unacceptable behavior for church leaders, and the community did not believe them.

For years he had been expressing concern about financial irregularities regarding the management of donations and projects. Howard Hospital had tens of thousands of dollars of unreconciled donations and hundreds of thousands of dollars of failed projects, yet there had not been a proper board meeting at Howard for months; nor a community advisory board for years. Minutes were scant, if written at all, and no action was forthcoming. Paul had turned a blind eye to these concerns, not wanting to disrupt the mission of Howard Hospital or lessen the reputation of the Salvation Army at home or abroad. He chose the better of two evils, praying that the issues of governance and finance would become self-evident and rectified with time, patience and the appointment of administration with experience and qualifications in hospital management. But when $20,000 worth of building materials allegedly went missing from the hospital after the Thistles' departure, and another $20,000 went unaccounted for in the community orphan program, he became deeply disturbed.

Paul was particularly upset that he and Pedrinah had been forced to violate their professional medical ethics in abandoning tens of thousands of patients with no arrangements made for their care; and that they had violated their covenant "to care for the poor, feed the hungry, clothe the naked, love the unlovable, and befriend those who have no friends." Their transfer had been poorly planned and badly managed; it did not address the underlying issue of governance of major health care institutions in the Army world. In fact, he emphasized, what they had created was a humanitarian crisis. He ended by stating what was clearly obvious to everyone but the deniers: if a team from International Headquarters had been on the ground in Zimbabwe to investigate firsthand, there would be no need for his letter.

But the letter failed to elicit any positive response. It was clear that to the Army the Thistles were nothing more than a problem that had to be handled and dealt with accordingly. The Army had made up its mind. From that point on, the shields were raised, the gates shut and the locks bolted.

And Dr. Thistle's name, along with 17 years of extraordinary service, would soon be wiped from the annals of the Army.

CHAPTER 12

Up Against Goliath

---

*First they ignore you, then they laugh at you,
then they fight you, then you win*

MAHATMA GANDHI

IN ADDITION TO HIS TEAM effort to support Dr. Thistle, Dr. Michael Silverman continued to work on Paul's behalf, writing to General Bond, phoning London headquarters, and appealing to anyone who was willing to talk to him. In an impassioned plea to the General, he wrote about his long association with Paul, praised his unswerving passion and dedication to his patients, his innovative approach to medicine and the initiatives he brought to Howard: programs to mandate breastfeeding two years ahead of the World Health Organization publishing their directive; prevention of mother to child transmission of HIV; and detection of TB. Silverman praised Paul's medical skills, citing his "great hands" and "God-given gift as a surgeon."

He emphasized Paul's holistic approach to medicine and commitment to the local people—the Thistles' attention to the care of local orphans and raising funds for their education, as well as other children in the community.

On August 18, Silverman received a response from Major Alison Cowling that was filled with denials: the Thistles had not been forced out, the hospital was open, would remain open and was adequately staffed "to address the health care needs of those that rely on it." Further, that "any project work that is funded by international sources is closely monitored by the International Development Office at The Salvation Army's International Headquarters in London."

In a three-page letter, Dr. Silverman refuted each of her arguments with tales of his own experience with funding, including the loss of a $250,000 Canadian government grant to fund HIV programs at Howard, due to the local Salvation Army's refusal to comply with the terms of the grant. He also took exception to Cowling's insistence that the Thistles had not been forced to leave Howard Hospital, citing that there is no real distinction between "being forced out" and "being ordered out." He offered his own conclusions for Dr. Thistle's prompt removal in the absence of any other reason than the standard "routine transfer." Paul's attempts to maintain the integrity of accounts had led him to be seen as an irritant by the local Territorial Command in Harare. Silverman wrapped up his letter by calling for an external investigation to be carried out immediately.

In early September, Dr. Silverman and four other members of the Interfaith Friends of Howard Hospital—Larry Gillman and his wife, Jennifer Reid, Brian Nichols and Sarah Zelcer—met with leaders of the Canadian Salvation Army at their headquarters in Toronto. When the team tried to ascertain the reason for Dr. Thistle's transfer, they were told that Paul didn't communicate well. But the most egregious and shocking accusation brought up at the meeting was the suggestion that Dr. Thistle "may not be qualified to perform some of the procedures necessary to treat patients"—this from Commissioner Brian Peddle, head of the Army's Canada and Bermuda territory.

Dr. Silverman immediately jumped in, assuring Peddle that there were numerous physicians who could testify to the contrary, verifying that Paul was indeed an exceptional surgeon, trained in numerous specialties. Ironically, Peddle's concern did not extend to the fact that with Thistle's departure, there was no qualified doctor to replace him. The meeting ended with the Army's Canadian leadership telling the IFHH that the final decision wasn't up to them, but was the responsibility of International Headquarters.

So Dr. Silverman flew to London to meet with Majors Dean and Eirwen Pallant. Dean Pallant was born and raised in Zimbabwe and holds a doctor of theology. His title is as long as he is tall: Under Secretary for Program Resources and International Health Services Coordinator. He is also a frequent user of social media sites to record his daily activities and his ego appears to equal his height. His wife, Eirwen, is a physician who specializes in the treatment of addictions.

During the discussions that extended to two meetings, five hours in total, Silverman tried to get a clearer picture of the situation and find out what possible grievance would cause the removal of Dr. Thistle from Howard Hospital, but no reason or explanation was given. The only mention of Thistle doing anything wrong was the Pallants' contention that Paul "didn't communicate well with the Army." To Silverman this comment didn't make sense since it was well known that telephone and internet service to and from Howard Hospital was unreliable. Silverman pointed out that Dr. Thistle was busy at what he does best and is trained to do—looking after his patients.

Thistle's title, as Silverman pointed out, was Chief Medical Officer, not Administrator, but since the administrator failed to secure funds to keep the hospital afloat, Paul had no choice but to look for funding elsewhere. To abandon his patients and their health care was unthinkable for any reason. All of Dr. Thistle's fundraising and administrative work was done after hours because there was no one else to do it. As Silverman suggested, the Pallants could have appointed an administrator to handle business and communications needs at Howard, instead of depending on Thistle to do it.

Silverman also said that since there was no emergency back in Canada requiring Thistle's presence, he should be allowed to continue working at the hospital until a replacement arrived.

The meetings concluded with a three-part agreement:

1. Dr. Thistle would stay in Zimbabwe until after the Salvation Army's investigative team arrived to conduct a review concerning missing monies and materials
2. A review would be done to see if Thistle could be re-instated during the investigation. Paul could remain pending the trial of the hospital's nurses, arrested in August
3. The reinstatement at Howard would have to follow after the review, but it would allow Thistle to return as a physician and surgeon, and a hospital administrator would be brought in to handle non-medical duties.

With all parties agreeing to the terms, the Pallants asked Dr. Silverman to please not discuss the contents of the meeting because of the media's continuous pressure on the Army to act. They wanted time to complete their internal investigations. Silverman agreed to this request and, despite his own pressure from the media, complied. For their part, the Pallants agreed to speak with Salvation Army THQ in Canada.

On September 20, Major Eirwen Pallant completed a clinical assessment of Howard Hospital. Her report concluded that the hospital continued to be functional: more than 200 babies had been born the previous month; maternal and child health service were operating normally; 4,000 outpatients had been treated in the past four weeks; there had been 1,756 inpatients treated and more than 100 operations in the theatre.

Upon the release of this sanitized assessment, Dr. Silverman knew that he had been lied to and forced to agree to terms that were clearly self-serving, including the Pallants extracting a promise from him to stay quiet and allow them to conduct their review. It was clear that the Army had finished their deliberations and had no intention of waiting for the review.

Silverman broke his silence. He felt that the public needed to know what was occurring in light of the significant public health implications; and the community needed to be informed and have a say about what was happening with their health care. While in London, he spoke to SW Radio Africa, an independent Zimbabwe radio station broadcasting from the United Kingdom. The station, staffed and run by Zimbabweans in exile, produces and present news and current affairs programs for broadcast in Zimbabwe via short wave and the internet. Its aim is to promote democracy and free speech and to counter mis-information and hate speech reported by state-controlled media outlets in Zimbabwe. Unfortunately, in August 2014, SW Radio Africa was forced to shut down. Throughout its 13 years of broadcasting from the U.K. the station had encountered its share of troubles, including the Mugabe government jamming its broadcasts and the loss of donations to keep it going.

Dr. Silverman revealed that the Army was intent on turning Howard Hospital into a "primary care" model. The replacement CMO would not be a surgeon, despite the fact that Howard had always been a surgical facility. A primary care health center would do nothing for those patients who required surgery. The cessation of surgery was an arbitrary decision by the Army that was not discussed with the surrounding community.

―――

At the same time, Paul Thistle continued to correspond with THQ in Toronto. The Canadian headquarters' responses were always the same. They began with pleasantries, but the single line of politeness was merely a thin veneer to disguise the missile that followed. Commissioner Brian Peddle's letter dated September 12, cemented the Army's decision: they had supported the September lst departure date, but several weeks had passed and they could not support any reconsideration of his appointment in Zimbabwe, nor agree to a further extension. The decision was final. Period. Amen.

The letter was filled with petty grievances. They objected to his continued involvement with the Friends of Howard Hospital and the Chiweshe community. Peddle appeared to be upset by any statement made by others supporting Paul and/or condemning the situation at Howard. He again asked for confirmation of Paul's intentions, even though his intentions had been clearly stated with each communication. It just wasn't the answer they wanted to hear.

Once again, Peddle mentioned that "as we have not been able to speak with you by phone, the provision of a number would enable the Chief Secretary to be in touch." He also cited the fact that they continued to support him financially—albeit the lordly sum of $600 deposited into his Canadian account.

Paul was told to leave the country by October 5. The only thing missing from the letter was any mention of the three-part agreement in London or any concern for the people of Chiweshe as a result of his forced removal.

In his reply, Paul reminded Peddle that telephone and e-mail reception in Zimbabwe was erratic. Paul was also aware that there was a fresh initiative at International Headquarters that might bring a resolution to the crisis at Howard and requested that the family be allowed to stay in Zimbabwe while awaiting this development.

It was evident from their correspondence that the Army's frustration was mounting. Their next attempt to persuade Thistle to leave was to have him meet with Major Critch who was visiting Zimbabwe. Following the meeting, Paul launched another appeal to Colonel Tidd in Toronto on behalf of his children, whom he felt should be allowed to finish out their school year. He also reminded Tidd that the idea of a one-year transition was first proposed by Commissioner Hodder, International Secretary for Personnel, during a meeting at Howard Hospital on July 19—a day after the Thistles received their transfer notice. This proposal had been agreed to by everyone in attendance, but later rejected by the Army without explanation. Thistle requested a special leave, unpaid or otherwise, until June 2013. With the Army's permission, he and Pedrinah would like to volunteer their services as clinicians/teachers at the University of Harare, where Paul had been an Honorary Lecturer for the past decade.

On October l, he sent a formal request for the leave of absence to the attention of the Officer Review Board in care of Commissioner Brian Peddle, Territorial Commander for Canada and Bermuda Territory.

A telephone conversation between Paul, Commissioner Peddle and Major Rice followed on October 24. Although all parties shared their concerns with mutual respect and what appeared to be a greater understanding of the situation, the Thistles were now faced with the possibility that their officership was in jeopardy. Surely, Paul stated in his follow-up letter the next day, there must be a way forward that could prevent such a grave decision. He further suggested a leave of absence that would allow the family to return to Canada over the Christmas break. In January the boys would return to Zimbabwe to continue school in Harare, while the parents remained in Canada.

Once again, Thistle's pleas fell on deaf ears.

Meanwhile, the Zimbabwean wheels of justice progressed at a turtle's pace. After further delays, allegedly to give the prosecution time to gather evidence, the Howard Hospital nurses' trial was rescheduled for October 5 and finally got underway on October 8. The four Salvation Army officials—Majors Makiwa, Nyahuma, Lt-Col. Ncube and Colonel Moyo—who testified against the nurses provided conflicting information about events during the protest. In fact, one of the nurses accused of overturning the officers' vehicle was at work inside the hospital at the time.

Other staff used the opportunity to speak to reporters who were covering the trial.

One unidentified staff member told SW Africa reporter, Tererai Karimakwenda, that the accused villagers were innocent people whose only crime was sympathizing with Dr. Thistle. They were arrested at random, he said, and police then made up charges to support their actions. Paul told the press that "nurses are people who treat and care for the victims of trauma and don't create it."

The case was again remanded to October 19, when 16 of the group of 20 Chiweshe residents, including seven of the eight nurses, were acquitted due to lack of evidence. The four others' next court date was scheduled for November 2, but the case was remanded again until the following week.

———

On October 26, Salvation Army IHQ issued a press release stating that according to the fact-finding team they sent to Howard Hospital in Zimbabwe to examine the processing and use of donations to the hospital, they could report that:

- *There was no sign that goods or funds donated directly to The Salvation Army in Canada for use by the Howard Hospital were diverted from their original purpose.*
- *The hospital continues to operate with qualified medical personnel serving thousands of people each month.*
- *Media reports that the hospital is functioning at 10% are false. Patients continue to be treated at Howard and more difficult cases are being referred to other facilities.*

The Army also reported that they remained committed to the work of Howard Hospital, stating that over the past week and months, the organization had:

- *paid for a shipment of medical supplies worth $300,000*
- *paid overdue bills totaling $30,000 to keep the electricity on*
- *paid $15,000 for much-need pharmaceutical supplies"*

In truth, the first and third items are the same. The Army paid the shipping cost of $15,000 for the donated $300,000 worth of medical supplies. This is consistent with the one thing the Army has always done: cover the cost for shipping on containers of donated goods and supplies from other sources.

The Army's statement infers that paying to keep the electricity on is an extraordinary expense, when, in fact, it is a necessary expenditure to keep the hospital running. No hospital could function without it. Rather than paying $30,000 to keep the electricity on, Thistle and his staff made arrangements to help the hospital pay down the debt over time.

And the only reason The Salvation Army ended up paying for much-needed pharmaceutical supplies is because they had no choice, now that the flow of funds that previously paid for them had stopped.

During a question and answer period following the press release, Major Dean Pallant stuck to the official spin that had been created in the board room of the Army's gleaming glass headquarters in London and woven into the very fabric of his uniform:

- Dr. Thistle's removal was a "regular" transfer
- The Army was in the process of appointing a new acting Chief Medical Officer at Howard Hospital, a Zimbabwean, Dr. Aaron Museka.

Dr. Thistle, he assured reporters, was being transferred back to Canada, even though Pallant knew that the last official transfer date had come and gone and Paul was still fighting to stay where he was.

As reporters clambered for answers, particularly about the need to bring in outside auditors, Pallant's defense appeared weak—one moment calling it an "audit", the next a "fact-finding" mission. Whatever the Army's probing amounted to, one thing was certain: "there was no misuse of donated goods or no sign of donated funds being diverted."

The Army's press release was the writing on the wall. The Thistles' friends and supporters urged them to seek legal advice.

CHAPTER 13

The Brick Wall

―

Each time a man stands up for an ideal, or acts to improve the lot of others, or strikes out against injustice, he sends forth a tiny ripple of hope, and crossing each other from a million different centers of energy and daring, those ripples build a current that can sweep down the mightiest walls of oppression and resistance ...

ROBERT KENNEDY

ON OCTOBER 29, 2012, PAUL and Pedrinah sent a formal letter to General Linda Bond in London requesting an independent tribunal to examine their recent marching orders.

As expected, no reply was received. To the Army, the Thistles were nothing more than a problem that had to be handled and the best strategy they could come up with was to ignore them. The Thistles' supporters had other ideas.

On November l, General Bond appeared in Toronto to take part in a public Salvation Army rally on November 2. When Interfaith Friends of Howard Hospital (IFFHH) learned of the General's appearance, they issued a news release announcing their intention to present a petition to her at the Metro Convention Centre in downtown Toronto. The petition, containing signatures from around the world, appealed to the Army to reverse their decision to remove the Thistles from Howard Hospital and to restore health and hope to the people of Chiweshe. The Army, upon learning of the planned intervention, asked IFFHH to cancel it. In exchange they offered the group a chance to meet one-on-one with General Bond. Not wanting to appear unreasonable, Dr. Silverman and the others—Sarah Zelcer, of Ve'ahavta, Larry Gillman, President of Beth Israel Synagogue in Peterborough and Ray Richardson, representing the Rotary Club of Whitby, Ontario—agreed to the meeting. They met General Bond, Commissioner Peddle and other unidentified officers in the chapel at Toronto's Pearson International Airport. This was an odd place to meet, since it is open to the public and there were other people in the chapel who had no relationship to either the Army or the IFFHH.

This didn't seem to matter to General Bond who proceeded to lecture and yell at them in front of onlookers in the airport chapel. Refusing to listen to anything they had to say, she launched into her own verbal assault—angry and defensive about the flood of negative publicity that denigrated The Salvation Army and publicly maligned their practices. According to the General, "nothing they could say would change IHQ's decision to remove Paul Thistle from Howard Hospital."

Dr. Silverman and the others were appalled by the General's behavior—deeming it a disgraceful display by any person, but particularly shameful in a person who is head of a church.

The meeting had barely begun when the General's handler stepped in and put an end to it. The group then spent another 20 minutes with Commissioner Brian Peddle, who stated that the hospital was functioning at much higher than the 10% capacity reported in the media. Although the pharmacy cupboards may be bare and the electricity may be cut off, he assured the team that a container of medications from health partners, as well as funds to pay the outstanding electricity bill were forthcoming. He also stated that the goods purported to be stolen were actually sitting onsite in a container at the hospital, but he failed to explain where they had been or how they suddenly reappeared. Peddle and his team blamed Dr. Thistle for a host of things, including the lights being out. The Commissioner said the Army had no idea of the scope of the projects he was running, the funds he was raising, nor the partnerships he had developed.

This revelation was shocking but entirely in line with their handling of the issue, given their lack of knowledge or understanding about other community-based programs initiated and developed by Thistle, such as the home care programs to support patients on antiretroviral therapy. Despite assuring Dr. Silverman and the others that they were committed to the survival of Howard Hospital and that the community continued to receive medical care, the group appeared to have little insight into the potential impact of their actions on the entire community of Chiweshe. Peddle said that they originally decided to move Paul because his safety was in jeopardy, but the Commissioner didn't explain what those safety concerns were. They said they had another doctor to replace Thistle, but the plan fell through because that person was no longer willing to take the appointment. However, they would not consider having Paul there in the interim before a new CMO arrived. According to them, the doctors on site were handling things.

On November 8, the Salvation Army in Canada issued the same press release that International Headquarters in London had released earlier.

Two days earlier, Paul had received a letter from Commissioner Peddle admonishing him for a letter he had addressed to Rotarians, which had inadvertently been leaked to THQ Canada. Paul's letter informed the Rotarians that there had been no resolution to the crisis at Howard. He noted that, according to reports, the hospital was operating at 20 percent or less, and the issues of clinical governance and project management remained. He also stated that he and Pedrinah had been offered employment at Karanda Mission Hospital in Mt. Darwin, northeast of Harare. Howard Hospital and Karanda had always been closely aligned as referral hospitals and the Howard had been sponsoring children in the Karanda area for years. In thanking the Rotarians for the bicycle program to aid community care, he was confident that Karanda would be a welcome recipient of the bicycles.

Tidd was not pleased. According to his reply, he saw this as an undermining of the "ministry and mission of Howard Hospital" and delivered a further slap on the wrist: "to say that this is inappropriate behavior as covenanted officers is an understatement." His message ended with his "disappointment and lack of confidence in the integrity of our exchange thus far", and "given your obvious access to email, I assume a 24-hour period (to respond) is appropriate."

Tidd got his wish. In response to the Colonel's harping on communications issues, Paul expressed puzzlement as to why Tidd was unable to reach him by phone, when other Canadians were able to call regularly. Tidd appeared to be unaware or chose to ignore the fact that it is far easier to reach Zimbabwe from Canada than attempting outgoing calls from Zimbabwe, which is often impossible and enormously expensive. Paul had been able to reach Tidd, though with difficulty. He told the Colonel that he felt there was a lack of sympathy for his family's extraordinary circumstances. Also, a disheartening inability to see the full story surrounding their departure from Howard, given the local, national and international outcry that ensued. Despite the many conversations and letters exchanged, he felt that they had not been listened to. Their exchanges had not been dialogues, but directives. He stated that the situation was unnecessary and preventable if the Army had followed recommendations from the government of Zimbabwe and community leaders in Chiweshe to implement a thorough transition plan.

He also pointed out that at the end of his telephone conversation on October 24, he overheard Major Rice in the background, saying that "Paul is 'passive aggressive' "—a comment that he considered to be unprofessional and unhealthy. There was little sense of appreciation for his years of dedication to their ministry, and little concern over the sudden loss of health care for the people of Chiweshe, and the suffering that followed.

He and Pedrinah, he wrote, would not resign from officership. They had done nothing wrong, except being forced to abandon their patients. Their failure to comply with earlier repatriation orders and subsequent request for a leave of absence was reflected in concern for their children and the desire to support the nursing staff in their ongoing trial by the Salvation Army.

In the meantime, offers of employment in other areas of Zimbabwe poured in, including a chance to work at various government posts by the Ministry of Health. There were also investors who wanted the Thistles to manage Whitecliff Hospital, but they felt that Whitecliff was too close to Howard for comfort. They were leaning towards a voluntary appointment at Karanda Mission Hospital, but would not accept any formal employment until they were sure of their status with the Salvation Army. It appeared obvious that the Canadian Territory wanted to terminate their officership and it wasn't clear if they would be allowed to volunteer in any capacity. As he told Dr. Watt, to trust the Army's leaders that the Howard debacle would not happen again to them or any other CMO at another Army-run facility, would be a great leap of faith. Considering how he was treated, any doctor would be mad to sign on as the new CMO at Howard.

Supporters in Canada, although not sure where Paul and Pedrinah would end up working, pledged their support wherever he chose to work. Larry Gillman of Peterborough assured Paul that wherever he chose to work, the Peterborough group was solidly behind them. The Rotary Clubs in Toronto and Langley, B.C. also extended their continuing support.

―――

On November 10, 2012, Julie Kirkpatrick, a lawyer from Port Hope, Ontario, who had volunteered at Howard, wrote a letter to Commissioner Brian Peddle advising that she had been retained by the Thistles regarding his repatriation. She pointed out that as officers of the Salvation Army, they were bound to abide by lawful orders and regulations. However, as a medical doctor, Thistle had a paramount duty to his patients, as stated in the Hippocratic Oath, a copy of which she provided.

After outlining the Thistles' position, she asked to be contacted by counsel for the Salvation Army. Her request did not receive a response. Instead, on November 23, the Thistles received a letter from Chief Secretary, Colonel Floyd Tidd advising them that their officership was terminated effective immediately, due to their 'persistent refusal to carry out lawful orders and instructions' as required of all officers of The Salvation Army.

On December 6, Julie Kirkpatrick sent a letter addressed to both Colonel Tidd and Commissioner Peddle. After reviewing the letter of termination, along with the Orders and Regulations of the Salvation Army, she noted that the letter did not meet the requirements set out in the first paragraph of the Action List for Paragraph 12 Cases, which specified that clients be informed of the date, time and venue of a review meeting at which their case would be considered. Secondly, it failed to enclose copies of all relevant documents that were available to the board, or an explanation of the arrangement made for these and any further documents received, to be read, and as required, copied by the officer before the meeting.

Judging by the contents of the Lt. Colonel's e-mail, there appeared to have been an earlier Officer Review Board meeting held without notice to the Thistles. As Kirkpatrick pointed out, this was again contrary to the explicit requirement of paragraph 1 of the Action List for Paragraph 12 Cases. Therefore, she noted, any decision of the Officer Review Board was invalid, in breach of the Orders & Regulations of the Salvation Army, and in violation of the principles of fairness and natural justice.

She also noted that in correspondence to Colonel Rice on November 14, 2012, she had requested to hear from the Army counsel by no later than November 16, but no response was forthcoming until November 21, when she received correspondence from Christine E. LeBlanc, Associate Legal Counsel for the Army. At no time, Kirkpatrick added, was she or her clients informed of the date and time of a meeting of the Review Board.

Paragraph 5 of the Action List calls for the Territorial Commander to provide the minutes of the meeting to the officer under review: *"the officer must be informed that if the facts of the case are still disputed, he/she has the right to a Commission of Inquiry, and that any request or such a commission must be made to the territorial commander within 14 days."*

Kirkpatrick further noted:

At no time after the meeting of the review board were her clients informed of their right to a Commission of Inquiry or that the request must be made to the Territorial Commander within 14 days.

Her clients' termination letter was sent ten days following the letter from Colonel Rice, and at best guess, three days after the meeting of the review board apparently occurred. This, she stated, rendered the decision of the Territorial Commander invalid and in violation of the principles of fairness and natural justice.

In reviewing the Memorandum for Guidance for the Application of O & R Governing Discipline, she noted that the actions of The Salvation Army in this case were clearly in violation of several portions of the guidelines.

Paragraph 7 of the Action List for Paragraph 12 Cases provides that *"notice in writing of an intention to appeal the dismissal to the Chief of Staff must be lodged with the Territorial Commander within 14 days of the day on which the notice of dismissal was delivered."*

Kirkpatrick asked for the Army to provide copies of all relevant documents that were available to the Board, and the dates, times, locations and Minutes of all meetings of the Officer Review Board pertaining to the matter.

This letter, she advised, was to be considered notice of the Thistles' intention to appeal. A further formal Notice/Statement of Appeal would be delivered within 42 days of the Termination Letter of November 23, as required.

She ended the letter by chiding the Army for their cavalier approach to their own Order and Regulations, in matters of such importance that had caused significant pain and mental anguish for her clients.

The only reply she received was a curt letter from the Army's counsel, Christine LeBlanc: *"My clients consider the dispute between The Salvation Army and Paul and Pedrinah Thistle to be an ecclesiastical matter, not a legal matter. Accordingly, The Salvation Army will be corresponding directly with the Thistles regarding their officership. I wanted you to be aware of The Salvation Army's position."*

Paul and Pedrinah took the Army at its word, and with no other option, sent a letter to Colonel Floyd Tidd in Toronto requesting a Commission of Inquiry and Appeal to examine all of the documentary evidence leading up to their termination as officers.

On December 20, 2012, Tidd replied that before any inquiry or appeal could take place, the Thistles would have to return to Canada immediately for reassignment. However, he was most emphatic that any future reassignment would not include a return to Howard Hospital.

Clearly, even to a layman, The Army's position appeared to tiptoe through the legal minefield—quoting precedents, but completely avoiding the sticky parts of their own regulations they had failed to abide by. When it was necessary, when Christmas kettles were evident on every street corner, they adopted a benevolent smile and swung into collection mode. When taxes and fiscal accountability were the issue, they fled to their glass tower and hid behind the Red Shield. But when it came to control in any situation, they were masters of solidarity. Nothing could penetrate their armor, not even consideration for one of their own, let alone 270,000 people abandoned on a whim.

They had little to fear from Dr. Thistle, a man of humble means, with little or nothing to fight with but commitment to his ethical and moral obligations. Nor from the people of Chiweshe, the rural poor, the sick and the hungry, left with nothing but their last thread of hope.

For Paul it was the end of the road with any hope of reconciliation with the Salvation Army, but not the end of his mission to help the people of Zimbabwe. The Army might be through with him, his name may be persona non grata among the upper echelon of Salvation Army brass, but to patients, friends and supporters around the world, he would not be forgotten.

As for the Army, they had created one fine mess that would not go away.

CHAPTER 14

Aftermath - A Humanitarian Crisis

The world is a dangerous place, not because of those who do evil, but because of those who look on and do nothing ...

ALBERT EINSTEIN

DESPITE THE SALVATION ARMY'S INSISTENCE that all was well at Howard, and despite threats to staff and attempts to bar the media, reports still trickled out.

Reporters from the Zimbabwe Sunday Mail and Guardian newspapers found that the wards were generally dirty, lacked fresh air and were mostly empty. The few patients found in the wards were awaiting transfer or discharge. The hospital was left with only two young doctors that nurses said were not experienced enough to carry out major surgery or equipped to handle the entire medical workload.

Hospital staff told reporters that conditions had deteriorated seriously following Dr. Thistle's dismissal. Patients interviewed confirmed their findings.

"We are deeply pained because this is the hospital that we used to rely on," said Shelly Mhundwa, a Chiweshe resident, who was seeking treatment for a broken leg. "Many of us are very poor in this area.

Many people are farm labourers. Getting money for treatment elsewhere is something we cannot afford," Mhundwa said. "During Dr. Thistle's time, there was nothing this hospital couldn't offer. It was even better than Parirenyatwa Hospital … we are very worried about how we are going to survive."

The first report of the death of one of Howard's former patients was of a 40-year-old respected mother who had arrived at the hospital at the appointed time to check on her colostomy. This was for a partial bowel resection that Dr. Thistle had done to save her life. Upon arrival, she and her children found that the good doctor had been removed with 24-hours' notice. Angry and frustrated, her children appealed to the Provincial Governor who intervened and provided transportation to Bindura Hospital. The doctors there, who were not specialists and had no knowledge of her history, did what they thought was right, opening her up and reconnecting the bowel. But when the woman was discharged, on the way home in a car the wound broke open and her intestines spilled out. Paul, who was back at work on August 13, did a further operation to repair the damage, but on August 26 she died of shock.

Wards that had previously been filled to capacity, were now down to a trickle of patients—4 or 5 patients in each of the male and female wards—and deaths continuing to climb.

Conditions at Howard Hospital continued to deteriorate. According to Chief Negomo, 50 deaths had been attributed to the acute reduction of health care services at Howard. His sons were leading the fight for full restoration of health services at the hospital. The community, Paul was told, was examining the possibility of a class action suit against the Salvation Army, but lack of funds made it impossible to proceed. Unless a lawyer who was interested in civil rights would take the case pro bono, the idea would have to be forgotten.

Local people reported that the gardens at Howard were full of weeds, the paint was peeling, and the place was dirty. They also confirmed that there were few patients in the wards. A first-hand report from staff at the hospital on November 9, 2012 confirmed that the hospital was running at a fraction of its capacity. Out of a total of 144 beds, only 5 of 32 beds in the male ward were occupied, 7 out of 32 beds in the female ward and 20 out of 40 beds in the Children's and Therapeutic wards,

In late November 2012, Doug McLellan, a photojournalist from Windsor, Ontario visited Howard Hospital, but was denied permission to photograph the premises, despite having taken photos previously, in 2001, 2006, 2008 and 2010. In fact, his photos inspired many doctors to volunteer their services and raised thousands of dollars from donors. In the past, the Salvation Army had been only too happy to publish McLellan's photos in their magazines and books in four countries. Even though he was willing to photograph only the areas of their choice, he was still not allowed to enter the hospital or photograph the grounds.

McLellan paid four visits to the hospital compound. There were few cars, a couple of security guards and a few people milling about, on average about seven people lined up outside the Outpatients ward. There was no doctor to be seen in Paul's old office, nor any patients lined up outside. McLellan reported that his sense of being closely watched was confirmed by an Army official's knowledge of the previous day's photos. Testimony from the people he met—staff, nurses, community leaders, patients and others—also confirmed that they wanted their doctor back. More than one person suggested that Thistle's homecoming would be bigger than a visit by the president.

The overwhelming impression was that the local people were indeed suffering. An orderly who fell off his motorcycle and was treated at Howard, had a hard time finding medicine for pain relief. Another woman, who depended on the outreach program, was reduced to eating boiled vegetables only. McLellan donated $10 to buy her some cooking oil. As he observed, Howard Hospital was transformed from a place brimming with life and activity to a place filled with sorrow and regret. One man, Katumbe, well known to McLellan, likened it to a home following a death—the home may look the same, but it felt differently.

Outside, before he was ordered to stop, he was able to snap one photo that provided proof of the changes. On a normal day, under Paul's leadership, 200 to 300 people would be lined up outside the hospital, patiently waiting to be seen. On a slow day, the number might be down to 100, but on this particular morning, only thirty people waited for the Outpatient Clinic to open. McLellan's parting impression was that the hospital was in an emergency situation. In other words, they were keeping the doors open, but limiting media coverage.

Howard Hospital, which had always been considered a public hospital was now being treated like Fort Knox, or a prison compound, with those who work there barred from speaking to or fraternizing with the inmates and visitors and the press barred as well.

Besides the changes at the hospital, there were changes on the administrative side. On October 6, 2012, Commissioner Venice Chigariro received her own transfer orders to report to the Kenya East Territory as Territorial Commander of that region effective January 1, 2013. And on the same day Commissioner Kenneth Hodder, International Secretary for Personnel was dispatched as Territorial Commander of Kenya's West Territory. As well, Commissioner Amos Makina, who had served of Territorial Commander of Zimbabwe announced his retirement effective January 1, 2013.

In late November, 2012, Major Gillian Brown, Director of World Missions for the Canada and Bermuda headquarters issued an update of her recent visit to Howard Hospital stating that the Army was rebuilding relationships with the Chiweshe headmen. In fact, the headman's sons had been trying to raise a petition to reinstate Dr. Thistle, but after being threatened with arrest, they had abandoned the idea. Brown went on to state that Howard Hospital "had not been financially sustainable over many years," but she failed to offer a reason why. She advised that over the next six months, changes would be forthcoming, including a plan to stabilize the hospital through "long term institutional support," claiming that many other Salvation Army missions were supported in this manner. Brown's report also took credit for a new ambulance that was delivered to Howard Hospital on November 19 from the Rotary Club in Canada, stating that this was one of "many signs" that underlined the continuing support of donors to Howard Hospital and the international Salvation Army.

What she neglected to include in her report was that this was the same ambulance that was due for delivery three months before, in the midst of the August protests. The ambulance was donated by the Rotary Club in Langley, B.C., but was held back due to Paul Thistle's removal. According to Brown, everything at Howard was running smoothly. The Army had the support of the majority of the hospital staff; and the community, as well as the local church congregation, most of whom were involved in the protests over Thistle's dismissal, was thriving once again. Brown concluded with assurances that International Headquarters was committed to Howard Hospital and would continue to "provide a ministry that was expert and compassionate," overlooking the fact that a replacement for Dr. Thistle had still not arrived.

On December 6, departing Commissioner Chigariro, in a last ditch attempt to bolster her image and that of the Army, made a donation of anesthetic and surgical equipment to another Salvation Army hospital in Zimbabwe. According to an article that appeared in the

Zimbabwe Chronical, Tshelanyemba Hospital, another hospital run by the Army in Matobo District, Western Zimbabwe, received an anesthetic machine and surgical LED light. The machines, valued at $49,000 US, were donated at a farewell ceremony held in Bulawayo. In presenting the state-of-the-art equipment, Chigariro said it was part of "the church's vision to provide affordable and quality healthcare to all."

As if to put a lid on the happenings at Howard in the previous year, the Army shut down the Howard Hospital website, advising people to contact The Salvation Army directly.

But an article by SW Radio's Alex Bell on February 7, 2013, reported that local police had clamped down on the community itself, stopping them from protesting, speaking to the media, or even from signing a petition that was started in 2012. The petition, intended for delivery to the government urging them to intervene, never saw the light of day. Talk of a class action suit to be filed by the headmen on behalf of the people of Chiweshe also never materialized. What the group needed was the interest of a human rights lawyer willing to take on their case, but there was none to be found in Zimbabwe.

SW Radio Africa reported that a local workers' committee was attempting to file an appeal. They also reported that no chief surgeon had yet been appointed to replace Dr. Thistle. The local community was being actively silenced, with a heavy police presence in the area preventing people from protesting. So, not only had Dr. Thistle been forced to remain silent under threat of political retaliation, the local community was being actively silenced by a heavy police presence.

Stephen Lewis, former Canadian Ambassador to the United Nationals and UN Special Envoy for HIV/AIDS in Africa, and Head of the Stephen Lewis Foundation, has a particular interest in Howard. Since 2003, his foundation has been involved in fighting the scourge of HIV/AIDS in Africa and has supported Howard Hospital in their prevention efforts. When he asked General Bond about the plight of the nurses, she replied, "They were inciting violence." In response to any question concerning Howard Hospital, the words did not differ. The same song reverberated through all the levels of bureaucracy. If nothing else, the official Salvation Army spin was intact, even though few believed it.

Part III
Truth and Consequences

CHAPTER 15

We Accuse ... The Case Against Paul Thistle

---

*I have decided to stick with love ... Hate
is too great a burden to bear*

MARTIN LUTHER KING JR.

WHEN PAUL THISTLE ARRIVED IN Africa to begin his life's mission, he was prepared for any danger, but he never imagined the real peril would come from within his own church. After 17 years of service, the idea of being made a scapegoat for the failings of that church was not in the cards.

How, then, was this allowed to happen? What exactly had Dr. Thistle done wrong? What sins had he committed in his desire to do right by the people of Chiweshe? By abiding to his Christian principles and upholding the oath that he had sworn as a medical doctor?

According to the Army, he was guilty of **not following strict Salvation Army protocols regarding donation remittance.** What they neglected to mention in their long list of grievances is the fact that the very people accusing Dr. Thistle, Commissioner Chigariro and company, were also guilty of not abiding by the Army's protocol.

They also accused him **of not following Canada Revenue Agency guidelines pertaining to monies donated by IFHH and other Canadian donor groups**, but Canadian officials were aware of the circumstances pertaining to these donations and there were no complaints registered by any of the donor groups during Dr. Thistle's tenure because the money was allocated to and used for the purpose to which it was given. It was only after his departure, when recently donated funds disappeared, that donors raised questions and asked for explanations. The Army was also patently aware of how donations were raised and how they arrived. Howard Hospital's 2010 Annual Report shows two options for sending donations: either through Canada and Bermuda Territories or directly to Howard Hospital, so the Army cannot possibly claim that they did not know. Commissioner Chigariro, in fact, failed to adhere to Canadian government guidelines that resulted in the cancellation of the Canadian International Development Agency (CIDA) grant.

Not communicating with International Headquarters. The fact that all correspondence with IHQ as well as any other paperwork such as annual reports passed through Commissioner Makina's hands first, makes this accusation suspect. A case in point was Makina's letter of July 15, 2012 to Dr. Thistle, confirming his transfer back to Canada. The letter was sent from Makina's office at International Headquarters in London but copied to no one else but Commissioner Chigariro in Harare. So, was this letter composed in consultation with other personnel at International Headquarters or did it bypass scrutiny of other decision-makers involved in the transfer of Dr. Thistle?

Then there were the personal insults.

Dr. Thistle was stubborn, arrogant and unable to get along with people. This opinion is in stark contrast to those who know him personally—staff who worked alongside him on a daily basis, volunteers who willingly gave of their time and talent to travel halfway around the world to volunteer at Howard Hospital, medical colleagues who praised his exceptional skills and tenacity in spite of the Army's meager support. Without exceptional people skills, Dr. Thistle would never have been able to attract and inspire volunteers to contribute their time, skills or money required to keep the hospital afloat. If his accusers in Toronto or London had ever bothered to meet Dr. Thistle and view his work, things might have turned out differently for all concerned, most especially for Dr. Thistle and the people of Chiweshe. Instead, they chose to sit comfortably at their desks, content to believe the word of the very people intent on getting rid of him.

He was also **too big for his boots and went too far.** If taking matters into your own hands in order to keep donations out of the hands of others was going too far, this accusation is true, but it had nothing to do with pride. If presenting to the world the needs of the poor to keep the hospital running and in good financial standing can be construed as being too big for his boots, then Dr. Thistle is guilty as charged. But no one who knows him would recognize the person the Army described. Other words spring to mind: hero, champion of human rights, loyal, determined, focused, and brave. Dr. John Sullivan, former officer and minister in the United Church goes further, describing Paul as "Christ-like."

As if the personal damage was not enough, they also attacked his professional reputation by accusing him of using outdated drugs, thereby endangering the lives of patients. As Dr. Thistle stated, surely this is a medical call, best left to authorities on the subject and not to the judgement of administrators with no medical expertise.

A research study conducted by the US Food and drug administration, on behalf of the US military, concluded that there is no danger. Most drugs, even years past their expiry date, still retain their potency. Harvard University drew the same conclusion, allowing that while the effectiveness of a drug may decrease over time, much of the original potency remains as long as a decade after the expiration date. The rare exceptions are drugs such as tetracycline, nitroglycerin, insulin and liquid antibiotics—drugs that were not in use at Howard Hospital.

As far as Paul Thistle was concerned, he would rather give an outdated, still potent, drug, than no drugs at all. Since the Army paid for the shipments of containers of drugs and medical supplies, Dr. Thistle had no control over their delivery. One of the containers of drugs bound for Howard was labeled "near expiry date" and failed to reach the hospital, having been "disposed of." Once again, someone with no medical knowledge and without consultation with the hospital's Chief Medical Officer made the decision to divert an entire container of much-needed medicine to some other destination or garbage heap.

- Performing complex procedures which the Army could not afford to cover in case of a malpractice suit—the same sorry excuse brought up in front of Dr. Silverman.
- Turning the hospital from its origins as a primary care model to that of a surgical specialist facility.

These accusations are patently false on both counts.

As far back as 1918, before Howard Hospital existed, Major Bradley treated villagers with prayer and simple medicines, although their recovery probably had more to do with prayer than medicine, considering the few medicines that were available. With the arrival of the Kirbys at the mission site in 1923, they carried on the same level of care, tending to the sick and wounded within the community. The opening of the hospital merely provided a structure to what others had been doing all along.

From its humble beginnings, under the guidance of its first doctor, Jock Cook, the hospital was able to provide total care. Dr. Cook took pride in the fact that in addition to the complex surgery that he provided, the hospital offered dental, surgical orthopedic, obstetric and eye surgery utilizing the skills of visiting doctors. He sent few cases to Harare. During Dr. Watt's time, he sent only bowel resections and cancer cases to Harare, as the cost of sending patients there was too great. Visiting specialists would do the non-emergency work, like plastics and cataracts. University doctors would do rounds on puzzling medical conditions. Schizophrenic and other psychiatric conditions were treated as well.

Contrary to the perceptions at International Headquarters, surgery is not the culprit. It rarely needs expensive drugs or blood—it's all in the skill of the surgeon.

Dr. Thistle, in collaboration with Dr. Michael Silverman and universities in Canada, has been at the forefront of preventive medicine, especially pertaining to HIV and TB. Most of those initiatives, including a mobile educational team that visited schools and beer halls using puppetry to explain prevention, have been abandoned.

- Attracting patients from all over Africa instead of concentrating on his own community

This was duplicity at its best, from the very people who were masters at concentrating on everything but their own community. The reasons why people came to Howard were obvious. Prior to Dr. Thistle's forced departure, the hospital had an impeccable reputation for providing quality care at an affordable cost. For the local population, the hospital was their lifeline, somewhere they could go for medical care, regardless of their economic circumstances. Locals who could pay were charged reasonable rates based on their ability to pay; those who could not afford to pay with cash were given the option of contributing produce instead, but no one in need was turned away. Patients from other parts of Africa who mistrusted government-run facilities and who could afford to pay more, were charged more. This model, which applied fees based on affordability, worked well and ensured a steady flow of income for the hospital. It is a universal model that is no different than proposals being considered by various provinces in Canada and other countries around the world, where publicly-funded medicine goes hand in hand with private treatment for those who can afford it.

Finally, that he **disobeyed orders from THQ and IHQ**. This charge is not disputed. It was Army officials in Harare who were keen on turning Howard into a profit-based private hospital. By resisting their attempts, Dr. Thistle was able to maintain affordable fees for the poor. He also spoke out for the welfare of his staff, guaranteeing sustainable salaries and preventing Harare THQ from demanding arbitrary payment from hospital employees. After his dismissal, lower level employee salaries were cut by over 50%, wages were delayed and employees were required to contribute to THQ meetings held at Victoria Falls.

If THQ Harare had safe-guarded and administered the use of donations and salaries with due fiscal governance, there would have been no need for Dr. Thistle to involve himself in these matters at all; but when donations had a habit of being delayed or disappearing altogether, and staff salaries were cut-back, delayed or not paid at all, in all good conscience, he could not allow the situation to continue.

To add to the problem, donors can attest to Commissioner Chigariro assessing a 30% fee against designated funds coming through her office specifically earmarked for mission-based projects in Zimbabwe. This was in addition to the 10% assessment fee that was automatically levied on incoming donations to Harare territorial headquarters.

By the time donations arrived at Howard Hospital, the original donation would be reduced by some 40%.

So, despite the demands of his medical work, Dr. Thistle was forced to rely on direct donations to keep the hospital operational. In some instances they were hand-delivered by volunteers or passed over to him at fundraising events during his furloughs in Canada. All direct donations were deposited into the Howard Hospital operating account, bypassing fees assessed by the various Salvation Army headquarters along the official donation chain.

Ironically, although they had a long list of grievances towards Dr. Thistle, none of these accusations were ever shared with him. But while he was forced to remain silent, the people who could not speak about personnel matters, according to those who asked, nevertheless spoke openly about them. And Commissioner Chigariro spearheaded the campaign, never missing an opportunity to defame Dr. Thistle and those who supported him. With Thistle out of the way, out of her jurisdiction, Chigariro let loose a torrent of vindictive statements to the press, safe in the knowledge that whatever falsehoods she uttered would be backed up by the uniforms behind her.

Commissioner Chigariro could not be described as a bright woman. The most you could surmise from her behaviour, witnessed by people who have crossed her path, is that she is cunning, and vindictive when she doesn't get her own way. Based on her behavior, she relied on her belief that if she issued receipts for the money received, the donors would be satisfied and go on their merry way. What she didn't count on was how deeply donors and volunteers cared for the people of Chiweshe, through their efforts to raise funds and protect the programs they believed they were paying for. On their behalf, Dr. Thistle followed the money trail and all roads led to the Commissioner—and if she couldn't get her way, Dr. Thistle and his "band of supporters" were going to shoulder the blame.

But in her rabid desire to get rid of Dr. Thistle, Chigariro effectively killed the engineer who drove the train, and ran it off the track. Regardless of her dislike for the man himself, the Commissioner failed to consider how she intended to keep the hospital operating without the donor money and free help that her target brought in. In reality, the funds that kept the hospital running came not from the Salvation Army, who claim to operate the hospital, though contribute little, but from other faiths and denominations. Yet, instead of thanking the donors and showing appreciation for their efforts on the Army's behalf, these groups are now denigrated and denied access to the hospital or any mention of Howard. Now they are spoken of in derogatory terms as "Paul's followers."

Allan Bacon, retired Director of Overseas Development for the Salvation Army Canada and Bermuda Territories, had this to say about the treatment of volunteers: "The great irony in all of this is that it is the non-Salvationists who have supported Paul's work who are rallying to his support and protesting his removal. These donors have had no problems with Paul's accountability over the years. What does the public think when it sees Jewish groups, the United Church of Canada and other steadfast in their support of Paul and his work and yet witness the complete failure to give him support within his own church?"

Jealousy was another factor that played a pivotal role. Dr. Thistle's reputation locally and abroad, his high regard amongst patients and community elders was considered by Chigariro to be more of a liability than an asset and bolstered her arguments against him. No officer was supposed to stand out. A lowly Captain could never trump a Commissioner. Obedient and compliant officers survived and those who rose above the crowd could easily be brought down with a few whispers in the ears of higher ranks.

The plot to get rid of Dr. Thistle wasn't a sudden decision, but a series of slanders cooked up by Commissioners Chigariro and Makina in Zimbabwe and served on a platter to IHQ in London. This slow death by a thousand cuts began when medical students who volunteered at Howard Hospital in 2010 and 2011 reported hearing high-ranking officers making disparaging remarks about Dr. Thistle and being very upset by what they heard. According to the whispers, he had been a "thorn in the side for a long time and had better toe the line." Despite never having met Dr. Thistle, those in charge at IHQ appeared all too keen to believe whatever was said about him in order to curry favour with their African counterparts, who showered them with flattery, cheering crowds and dinners in their honour.

By August 2012, senior officers in London had heard enough slanderous accusations against Dr. Thistle, that all it took was a final nod in his direction for London to sanction his removal. There was obviously no thought to what would happen when the only surgeon was suddenly wrenched from the community with no replacement. When the local people protested, Paul was blamed for inciting violence. But the underlying issue still goes back to money.

Commissioner Chigariro worked up a case against Paul Thistle and someone at International Headquarters in London listened to her complaints and gave in to her demands that Paul be removed. Someone in that office issued the order for the Thistles to leave Zimbabwe by September 1, without consulting the Canadian Territory. However, the Commissioner was in Canada during the period of July 8-14, 2012 to attend the International Leaders' Conference. Although there is no confirmation, it is conceivable that she took this opportunity to plead her grievances to the Canadian Territorial Command at that time. The Thistles left Canada for Zimbabwe on July 13, and either by coincidence or design, their departure was immediately followed by the Commissioner's own return on July 14. It is hard to believe that the Canadian territory was unaware of her plans from the outset.

The Army's concern for the people of Chiweshe is civil but lukewarm, *"We consider the health of its patients and well-being of the staff at Howard Hospital to be of paramount importance."…Commissioner Brian Peddle, press release August 12, 2012.*

But actions speak louder than words, for when the local community—whose welfare was of "paramount importance" to the Army—rebelled, that incident presented the perfect opportunity to remove Dr. Thistle, not just from the territory controlled by the two local commissioners, but out of the country altogether. Now, the organization that was all about compassion, all about saving body and soul, was more about Army than Salvation.

This is the very antithesis of what The Salvation Army is all about. An organization that claims to be guided by the hand of God should recognize that there are others in the world who wish to demonstrate their own faith through compassion and hard work. But the Army today is more about corporate branding and preserving their image than fixing the wrongs within the organization. It is far easier to talk the talk than walk the walk, as commissioned officers who are sent to danger zones with little support from the corporation have discovered.

Dr. Thistle is a physician first, something the Army chose to overlook. His ethical obligation to his patients was sadly ignored by his superiors and the people who should have supported him. As Dr. Silverman pointed out, if a competent administrator had been assigned to Howard Hospital, there would have been no need for Paul to involve himself in the hospital's finances. He would have been free to concentrate on his medical work and the job he was assigned to do, that of Chief Medical Officer. With 100 staff and some 300 patients a day, his workload would have broken an ordinary man. Add to that all the fund-raising he willingly executed, it is a wonder that his own health didn't fail.

Had there been any mention of the wear and tear that years of long hours and interrupted sleep does to a physician, particularly in a hospital with little funding and inadequate staffing, the decision to move him out of that situation for rest and respite would have been understandable. But neither his physical or mental state figured into the equation.

There is no excuse or reasonable explanation for the Salvation Army's actions. Nor can they be excused for being politically naïve. The organization has a long history of dealing with the political situation in Zimbabwe. Missionaries have been on the ground since the country was formed, with many of its senior officers born and raised in Zimbabwe. Mugabe has been in power for more than 30 years, so pleading ignorance doesn't wash.

The Army also has considerable experience in the health care field. They operate 27 hospitals in a variety of countries. Howard Hospital is not the only hospital that the Army operates in Africa, including the three facilities in Zimbabwe. And, to claim ignorance of financial irregularities at Howard, says more about their governance or lack thereof than they care to admit.

The Salvation Army's response to any form of criticism is indicative of the behaviour of other faith groups who come under fire: first denying the problem exists, then failing to take the necessary steps to correct it; but no problem can be fixed until it is first acknowledged.

Had the people who approved his removal got up from behind their desks and traveled to Howard Hospital when Paul Thistle first raised concerns over funding, had they learned about the Shona culture and how seamlessly he fit into it, they would have been able to see for themselves what a void his departure would leave. Instead they were more focused on their own agenda, saving face, and were blindsided by the uproar Thistle's departure caused. Had they studied the situation before leaving the local population without proper medical care, they could have avoided the tsunami of shock and anger that followed his abrupt departure, not to mention the ensuing damage to their reputation.

CHAPTER 16

The Money Trail

*A man is rich in proportion to the things
he can afford to let alone*

HENRY DAVID THOREAU

THERE'S A CATCHPHRASE MADE POPULAR by the Watergate film *All the President's Men*: "Follow the money and it will lead to the truth." In this case, the trail begins with funds raised in Canada through the efforts of Dr. Thistle and the supporters of Howard Hospital which were then donated to The Salvation Army.

At Howard Hospital, the money was destined to flow in a straight line that began with the influx of donations into the International Headquarters in London, where it was then distributed to individual territories, under the supervision of each Territory's Commander. But, starting in 2008, the rules changed and donations were sent directly to the Territorial International Commander in each region. From that point on, the trail began to twist and turn, leading to a labyrinth of lies and deceit as deep as the potholes on the road from Harare to Howard.

Cash flow problems were not new in Zimbabwe, nor unique to Howard Hospital. And Paul Thistle wasn't the first doctor to question authority. According to Dr. Thistle's predecessor, Dr. James Watt, following the country's independence in 1980, donations were handled with utmost transparency. In those days, Salvation Army finance officers were honest to the penny and Territorial Commanders were very supportive of medical work. IHQ provided a list that identified the donor, the amount donated and its intended use, if stated. Donors received a thank you note directly from the hospital and when the project was completed, they were sent another note with pictures, showing the result. In this way, the donors were always kept informed and shown appreciation for their gifts.

But on his return to Zimbabwe in 1994, money problems surfaced. The Children's Village in Calgary, where Dr. Watt had spent the last 10 years, had raised $7,000 for a play centre at Howard. The money was sent from THQ Canada to IHQ London, then on to THQ Harare, but the money didn't arrive. After a slew of correspondence passed back and forth from Zimbabwe to Canada, it suddenly appeared. With funds delayed up to a year and others not traceable, he began to ask a lot of questions.

In the late 1990s some US$42,000 disappeared from Howard Hospital's reserve account which held money for projects that were in process but not yet completed. All monies donated to the Zimbabwe Salvation Army were held at THQ Harare, including those for Howard Hospital and the loss occurred when THQ Harare changed banks. A bottom-line review was done, and while there was no overall loss in total monies held by The Salvation Army, the missing funds in Howard's reserve fund were dismissed as an error in accounting entries. The person who served as Hospital Administrator for part of that time was none other than Commissioner Chigariro. She was later appointed as Finance Officer at THQ Harare. On his return to Canada in 2000, Dr. Watt reported that the money had not been located or repaid and as of this writing, it is still missing.

Retired Salvation Army Officer, Major Dorothy Munday, in a letter to Commissioner Brian Peddle in Toronto, detailed her own experience working at Howard. Between 1987 and 1995, she served at Howard Hospital as the Nursing Instructor. She was appointed in 1987 to fill the gap created by another swift transfer that created a similar personnel problem. At the time, the hospital was also dealing with a serious internal fraud that extended across the entire territory. Staff lived from hand to mouth, never knowing if the hospital would survive another month. Basic supplies like sheets, blanket and towels were insufficient for daily needs. Only donations from Canada and Switzerland kept them afloat during those dark and difficult days.

SOMETHING WICKED COMES THIS WAY

Dr. Thistle's own troubles began when he clashed with Commissioner Chigariro over the way donated funds were handled and allocated. Although he had complained about missing funds since the Commissioner's appointment in 2008 and she had offered to assist, four years later nothing had changed. Donations were raised to fund specific programs, but the new Commissioner refused to abide by any rules that were not her own or to her advantage. Far too often the money was used for other purposes or disappeared altogether.

Under normal circumstances, the hospital is mostly self-run, requiring little intervention. Officially, the territorial headquarters oversees the hospital, which pays a certain amount each year for this "supervision." The hospital's books are kept by the administrator and a finance person, sometimes called the bursar. Regular finance meetings involving the Chief Medical Officer, the Matron, the Tutor, the Chaplain, as well as the bursar and the Hospital Administrator, are regularly held, often with someone from THQ in attendance. Purchases had to be agreed to before being made, except for routine food items. Then the receipts were signed to acknowledge that the goods had been received and were in use. Income from the Outpatient clerks and Dispensary was noted.

Around 2003, accountability slackened. The Chief Medical Officer was no longer involved and Paul noticed that despite the steady flow of funds into Howard, it became apparent that the local hospital basket had a giant hole in it. Increasingly, he was forced to look elsewhere for funding to keep the hospital going. That's when he started raising more direct donations—having to rely on aid sent directly to the hospital, often hand-delivered. All of these donations were recorded in the hospitals books. The books were audited regularly by THQ in Harare and the Hospital Administrator was in daily contact with that office.

When Vinece Chigariro was appointed as Territorial Commander in 2008, the entire operation of Howard Hospital changed. Her arrival, together with the Army's implementation of new funding rules, converged like the perfect storm, guaranteeing that incoming funds passed across her desk. As a result, all accountability in Zimbabwe vanished. Howard Hospital administration could not account for hundreds of thousands of dollars of failed projects. Board meetings were scant, held months apart. There had been no community advisory board for years. When a board meeting did occur, minutes were brief or non-existent and no action came out of it. Over the years, as the situation grew worse, Dr. Thistle continued to raise concerns about the management of donated funds, but they were also continually ignored.

Gay Pratt, a member of the Salvation Army's Ottawa Citadel Corps, spent six months at Howard Hospital in 2009. During that time her mother sent $10,000 through the Army's prescribed channels to fund Dr. Thistle's work at Howard. The trail stopped at Zimbabwe THQ, where the money disappeared, but following strenuous objections from Canada, it was quietly replaced with money that was conveniently available from THQ Canada's funds. The only way to safeguard donations and make sure that the money arrived safely and did not disappear was to have it hand-delivered by volunteers.

The Army's International Headquarters was supposed to be conducting annual audits, but it appears that the books were kept under close supervision by the Territorial Commander, who balked at any outside interference, even from London. Even though IHQ admitted several times that the books were not well kept, they apparently had no will to investigate whether this was the result of incompetency or dishonesty. So the Army's official statement that they found no evidence of financial misconduct is misleading.

This hands-off approach could also have its roots in politics. Following Independence from an oppressive white government, African leaders objected to anything smacking of white control. This perception and defiant attitude was very evident at THQ Zimbabwe, where even auditors from IHQ London were seen as neo-colonial. This attitude was particularly evident in both the International Secretary for Africa, Makina, and Territorial Commander, Chigariro (fellow Africans who are very good friends). The two worked well in tandem. Makina objected to any supervision of the new Howard Hospital and Chigariro insisted that all donations pass through her hands.

The Good Samaritans

In 2001, when Jennifer Reid, another of the Peterborough volunteers, travelled to Howard Hospital for the first time to teach clinical midwifery, she was struck by how old and dilapidated the buildings were. Right beside the old hospital sat the new Howard Hospital—a fine expansive building with fresh walls and new wiring and plumbing. But now, one year after the project began, Reid was told that the money had run out. The buildings sat there for five more years until, in 2006, Zimbabwean authorities declared it unfit for use. Yet, as she notes, there was not one word in any of the Salvation Army press releases about this new facility that was allowed to sit unfinished and in a deteriorating state for a dozen years. Reid was astounded by such massive waste and mismanagement of donor dollars while she was asking Howard's supporters to donate $4 so that the staff could administer antiretroviral drugs to women in labour to prevent spreading HIV to their babies. Without the available medication, it was likely that the mothers would die, but if the babies proved to be HIV negative, they were more likely to be adopted by other families.

Such was the situation that volunteers and staff faced all the time. There were always too many people to attend to, too many problems to be fixed and too little money to go around. But even more frustrating and unexplainable was the fact that every time hard-earned money flowed in, it somehow fell into a big black hole never to be seen again.

One of the largest and most steadfast contributors to Howard Hospital and its various programs is the group of volunteers from Peterborough, comprised of eight United Churches in the area. As a member of Donwood United Church, Brian Nichols can attest to how monies began to flow to Howard. In his letter of August 28, 2012 addressed to General Bond and Territorial Headquarters in Canada, he outlined his long history with Howard Hospital. Initially, the group sent money through Ve'ahavta, the Canadian Jewish Humanitarian and Relief Committee, but when that organization found it necessary to apply a 15% administration fee, they searched for other means of distribution while continuing a solid relationship with Ve'ahavta. By combining the money they raised with Rotary

International, they found that the funds could be doubled through various Canadian government programs. Because of the transparency of the Donwood United Church fund-raising efforts, other groups and individuals chose to combine their efforts with Donwood.

But since their involvement with Howard Hospital that began in 2003-04, hyper-inflation of the Zimbabwean dollar reduced the value of donations by half or more. In those days, it was illegal to use American currency in Zimbabwe and the only other choice was the black market. The other way around this dilemma was to deliver it by hand and that is what Brian chose to do.

His pattern when he arrived at Hospital was to meet with senior administration, tell them what money he was able to bring and confirm that the plan agreed to the previous year was still the priority. If so, they would re-commit; if not, they changed the plan, communicating directly with hospital staff to best determine how to use their limited resources. The group's financial support extended beyond the hospital and into the community to God Knows Orphanage, Nyachuru Primary and Secondary Schools, helping individual families with school fees, funeral costs, hospital fees, roof repairs and much more.

Their level of commitment is boundless. The group was able to guarantee to donors that 100% of donations went directly to the work of Howard Hospital and its various projects. All of their overhead costs, including postage, are paid for by the volunteers themselves, who followed the money to see directly how it was spent. The testimonies these volunteers brought back from Howard, about how the money was used, ensured that people continued to donate. Money for school fees went directly to the school and donors were provided with receipts.

Over the years, they have built close relationships inside and outside the community to ensure that the needs of the Chiweshe community are met. Whenever possible, materials were purchased in Zimbabwe and labour paid for on site.

This arrangement could not be tolerated by the Territorial Commander who did everything in her power to subvert programs and make it difficult for staff and volunteers to do their job. Instead of being grateful for their efforts and helping in the completion of the various projects to improve conditions at Howard, she terminated the volunteer program that included volunteer doctors and nurses from Zimbabwe and abroad, and set about to get a more pliable doctor in charge of Howard.

In 2011, money raised in Canada arrived in Zimbabwe, specifically earmarked for a program to train individuals to become rehabilitation aides. Their duties were split between hospital activities— mobilizing in-patients, making crutches, cleaning the physiotherapy space, triaging and registering individuals as they came into the physiotherapy unit, helping transfer patients, ordering and picking up supplies, etc. As well, their off-hospital duties included biking to communities to provide home care for patients who couldn't make it to the hospital on a regular basis. For all of this work, they were to be paid $20 per month, but money earmarked for their training never reached the aides. A staff member reported that the aides received no pay for four months, from July 2011 until November 2011. The Salvation Army did not approve the program until September of 2011, but Paul and Pedrinah did not think it was fair to let the aides work without appreciation in the interim, or let them sit idle. So, against the wishes of the administrator, The Thistles paid them out of pocket until the funds were finally approved in September.

Amazingly, despite no compensation for their efforts, the aides continued to work. Paul Thistle arranged for them to be paid from other donations that were raised while he was on his annual furlough to Canada.

When Sarah LeBouthillier, the volunteer physiotherapist from Peterborough, Ontario arrived at the hospital in July 2011 approximately six months after the program was initiated in February 2011, the aides' bikes were in disrepair. New bikes had arrived in a shipping container, but had not been distributed to replace the old ones. When the head of the rehabilitation unit's bike was stolen, she was told that she was not allowed to have a new one because the administration had no proof that it had been stolen. Sarah's own request for a new bike, to enable her to accompany the rehabilitation aides on their field trips, was treated with equal disdain. The key to the container, she was informed, had been lost. Three weeks later, with Paul's intervention, the mysterious lost key was found and a bike was provided to Sarah for her last weeks of stay.

In November 2011, the aides also complained to the administration that their bike parts were wearing out and that they needed new tires and brakes. This maintenance was also included as part of the program. The administration promised to order new parts that week, but it took until March 25 of 2012 before new parts were purchased.

Other volunteers who spent time at Howard reported on the Salvation Army Canada and Bermuda Territories website that they have witnessed Salvation Army officers helping themselves to cash and other supplies.

Two Norwegian anesthetists who had volunteered at Howard every year since 2002, also organized a Norwegian aid program to pay the school fees of more than 100 children and young people. In their years at Howard, they got to know the hospital, the staff and members of the community, and were surprised to learn that the Salvation Army did not contribute economically to the hospital. Instead, the local Salvation Army drained money from it. In their comments posted to the Salvation Army's Canada and Bermuda Territories website on August 29, 2012, the doctors noted that they had witnessed the administrators and other Salvation Army officers stealing from the hospital. "We wrote a letter to International SA in London about this affair. Nothing was done. And now they have removed he who contributed and sacrificed." They also noted "they were glad to hear that SA Canada was sending medical supplies, but they hoped that they were necessary medicines and supplies, because a lot of what was sent was not usable."

Biting the Hand that Feeds You

But the last nail in the coffin came in early 2012, when Howard Hospital was granted $250,000 from the Canadian International Development Fund for HIV treatment. Grants of any kind, especially those awarded by governments are hard to come by. They are extremely competitive and an enormous amount of work by Canadian volunteers went into winning this competition. CIDA's condition for the awarding of the grant was that the money be used specifically to fund a new HIV program at Howard, but, as Dr. Michael Silverman reports, the Territorial Command in Harare were not only extremely unhelpful but overtly obstructive, insisting that the money would be used "at their discretion," with no guarantee that Howard Hospital would see a penny of it. CIDA naturally would not comply with anything less than transparent accounting and strict adherence to guidelines laid out for the fund's use. Even after it was explained that the funds would be withdrawn if the local command did not comply with CIDA's rules, THQ Harare refused to co-operate. As Dr. Silverman observed, clearly their own demands and grip on authority were more important than the welfare of the poor and the sick. Their fists were clamped around the bundles of dollars that arrived from Canada on a regular basis and they were not about to let it go. One man stood in the way, so the Territorial Command demanded that he be removed and their request was accepted at face value. With the

Thistles removed, staff silenced and volunteers and the press barred from the premises, the territorial commanders were free to do with Howard Hospital as they wished.

Dividing the Spoils

Shortly after the Thistles' departure, building materials worth $18,000, along with $10,000 in cash, provided by St. Matthew's-Donwood United Church in Peterborough, Ontario, Canada went missing. The building materials sat for more than a year in a storage container at the hospital because a site plan could not or would not be approved by the Salvation Army territorial command in Harare. According to Brian Nichols, in a letter to the Salvation Army in Canada, the looting appears to have been done under the direction of the chief administrator, who was appointed in 2011, during the time the Thistle family was on furlough in Canada in the summer of 2012. Although Nichols received a receipt for this donation, it appears not to have been entered as receivables in the hospital's books. The Army contends that the money was "harder to track" because it had not gone through International Headquarters, but was passed to the hospital directly. However, if proper accounting procedures had been followed, an account of the money would have appeared on the books.

The Peterborough group were not the only ones to run up against the brick wall created at Howard. Dr. John Sullivan is a United Church Minister and former Salvation Army officer, whose parents served in Zimbabwe. Throughout the years, the United Church of Canada has made significant contributions to the work of Howard Hospital. In 2012, they donated another large sum that was handed directly to the hospital's administrator. The church's attempts to contact him to request that the money be returned until the issue with Dr. Thistle was resolved were unsuccessful. As Dr. Sullivan reports, "the only response to their request, and the heartfelt pleas of others who have appealed to the Salvation Army, is for the tambourine to be held out asking for more money." As he rightly asks: "Why would anyone in their right mind make a contribution, knowing that it would be sent on to IHQ, which would send it on to Zimbabwe Territorial Headquarters, with the knowledge that some of it would disappear before it reached the hospital?"

Another of the organizations involved with Howard Hospital is SHUMBA, a Canadian registered charity involved in augmenting the work of hospitals in southern Africa with short term medical volunteers. SHUMBA had earlier donated specialist equipment and delivered it to Howard Hospital for the express use of scheduled volunteers. Since the volunteer program was subsequently cancelled and the equipment was there on a temporary basis, the equipment had to be returned to SHUMBA.

To that end, Dr. Norman Fenton, SHUMBA's Medical Director, and also a frequent donor and volunteer, received permission from the Territorial Command in Harare to retrieve the equipment. On February 3, 2013, he met with THQ's Secretary, Lt.-Col. Varughese and Major Angeline Kapere in Harare to collect the equipment. However, the equipment he was shown was not the complete collection of instruments. All of them were of significant vintage, poor quality and complexity—obviously not the original SHUMBA set. It was agreed that he could travel to Howard Hospital the following Monday to collect the remaining instruments. He was informed that Major Gillian Brown from the Salvation Army in Toronto would be there at the time. But, once again, the equipment that Dr. Fenton came to collect appeared to be missing. A complete set of nasal instruments, plus five rigid scopes, two laryngoscopes and two esophagoscopes were not located. It was evident that the Sister in charge of the operating room was unable to identify nasal instruments. A further inspection of three sets of instruments from the operating room were opened, yet revealed none of the missing instruments worth about $7,000. Dr. Fenton pointed out that the nasal instruments provided by SHUMBA were easily identifiable by the labels "Jed Med" and "Made in the USA." In order to prove his point, Dr. Fenton took a photo that the Howard Hospital staff tried to pass off as instruments supplied by SHUMBA, which were in no way similar to the originals.

The fact that the original equipment was never found flies in the face of Major Gillian Brown's report and the official Salvation Army version that she found no evidence of missing equipment. The fact that International Headquarters in London has admitted that the books are not well kept reveals enough evidence of incompetency to warrant regular audits. Had IHQ intervened sooner and demanded fiscal accountability, the crisis in Chiweshe would never have occurred.

Dr. Fenton was asked by Major Dean Pallant not to wander around the hospital premises as there had been a lot of mistruths spread about the hospital situation, and with the overall sensitive nature of his visit, it was better that way. Dr. Fenton was naturally disappointed. With his visit curtailed, this meant that he would have to forego seeing a lot of people he had intended to visit.

However, his driver, who walked through parts of the hospital, noted that there were about two and five patients in the male and female wards respectively, and a scattering of patients in the children's ward. More noticeable was the lack of booths and people hanging around on the road alongside the front entrance of the hospital—the marketplace—and the courtyard of the hospital. Dr. Fenton took pictures which he later posted to a website for former Salvation Officers, Former Salvation Officers Fellowship (FSAOF).

As with most other charities, the Salvation Army is a clearing house for other people's money—a giant administrative machine that collects donations from various sources and spreads them around where it is most needed. It is also one of the most respected organizations in the world and the recipient of some of the most generous donations ever awarded. But for supporters who recognize the great need and are willing to give so generously of their time and money, the very least they expect is honesty and accountability and for their donations to reach their intended purpose. And if the money falls off that straight and narrow path, they want to know the reason why and how to get it back.

CHAPTER 17

The Strange Marriage of Church and State

Every new & successful example therefore of a perfect separation between ecclesiastical and civil matters, is of importance. And I have no doubt that every new example will succeed, as every past one has done, in showing that religion and government will both exist in greater purity, the less they are mixed together ...

JAMES MADISON, JULY 10, 1822

THERE'S AN OLD ADAGE ABOUT church and state making strange bedfellows—and none more so than in Zimbabwe where the relationship between the two could also be compared to a bad marriage, with each partner complaining about the other while continuing the relationship and using the other for mutual convenience.

In Zimbabwe, where church and state are intertwined, many people use the Army affiliation and uniform to gain trust and further their own purposes and political ambitions. Although every officer in each territory signs a covenant, in Zimbabwe that covenant is often ignored or sidestepped where political alliances forge the greater bond.

Former Territorial Commander, Commissioner Vinece Chigariro, is a close friend of Joice Mujuru, a member of ZANU-PF and the country's first female Vice-President under Robert Mugabe. Mujuru's association with the Army goes back a long way. She attended the Howard Secondary School during Dr. Watt's tenure. Indeed, she was a student in his wife, Bette's, English class, but left in mid-term to cross the border and join the guerillas in the country's fight for independence from the Rhodesian regime.

Mujuru lives on a 3,500 acre farm south of Harare, which the Zimbabwe Supreme Court found to be illegally seized from the farm's owner. She has also been implicated in the sale of 3.5 tonnes of gold from the Democratic Republic of Congo to a European company, contravening European Union sanctions. She and her husband, now deceased, are among the wealthiest and most powerful people in Zimbabwe with extensive interests in mining. According to BBC News, she is one of 200 Zimbabweans hit with European Union sanctions, accusing them of human rights issues.

Mujuru is not immune to using her political status to influence the local population. According to various press reports, Mujuru is listed as a "senior Captain" (a designation no longer listed in the current rank structure) in The Salvation Army and is often photographed wearing her uniform to various social and political events. More likely, she is a senior soldier, with no official rank.

In August 2005, when General and Mrs. John Larsson attended the first ever All Africa Congress, Mujuru was there to welcome them along with the acting Mayor of Harare and the town clerk, both of whom are Salvationists.

In November 2009, General and Mrs. Shaw Clifton led the Zimbabwean Congress in Harare. According to a Salvation Army newsletter, "the General paid a pastoral visit to the acting President of Zimbabwe, the Honourable Vice-President Joice Mujuru, who commended the role being played by The Salvation Army in Zimbabwe in the field of education health and community development," adding that the General's visit "cemented the relationship between the peoples of Zimbabwe and the Army." The article also mentioned that Mujuru hosted a private farewell dinner for the General and his wife, Salvation Army cabinet members and government officials.

As part of its campaign strategy during the latest Zimbabwean elections in July 2013, ZANU-PF members approached local churches in an attempt to woo voters to reverse the loss of votes suffered by President Mugabe in the 2008 election that went to Prime Minister Morgan Tsvangirai and the rival MDC party,

The worsening infighting amongst ZANU-PF members over the future leadership of the party is also rumored to have influenced the clampdown at Howard Hospital. Since Chiweshe is said to be a stronghold of Mujuru's rival, Emmerson Mnangagwa, her attempts to control the hospital are linked to her attempts to control the entire region.

In fact, as reported in The Zimbabwe Independent, a weekly broadsheet, some churches in Zimbabwe had postponed their annual gatherings, generally held between July and August, fearing that their events would be hijacked by politicians as the election set for July 31 approached. The Salvation Army cancelled their July meeting in Gweru, based on the fear that Mujuru would likely attend the meeting accompanied by her party's supporters, which had happened at previous events.

Other newspapers were bolder, alleging that Mujuru had a hand in Dr. Thistle's removal from Howard Hospital. Since Commissioner Vinece Chigariro is a good friend of Joice Mujuru, the suspicion is not unfounded. One of Mujuru's former jobs was serving as Finance Officer for Zimbabwe. The general consensus is that she has disliked Paul Thistle since the American Ambassador exposed the massacres that occurred in the Chaona area of Chiweshe in March 2008. The incident occurred three days after the Mugabe regime released the results of that year's presidential election in which MDC opponent Morgan Tsvangirai beat Mugabe. Over 200 ZANU-PF militia, accompanied by rogue army units, rampaged through the village killing 14 MDC supporters. Women were stripped and beaten so viciously that whole sections of flesh fell away from their buttocks. The militias also resorted to genital mutilation in their attacks. One post-mortem listed, 'crushed genitals' as one of the causes of death. Paul Thistle had nothing to do with the Ambassador's visit, but Mujuru may have suspected he did. Mujuru prefers silence and anonymity on most subjects, choosing to work through intermediaries. She is also aware of Paul Thistle's popularity, so she's careful not to alienate people who supported him and wanted him to stay. Following his removal from Howard Hospital, she offered the Thistles employment in the Ministry of Health at a government institution.

Chigariro also has a lengthy history with Howard Hospital, having served as hospital administrator during Dr. Watt's time. At the 2012 International Conference of Leaders, she gave a speech on "Integrated Mission," which emphasized the concept of 'ministering to the whole person' as the core business of 'One Army.' On the subject of hope, she described it as a "beacon of our faith, especially in difficult situation and challenges." She ended with this final thought, "It is the leader's responsibility to provide hope," which in the context of Howard Hospital is particularly ironic.

The speech was not typical of others she had given and quite a few Salvationists suspect that the script was penned by someone else, as she has never appeared to be an educated woman. Most of her sermons prior to this focused on the subject of how to wear the Army's uniform.

When she officiated at Paul and Pedrinah's wedding in 1998, the ceremony dragged on for much longer than expected because of her many speeches, which appeared to be more like sermons, as she turned and faced the crowd while speaking. But in spite of her shortcomings, she has risen to the rank of Commissioner and appears to have considerable clout and influence within Salvation Army ranks.

Dr. Tineshe Gede, in an opinion piece that appeared in the online news magazine *www.newzimbabwe.com/opinion* shared his take on the marriage of church and state. "In perhaps the only funny part of this whole ordeal, the Mash Central province is on record as saying the 'government does not interfere in the activities of the church'. I must confess, when I first read this, I laughed uncontrollably. Is he seriously living in Zimbabwe? Everyone but the village idiot knows how hard the government fought to protect Kunonga when he was ex-communicated for insubordination by the Anglican Church. Taxpayers' money was used to rent riot police for the Bishop's use."

Nolbert Kunonga is a man of dubious credentials. No one is quite sure whether his PhD designation is legitimate. As for his ability to lead a church, he was supposedly studying theology, but had little knowledge of the bible. Nonetheless, in 1997, he was ordained as the Anglican Bishop of Harare. He was also recruited by ZANU-PF as part of a project to rally Anglicans in Zimbabwe to guarantee a steady basis of support.

Everything went smoothly as long as Mugabe's hold on power was firm, but when the MDC party formed in 1999, politics became polarized. In his desperation to prove his loyalty to Mugabe and his party, Kunonga repeatedly abused the pulpit to preach politics—demonizing the opposition, western nations and homosexuals in his sermons.

The Bishop's power went to his head and he got greedy. He and his followers began grabbing hordes of church properties across the country. Churches, hospitals, even a shrine belonging to the Anglican Church were seized, with some converted into private homes for the faithful, while others were run as commercial enterprises.

But in 2011, a High Court ruling determined that, since Kunonga had left the church three years earlier, he could not claim ownership of Anglican property in Zimbabwe. Legitimate Anglican congregants rebelled, further destroying ZANU-PF's reputation and credibility.

It was the final straw for Mugabe, who complained that Kunonga was not taking the party anywhere and objected to the Bishop's personal gains from the assignment. Kunonga had become a burden, therefore, he had to go.

For Salvation Army members in Zimbabwe, the situation at Howard Hospital had a familiar ring. At a Salvation Army training camp, Commissioner Makina was booed when he tried to give a lecture to cadets. Similarly, when an officer ordered congregants at Harare City Corps not to discuss the situation at Howard, the congregation walked out.

CHAPTER 18

Bending the Rules

I have principles...if you don't like them, I have others.....

GROUCHO MARX

IN HIS FORMER POSITION AS Director of Overseas Development for the Salvation Army Canada and Bermuda Territory, and now retired, Allan Bacon's job was to travel the world to monitor ongoing projects. On his travels, he had the privilege and pleasure of working with many fine Salvation Army personnel around the world—dedicated, hard-working, and scrupulously honest people, committed to making a difference within the deprived communities they served.

There was Captain Leonor Zelaya, a diminutive young female officer who ran a school and daycare centre in Viacha, Bolivia, a village high up on a plateau above La Paz. During the two years of her appointment, she recounted how she had used her salary to reimburse funds that had been misappropriated by her predecessor. She had lived on a meagre inheritance from her father to sustain her. The local territory in Bolivia refused to accept any responsibility for the misuse of funds, but Captain Zelaya was doing a fine job, and on subsequent visits Allan was able to witness the tremendous transformation she had made with funds that he managed to solicit from generous donors in Ontario.

Although some of the most successful development work occurred in Ecuador and Bolivia, one of Allan's visits to Ecuador was greeted with instructions from the Territorial Commander in Santiago, Chile, instructing the host, a Division Commander, "not to discuss any new project proposal or ideas" with Allan during his visit. The Division Commander showed him the letter, which they both ignored.

The Territorial Commander had also arranged for Captain Darlene Harvey, an American officer, to be recalled back to the USA, with no explanation, even though she was doing a fine job. Captain Harvey was replaced by the TC's daughter who had no experience in development work. Her assistant was also replaced, despite the fact that Allan had arranged and funded training seminars for officers in that Territory so that a local officer could assume responsibility once the Captain was ultimately reassigned. When notified about the obvious conflict of interest, IHQ rolled out the standard answer, asserting that each Territory was independent and London could not interfere.

During his seven years of work with the Salvation Army, Bacon was also a member of a Development Consultancy Group that met regularly at International Headquarters, or sometimes in other locations such as Brussels to attend meetings with European Union development officials whose primary function was to advise International Headquarters on development issues. At that time, he became aware not only of the tremendous successes being achieved around the world, but also of the many problems within the Army and its operations—the rigidity and inflexibility of the system, policies and procedures that hindered rather than helped, opportunities for corruption within the system, as well as the lack of trust and insistence on control.

Corruption was such a big concern for the Consultancy Group that officers in the Army's Australian territory were asked to prepare papers on the subject.

In March 1998, Commissioner Ronald G. Irwin, who was retiring, presented a paper at the International Conference for Salvation Army Leaders in Melbourne, Australia.

The Commissioner's report, entitled "Breaking Out of Boxes" concentrated on key points:

- *Control –rigid inflexibility, competence over position, failure to delegate, and a tendency to micro-manage.*
- *Trust – implies integrity and practices and policies that impede progress need to be eliminated*
- *Leadership – implies care, but there is a strong impression that the army shoots its wounded and that leaders have a callous, unconcerned attitude about officers and lay employees.*

As Allan Bacon states, sadly Commissioner Irwin's calls for change have not been heeded. Since his retirement in 2003, nothing has changed. The Army, he fears, is rapidly losing sight of its mission and becoming more like a cult than a church.

On his travels, Bacon encountered many examples that cemented the Commissioner's findings: financial irregularities, failure of policies and procedures coupled with poor leadership, and people using their position for personal gain; and failure to abide by undertakings and agreements in every corner of the world.

Kenya and Zambia

In October 1996, when Bacon assumed the position of Assistant Director of Overseas Development for the Army's Canada and Bermuda Territory, he inherited a number of ongoing development projects, including two that totalled some $240,000 (two-thirds contributed by CIDA, the Canadian International Development Agency and one-third by the Canadian Salvation Army.) When Bacon's predecessor, Captain Ivor Telfer, handed over the file, he advised that a visit to Kenya to monitor the projects was a must. The Army's agreement with CIDA mandated such a visit and they expected reports on the projects in question.

What followed was a series of ducks and dives by both territories, designed to avoid being audited. Prior to his departure, Allan received a fax from the Territorial Commander in Kenya stating that "the proposed dates for the visit are not convenient for the East Africa Territory," adding that "it was unlikely that he would be able to accept such a visit at any time that year." Bacon went anyway. He found that no separate accounts had been maintained for the CIDA projects. And reports submitted from Kenya Territorial Headquarters were fictitious. He also discovered that other than the most recent payment, the project funds had disappeared.

Bacon reported these irregularities to International Headquarters, but it was not until the year 2000, following a visit by the International Auditor to Kenya, when it was revealed that in November 1997, Colonel Colin Tucker had signed his name to a financial report of the project indicating that all the funds had been expended properly.

A year later, in October 2001, when Price Waterhouse Coopers informed Allan that they had been asked by CIDA to carry out a possible audit of the Kenya Projects, together with a project from Zambia, they faced the same obstacles and obfuscation. Despite numerous requests for Zambia to forward project documentation to Kenya, their requests were ignored.

Allan documented the events in a full report compiled on February 10, 2003, in which he laid out in detail the game playing, the evasion, and the lies surrounding the unsuccessful attempt by the

PWC auditors to carry out their task. In brief, the auditors discovered that all documentation in respect to the Home League Project had been shredded in the six days prior to their visit to THQ Nairobi. They were told this was in accordance with THQ policy, despite the fact that THQ were aware of the audit and had also signed an agreement to retain all documentation for seven years, in accordance with Government of Canada requirements for income tax purposes

To make matters worse, THQ Zambia had refused to send any documentation to Nairobi, claiming that they were unaware of this requirement. Allan had worked with David Bell, a New Zealander, who was the Project Officer in Zambia for some time and had absolute trust in him. Bell informed Bacon in an e-mail that "the TC is upset about the request that documents be sent to Nairobi and if they want them they can come here." This was the same territorial Commander (and his Chief Secretary) who claimed that they had no knowledge of this requirement, even though they had been clearly informed about the audit. Allan later received an e-mail from his Australian counterpart, confirming that no preparations had been made for an audit and, furthermore, the project in question had never taken place. In fact the funds had been used to buy personal vehicles for the TC and Chief Secretary, valued at $20,000 and $7,000 respectively. The Territorial Commander was from Zimbabwe and the Chief Secretary from the U.K. The project had been in place prior to David Bell's arrival in Zambia.

The Zambia territory also did everything in its power to stop the audit, claiming not to know that documents were to be forwarded to Price Waterhouse Coopers in Nairobi.

Although the PWC auditors were unable to conduct the audit at that time, they gave Zambia one final opportunity to produce documentation when Allan visited there in July 2002. Once again, the paperwork never arrived, nor had it ever been sent. Subsequently, on August 20, 2002, Price Waterhouse Coopers informed Allan that they had no option but to report to CIDA that it had not been possible to conduct an audit on funds remitted to Kenya and Zambia for the period 1995-1996.

In a further twist of irony, on October 15, 2002, Allan received an e-mail from the Chief Secretary in Zambia complaining that he and the Territorial Commander had only just discovered that further funds from Canada had been suspended.

It came as no surprise that, for all of the above reasons and more, TSA Canada subsequently lost its CIDA funding.

ZIMBABWE

Allan inherited the Mirimi Farm Training Centre project from Captain Ivor Telfer in October 1996. There were no reports on file regarding this project and requests for narrative and financial reports were unsuccessful, in part because of difficulties in communication and partly because of the political instability. On his visits to Zimbabwe, at no time was he granted a meeting with the Territorial Commander (at first an American and later a native Zimbabwean), so he was never able to gain access to the territorial headquarters in order to meet with finance staff. Of the five small projects funded by CIDA and TSA Canada, he was only able to view two. The first showed little progress and few signs of activity related to the project. The second, an agriculture development incentive, was proceeding very well and the women involved were enthusiastic and proud to be able to improve their economic situation. The other projects were undermined by the unstable political situation at the time. Promises were made to forward narrative and finance reports on all the projects to Allan's office through the usual channels, but none were ever received.

His visits to Howard Hospital, hosted by Major Jim Watt, involved lengthy discussions regarding the needs of the hospital and future project funding. During these visits he also met Dr. Paul Thistle and his wife. In March 2001, at an IHQ Consultancy Meeting in Brussels, Allan reported on the situation on Zimbabwe: "I am experiencing some difficulties with the use of project funds in Zimbabwe. This is compounded by severe problems with communications in this Territory." As he states, "when I retired in December 2003, these problems still had not been resolved."

As everyone associated with humanitarian aid in Zimbabwe discovered, the problems only got worse when Commissioner Vinece Chigariro took over as Territorial Commander in 2008.

Ghana

If Kenya, Zambia and Zimbabwe clearly illustrate the misuse and disappearance of funds, Allan's experience in Ghana defies logic.

During his visit in March 1999, he was forced to confront the Finance Secretary, a young officer fresh out of the U.K., who insisted on issuing cheques to project staff for use on project needs. The project component in question was in a very remote area of Ghana and the nearest banks were several hundred miles away. Even in Accra, the capital, cheques took a minimum of six weeks to clear, so Allan arranged that all payments be made in cash. The officer did not take kindly to Allan's changes, but his actions were a clear example of how policies and procedures prescribed by IHQ in London don't work in remote areas.

Another example was the need for wells. At the conclusion of his visit in March 1999, Allan was handed a proposal for wells amounting to approximately $8,000. On his return to Canada, he received a proposal for wells totally $83,000. Apart from the excessive amount which was way beyond available resources, Allan was aware that some of the suggested locations were inaccessible to drilling equipment and too far away from populated areas to do any good. The TC in Ghana fired off an angry letter alleging that the topic had been discussed with Allan during his visit (when no such discussion took place) and that Allan had stated there'd be "no problem" in providing funding. In his response, Allan rejected the claim, pointing out that he was still waiting for a report on a well project funded two years earlier.

On another project, the number of staff authorized in the proposal had expanded from 6 to 15 without his authorization. As well, renovation work at Begoro Clinic/Hospital was "deeply disappointing and disturbing." The roof had not been repaired, there were leaks and damage to walls, the pitted floor had not been replaced as required, the painting was appallingly poor in quality and not according to specifications. In Allan's estimation, 80% of the $75,000 allotted could not be accounted for.

He was taken to an Officers Training College, on the outskirts of Accra that had a large hall with seating for a 100 people, complete with beautiful wooden pews and ceiling fans. It was used once a year for commissioning and by a small group for service on Sunday mornings. The costs of upkeep and maintenance were far beyond the resources of the Territory, but a previous TC had insisted on the hall being built "as his legacy."

Pakistan

In October 1996, Allan inherited four ongoing projects in Pakistan. The first three, involving primary health care, community development through Adult Literacy for Women and one for skills training and income generation, proceeded with great success. Financial and narrative reports were submitted on time, along with full disclosure of all information being supplied at THQ meetings in Lahore.

The fourth project was to provide clean drinking water to a Boys' Home in Karachi. The water in the area had a high saline content and was unsuitable for drinking, a fact well known to local officials. Reports submitted attested to "progress" drilling, describing various depths reached, but with no success in finding clean water. All of these reports proved to be fictitious; the "hundreds of feet drilled" turned out to be less than 10 feet. After a full investigation, Allan instructed the officials on the spot to use the remaining funds to pay for a link to the city water supply pipes that were only several hundred feet from the Home.

Although a subsequent CIDA audit produced a favourable report on the first three projects, there were other signs of danger within the territory. When an earlier Territorial Commander uncovered corruption, he was forced to leave the country in a matter of hours after his life was threatened by senior THQ staff. On September 27, 2007, the Territorial Commander, Colonel Bo Brekke, a Norwegian, was murdered at the Territorial Headquarters Lahore. A Division Commander, Major Mark Younis Joseph, was arrested as the prime suspect. After being allowed to escape custody, he was subsequently tried with four others, but was acquitted on January 14, 2010. The Salvation Army remained silent on the case, but it is understood that Colonel Brekke had uncovered financial irregularities by the Divisional Commander relating to the use of Army funds to purchase land.

Haiti

Following a visit to Haiti in September 1999, Allan uncovered serious issues relating to finance. 10% was being deducted from project funds by the Divisional Headquarters, a policy that is strictly forbidden.

In addition, they were demanding a percentage from a clinic in Port au Prince at the Divisional Headquarters site, and seeking contributions towards the general's visit. Since the clinic is self-supporting and independent of DHQ who provide no financial support and, therefore, have no responsibilities towards the clinic's work, they were given instructions to stop this practice.

Major Haefeli, a Swiss officer, has served in Haiti for 35 years. Over the years, she has brought in hundreds of thousands of dollars to Haiti that territorial headquarters has consistently relied upon to fund schools, clinics and programs These funds have not gone through the usual channels, but, as in Zimbabwe, sent directly to the location to fund specific projects. Funding for the projects that Allan was in Haiti to monitor had been sent from Canada 18 months prior to his visit, but no funds had arrived in Haiti. Calls to the Chief Secretary in Kingston, Jamaica, headquarters for the Caribbean Territory, elicited no explanations as to what had happened to the $14,225 and $10,000 donations or why the projects had not begun.

Costa Rica

A multi-faceted project inherited from Captain Telfer involved vocational training and income generation in various parts of Costa Rica. During six visits, Allan found very successful progress being made, with most aspects of the project generating income and completely sustainable. But over time, it became clear that there was a lack of financial reports, and narrative reports often contradicted earlier ones. There was a good deal of movement of funds within the project, without his authorization, as well as program activities being changed, also without his knowledge.

During intensive discussions with his colleagues from Australia and Switzerland, Allan discovered that apparently the three of them were paying for the same project (shoe and boot making) and had received photographs of the same machinery being employed. All three returned home and contacted Costa Rica Divisional headquarters seeking clarification. This resulted in a joint visit in March 2000 by Allan and Ty Morrissey from Salvation Army Australian Development Office for meetings with the Territorial and Division Commanders to deal with concerns about poor project and financial management by Costa Rica Division, characterized by evasion and obstruction.

In the meetings that followed, there was considerable enmity, with The Divisional Commander, Major Mike Sharpe from the USA, accusing Australia of "fabricating" the budget document and claiming that Captain Telfer had insisted on the project being the way it was. Other information, as required by the Agreement, proved impossible to locate. Major Sharpe remained unco-operative, stating that he was under no obligation to provide either man with reports. He would simply "adjust figures to meet their requirements." He seemed to find nothing wrong with changing budget line items, a serious concern not only for Bacon and Morrison, whose job it was to oversee the funds, but also for CIDA and AusAid. Both of these agencies could refuse to provide further funding.

In San Jose, Costa Rica's capital, territorial headquarters happily confirmed that some $300,000 of the funds received from Canada for relief purposes in the wake of Hurricane Mitch, one of the worst storms to hit Central America, was, in fact, spent on building new houses for Salvation Army officers. Although Allan reported this to both THQ in Canada and to IHQ, nothing was done.

He was also appalled to find a magnificent Officers Training College, complete with a swimming pool, a fine quarters for the Territorial Commander and a TV satellite dish on the roof, surrounded by hundreds of homes made out of rusting tin or tar paper, with no running water, sanitation or electricity available.

CANADA

It's surprising that CIDA would ever deal with the Army again, considering the amount of obfuscation and failure to comply with the agency's conditions.

One of the things that struck Allan when he began his work with the Army in October 1996, initially as Director of Overseas Development, was the number of trips overseas. Most of the visits were to countries where the Army had no project work. The reports, which were ostensibly to deal exclusively with monitoring projects funded by CIDA and The Salvation Army Canada, rarely mentioned anything about the projects. Officers' visits to Spain, Portugal and the Great Wall of China, though, were clearly enjoyed. Reports were filled with accounts of important people met, exotic foods consumed, and the comfortable beds in fine hotels. Meanwhile, the person who was, in fact, doing the work of overseeing the projects, was rarely allowed to travel and struggled to keep on top of the work from his Ottawa office.

At one point, Allan had planned a visit to Pakistan to begin monitoring of the four CIDA/TSA projects there. Instead, his superior insisted that she would go instead, even though she had no knowledge of the projects at all. Allan had spent some three weeks compiling extensive information on each project, to give her a good grasp of what was involved, what progress had been reported and the questions that needed to be answered in order to report to CIDA. It turned out that the Colonel's rationale for the visit was that two of her close friends were filling in for the Territorial Commander in Pakistan, who was on leave, and she wished to spend Christmas with them. In the lead-up to her departure, Allan was instructed to find out whether a frozen turkey would make it safely to Pakistan without spoiling. Anyone planning a similar trip can be assured that it did.

On her return, the Colonel produced no answers to any of the questions that Allan had given her. She had not visited any of the projects or produced any kind of report and he had difficulties with CIDA as a result. This was one of several reasons why CIDA withdrew funding from the Canadian branch of the Salvation Army. She had, however, had a wonderful Christmas with her friends and had even been a guest at a wedding. Allan subsequently had to make an extra trip to Pakistan to obtain the information for his report to CIDA.

―――

The parallels with the present climate, many years later, are hard to ignore. Once again, we see examples of stonewalling and outright lies. Much of Allan Bacon's observations still exist in today's Army, particularly as they relate to Dr. Paul Thistle and the situation at Howard Hospital and how it was mishandled.

General's Visits
But financial irregularities were not the only problems Bacon encountered on his visits to various territories within the Salvation Army's global network. The impact of the General's visits on poor and deprived nations were even more disturbing.

Kenya 2001
Visits by the General and IHQ staff are routinely paid for by the receiving Territory, placing an extra burden on their meager resources. In February 2001, Allan led a group of Canadian Farmers to Ethiopia and Kenya on a Canadian Foodgrains Bank food-study tour. One such visit was to an elementary school to witness the children being fed at lunchtime, for many children their only meal of the day. The meal consisted of a mixture of maize and soya beans, pre-cooked and

fortified with vitamins and minerals, widely used in relief work to feed malnourished children and adults. When lunchtime arrived and no feeding took place, Bacon was told that as the General was scheduled to visit, the Territorial Commander had forbidden "all normal activities" in preparation for the visit. Instead of being fed, the children were busy whitewashing stones that bordered the pathways of the compound. The following weekend, there was a command performance in the Nairobi Stadium with 35,000 Salvationists on hand to greet the General and every officer in the country was mandated to attend wearing a brand new white uniform.

Tanzania

When the General visited Tarime in northern Tanzania, special chefs and servers from Dar es Salaam (an arduous two-day journey) were brought in to cook and serve him, because the locals were not considered to be "good enough." The General travelled on paved roads, visiting specially-selected locations, avoiding the most impoverished villages many miles from the decent roads.

Haiti

In Haiti, one of the poorest countries in the word, Bacon encountered a similar situation. As part of the Salvation Army's Caribbean Territory, Haiti receives funding through Territorial Headquarters in Kingston, Jamaica. Payments to Haiti prior to 2003 varied between $2,000 and $10,000 US per month. When General Burrows visited at that time the visit cost $70,000 US, of which THQ Kingston promised to pay half. In reality, THQ never paid a cent and Haiti was forced to go without that amount from its yearly budget.

And yet, in 2010, when Haiti was hit with a catastrophic earthquake, the Salvation Army World Services Organization was quick to respond. Immediately, a clinic was set up to begin treating patients, together with a staging area in south Florida. Three days after the quake, as assessment team arrived in Port-au-Prince following a 16-hour cross-country journey. In conjunction with the Haiti government and U.S. military, relief flights were organized to bring and deliver supplies.

CHAPTER 19

The Truth, the Half-Truth and Anything But...So Help Me God

Nothing is covered up that will not be uncovered, and nothing secret that will not become known. Therefore, whatever you have said in the dark will be heard in the light and what you have whispered behind closed doors, will be proclaimed from the housetops,

Luke 12:1 – 3

NOTHING BRINGS COHESION TO LEADERS of religious organizations more than accusations of wrongdoing. From the outset of the Howard Hospital debacle, the hierarchy of the Salvation Army has clung together like fleas on a dog to quell any uncomfortable questions and put the matter to rest so that "everybody could move on." The Army's official statements are not just enigmas, but carefully-crafted denials. Although they have a laundry list of disclaimers and rebuttals that are put through their wash and spin cycle before being released, their sanitized version of events has failed to stop the cries for accountability and restitution.

THE SPIN IS IN

Back in August 2012, when Dr. Michael Silverman addressed his concerns in a letter to General Bond, he received a reply from Major Alison Cowling, at the Salvation Army's Toronto Territorial headquarters

Cowling's response stated: "We have been provided every assurance by our International Headquarters that Captains Paul and Pedrinah Thistle have not been forced out, the hospital is open, will remain open and will be adequately staffed to address the health care needs of those that rely on it."

In his reply, Dr. Silverman advised that this was not accurate, pointing out that the Thistles were originally ordered to leave September 1, then subsequently told to not only vacate Howard Hospital, but ordered to leave the country within 48 hours.

The hospital, he said, was not adequately staffed. As Dr. Thistle was the hospital's only surgeon, with his removal all surgery—elective and emergency—had to be stopped. Plus, there was no surgeon to replace him. As Dr. Thistle's primary role is a physician, he is bound by his sworn oath not to abandon his patients unless he could directly transfer care to another physician with the necessary skills to accept immediate responsibility. The Army, therefore, was forcing him to break that oath against his will. Since no reason was provided for his removal other than "determined by leadership", asking dedicated staff to break their principles for such an opaque and flimsy excuse was unacceptable practice for a humanitarian and religious organization.

Cowling's next statement was equally jaw-dropping.

"Any project work that is funded by international sources is closely monitored by the International Development Office at The Salvation Army's International Headquarters in London, the objective always being to provide a level of services that is both sustainable and within the definition of the international standards for Primary Health Care."

If the above statement were true, Silverman stated, then the Army's International Headquarters had a great deal to answer for, because supervision had clearly been inadequate. He pointed out that there had been serious allegations of improper use of funds and equipment by the Zimbabwe territorial office, a fact witnessed by many who had volunteered at the hospital. "Simply put, when they visit the Howard things 'go missing' and funds donated by them do not arrive or arrive late. I am personally aware of the very serious lapses in accounting at the national office and I will discuss this below."

Silverman explained that he had worked with Dr. Thistle since 1999. Because of the enormous trust he had for Thistle, Silverman had helped to co-ordinate several significant grants—all funded to Howard Hospital and well-managed. He then gave a detailed account of the process involved in obtaining the large grant of $250,000 from CIDA, the Canadian International Development Agency to fund a new HIV program at the hospital. Since this was an extremely competitive process, very few grants are awarded. An enormous amount of work by Canadian volunteers was involved to win this competition.

However, the Zimbabwean territorial command were not only unhelpful in the extreme but overtly obtrusive. Although he understood their insistence that all funds "be funneled" through their office and could accept the Army's policy of charging a transfer fee, Dr. Silverman and his colleagues were told that "there was no guarantee" that the funds would be transferred to Howard Hospital for their intended use—to fund the HIV project. The Army, they were told, may have "other priorities." The use of the funds was to be "at the discretion" of the national office. A request that Dr. Silverman and his colleagues made for open and transparent accounting process in the management of the funds, demanded by CIDA, was refused. When it was made clear to the local territorial division that CIDA would never accept these terms and that the Army's demands would mean cancellation of the CIDA grant, church officials remained adamant. Sadly, Dr. Silverman said, the grant was cancelled, effectively depriving women and children with the enormous benefit that the grant provided. The church had made it clear that maintaining opaque accounting processes and the right to direct funds within that context was more important than the welfare of the poor and sick.

Silverman added that he hoped the International Offices of the Salvation Army in London had not been overseeing this process. He stressed that he would be deeply disappointed if an organization for whom he had great respect had been complicit in this type of behaviour and called for an external investigation to be carried out immediately.

This exchange occurred a good month prior to any investigation—either internal or external—taking place, yet Cowling was insisting that everything was as it should be. Perhaps she was praying for divine intervention to cleanse the wounds of those affected by the Army's actions. More likely, she was praying, along with the rest of the Army brass, that Dr. Silverman and his ilk would just go away and stop asking questions that she had no stomach for answering.

Missing Donations and Goods

The Army's internal investigation a month later didn't change the tune. An official statement issued after the Army's own internal audit dismissed all claims about fiscal mismanagement and the loss of donated materials. According to their press release of October 26, 2012, "there was no sign that donated funds had been diverted from their original purpose" and that "donated goods, falsely reported to have gone missing, were all accounted for." But try telling that to the folks in Peterborough who donated the goods.

This statement was patently false. The $18,000 worth of building materials and $13,000 in cash donated by supporters at Donwood United Church in Peterborough, Canada were missing from the hospital. Roofing sheets were witnessed being removed and transported to Major Benhura's farm. Cement, paid for and receipted, never arrived at Howard. Even by the slightest stretch of the imagination, it is hard to believe that enough material to build a small house would go unnoticed. The Army claimed that the material was used to build new staff quarters, but you have to take their word for it because they have offered no evidence to back this up. Since the donation was to be used specifically for housing the volunteers and that program was abruptly cancelled, the donor asked for it to be returned. The fact that this volunteer program no longer exists is all the more reason to suspect that the Army's explanation is false. Rumours circulated around Chiweshe that the local population believed the materials had been transported to Commissioner Chigariro's farm nearby. The Army's claim that "no evidence was found" is purposely vague; that excuse would also apply if they never bothered to look.

The Army has consistently ignored the tens of thousands of dollars sent through the Zimbabwean territorial headquarters that never arrived at their destination. These have all been documented by donors, but far too often, requests for receipts were simply met with a "thank you." The only explanation given was that donations were intercepted by "sanctions." This is another falsehood because economic sanctions do not apply to charitable donations, even in heavily-sanctioned Zimbabwe.

Goose vs. Gander

As a religious organization that operates in 127 countries, the Salvation Army's national headquarters controls every territory, with checks and balances that are supposed to apply to every soldier.

So why were they not in place, why did they not apply to the Army's territory in Zimbabwe? Obviously, TC Chigariro circumvented accounting rules as they applied to donations. When outside auditors were sent in, they were barred from seeing the books. Again, it begs the question: why was this allowed? Why did International Headquarters in London and Territorial Headquarters in Canada sanction and support her actions?

More importantly, if Dr. Thistle was supposed to follow the commands of his superiors, why was his superior, Commissioner Chigariro, not required to follow the same rules? She too reports to a higher authority, be it God or her immediate superior, the General. Why was she allowed to bend and ignore the rules and create new ones of her own to gain control of incoming donations? Not only had she no respect for Dr. Thistle, but none for the staff or any appreciation of their hard work and need to survive. Patients were viewed as cash cows, even though they had little cash to give. She showed equal disdain for the hundreds of volunteers who, throughout the years, gave of their time and energy to collect dollars to keep the facility under her command afloat. Volunteers were seen as interlopers who had no business being there or exposed to the way the local Army did business. But she had no problem accepting and spending their money.

Her lofty title—Territorial Commander—that conjures up visions of a mighty Roman general, went to her head. For the people of Chiweshe, her "command" amounted to a reign of terror.

Despite all the evidence to the contrary, the tsunami of letters and e-mails and media coverage supporting Thistle and praising his skills, the Army refused to be swayed. Instead they concocted a series of cover-ups, half-truths and outright lies to change the landscape surrounding Howard Hospital to suit their purpose and paint their own version of events: the hospital, which had been a surgical facility for over 50 years, was actually a primary clinic, there was no fiscal malfeasance, no funds missing, no jealous Commissioner with a score to settle. This was the official Army line, repeated over and over again by every command.

If accusations of wrongdoing cause senior church officials to band together to contain the damage, there is nothing that causes derision among the rank and file more than denials and cover-ups. Church members, current, retired and former officers and supporters of Howard Hospital were disgusted and dismayed at the way the Army had handled the situation, or more to the point, mishandled it. People couldn't understand how their own church could abandon one of their own, abandon their principles, and worst of all abandon 270,000 people. Their loyalty as well as their faith in the church that they had pledged their lives to was shaken. Something was very wrong. Rot had set in and it started at the top. How could their church allow this to happen? There were so many questions, but very few answers. They appealed to the Army to do the right thing: call in independent auditors, apologize to Dr. Thistle and his family; admit their mistakes, reinstate him and restore proper health care to the region. Although their faith was solid, their search for the truth was just as strong.

The word of one individual, afraid of discovery and loss of position was taken as gospel and sanctioned by an investigation conducted by her peers. Instead of allowing outside auditors to open the books and determine what had taken place and address the concerns of donors, the Army closed ranks and barred the doors to all outsiders. Instead of disciplining the person suspected of fiscal mismanagement, and possible fraud, the Army chose its own method of correction that was way off course. Rather than deflect controversy, it invited more.

Exit Stage Left

On June 13, 2013, members of the Salvation Army were shocked to hear that General Linda Bond had resigned. No explanation was given for her resignation other than for "personal reasons," which were also not disclosed. This announcement resulted in a good deal of speculation by church members who aired their feelings on the Army's official website. The General's resignation came smack in the middle of a mess of scandals the Army was forced to deal with. She was Territorial Commander when charges of sexual abuse surfaced in the Australian Territory, but she did nothing about the charges. Her successor was left to handle the fall-out and, after a lengthy enquiry, offered a tearful apology to the 474 victims of abuse. The Army paid out $ 15.5 million in compensation to the victims. She was head of the church when the Howard Hospital situation erupted, but stayed out of the controversy, leaving the Territorial Commanders to solve it by themselves. The General was at the centre of all the controversies, so there was plenty of motivation to get her to retire. Another element for concern is that Miss Bond suddenly left a top administrative job once before. In August 2004, after about two years as leader of the Army's USA Western Territory, which covers 13 states and several U.S. Pacific island areas, she resigned, citing "personal reasons" and without giving notice.

Following General Bond's resignation, Commissioner Andre Cox, who acted as the Army's second in command, and the person who made the announcement, took over as acting General until a new leader could be appointed.

Taking it to the Streets

On July 11, 2013, while Paul and his family were on furlough in Canada, he learned that a group of former Salvation Army officers were intending to start an on-line protest regarding his dismissal.

They already had an established blog, Former Salvation Army Officers Fellowship (FSAOF). With over 700 members, they hoped that a discussion about the situation at Howard would generate enough traffic and responses to influence the Army, ahead of its planned meeting of its top soldiers in London. This meeting of the High Council was being held later that month in London to elect a new General, following the abrupt and unexplained resignation of the former General, Linda Bond.

The blog's creators planned a three-day blitz to focus attention on Howard Hospital, but the flood of responses rose beyond anything they had hoped for. With the amount of interest shown by former officers and others who were following the debacle at Howard Hospital, there was no reason to stop the flow of traffic by limiting the timespan of the coverage. It was evident from the responses that people were enraged at the treatment of Dr. Thistle and the Army's insensitivities and lack of compassion for the humanitarian crisis created by their decisions. But it was also apparent that although many current and former officers wished to express their anger at the church bureaucracy that had caused this mess, they wished to do so anonymously. Since gag orders had been imposed, many commenters were reluctant to reveal their identity and face the wrath of church leaders. Many of the original people who had first joined the protest on the Army's own website, registered their feelings once more. Paul's supporters from every corner of the globe joined the fray, sending a clear message to the Army that they were tired of the official spin and would not be satisfied until a full investigation by outside auditors was conducted and/or Dr. Thistle received an apology and was re-instated at Howard.

When the blog's administrators began to analyze the traffic, they noted that many of the people who logged in were, in fact, residents of the London area and many of them signed off as U.K. officers. Some admitted that they knew nothing about the tragic events that had unfolded at Howard, a clear indication that the people at Army headquarters were keeping a lid on the situation and an even tighter hold on the tongues of their own officers.

But others would not be silenced into posting anonymously. Dr. James Watt, Allan Bacon and a handful of other former and retired officers bravely spoke out, unafraid of displaying their names or their feelings.

By the time delegates arrived in London for the Army's High Council meeting the week of July 29, 2013, the blog was in full swing and members had prepared a written statement, outlining their mandate of accountability, with the intention of presenting it to the attendees. This meeting was a week-long affair, held at the swanky Renaissance Hotel's Heathrow Airport location in suburban London, replete with all the trappings and hoopla of a secular convention, but with less pomp and ceremony than a papal election. Only the top brass were invited—117 territorial commanders and senior officers flown in from a variety of nations, hand-picked to decide the fate of the candidates.

In attendance were several native Zimbabweans and officers born and raised there

> Commissioner Andre Cox, Chief of Staff – London Headquarters
> Commissioner Vinece Chigariro – former Territorial Commander of Zimbabwe
> Commissioner Amos Makina – International Secretary for the Africa Zone – London, England

And Major Dean Pallant, who was there in an advisory capacity, but without voting privileges.

Two of the group are Americans: Commissioners Barry Swanson and Kenneth Hodder, and two others are Canadians: former General

Linda Bond (who was not a member of the High Council and was not in attendance during the election procedure) and Commissioner Brian Peddle.

Effective January 1, 2013, the following shifts had been put into effect:

- Chigariro moved from Zimbabwe to become Territorial Commander of Kenya East Territory,
- Swanson, former Chief of Staff at IHQ London became Territorial Commander in the U.S. Eastern Territory,
- Hodder, former International Secretary for Personnel and Legal and Constitution Advisor to the General in London became Territorial Commander in the Kenya West Territory.
- Makina, former International Secretary for the Africa Zone and a former Territorial Commander of Zimbabwe retired.

A quick glance through the names reveals how many of the commissioners and attendees were directly involved in the removal of Paul and Pedrinah Thistle from Howard Hospital. Of this group, only Swanson was not directly involved. The Army claims that these appointments were already in progress prior to Dr. Thistle's transfer orders being issued, but the timing points to another expedient attempt to shift the focus from Howard Hospital and protect Commissioner Chigariro from further scrutiny when the situation in the Zimbabwe territory grew too hot to handle.

But the big question for the petitioners was how to get the document into the hands of the delegates. If the people delivering the petition tried to go anywhere near the hotel, they were in danger of being stopped. They decided instead to have individual copies delivered to each of the High Council members through their inboxes at the hotel's front desk.

High Council Protocol

The High Council meets for one purpose only—to elect a new general. However, high council members do not necessarily represent their particular territories or even their countries of origin. Only those with the requisite experience in both leadership and ministry will have risen through the ranks to become members of this council and nomination is restricted to those attending.

Nominees are usually given a set of questions put together by a committee. This particular set of questions is given to everyone who has accepted the nomination and, where appropriate, questions are also submitted to the nominees' spouses. The nominees prepare written responses which are then shared with the entire High Council.

Final voting is by secret ballot, requiring a two-thirds majority of members to win the election. Usually three rounds is enough to establish a majority, but if it goes to a fourth vote or more, a majority, regardless of percentage, will be enough. After each round, the nominee with the lowest number of votes drops out.

Since the High Council is a closed-door session, only those who attend are privy to how the voting progresses, but at the end of the week, a new leader is chosen. As the outgoing leader, General Bond's official function was to appear after the vote to congratulate the new leader.

The winning candidate in this case was Andre Cox, former Chief of Staff.

Open Windows

Back in 2004, at the opening of its new world headquarters in London—a gleaming glass structure within sight of St. Paul's Cathedral—one leader had declared that "its glass exterior communicates our transparency." If only that were true…

During an interview for an article in the Salvation Army's own magazine, General Cox was asked if he thinks the Army is inclusive and were there any areas that they needed to work on. His answer is telling in its opacity.

> *"Based on the feedback I've received, I think that sometimes people feel they are not listened to, that they have no say in the way the mission is shaped. I think there is still a myth within the Army that we have our military structures and all decisions are top down. I'm not sure that is the reality, but I'm not sure we've always done it right. It's trying to ensure that we hear as many voices as possible and that people feel that they have a stake in The Salvation Army and the mission going forward. That's the way I've always worked with colleagues and something I hope we will continue."*

His comment, that they are trying to ensure that as many voices as possible are heard, rings hollow in the face of the outcry at Howard Hospital, where so many have spoken up, but are still waiting for answers. Not only was Dr. Thistle not heard, his pleas for his family and the welfare of his patients either ignored or dismissed, but the collective outcry from the church's own members failed to sway any of the decision-makers, either top down or bottom up.

Although the completion of the new buildings may be seen as an attempt to make amends, failure to provide a surgeon and an almost total lack of needed medicines have forced patients to seek help elsewhere or simply die at home—a far cry from what Howard Hospital had achieved in the past.

Hope and Misdirected Glory

In September 2013, the Army's website featured an article on Howard Hospital entitled "Tariro—An Ongoing Story of Hope." The article was released following a visit by two officers, Major Sandra Welch from IHQ London and Major John Murray from THQ Toronto. Although the article outlines Howard Hospital's services, and its continuous history of providing exemplary care in a rural setting, there is not one mention of the former Chief Medical Officers who helped to establish these services. Accompanying the article is a series of pictures taken by one of the two officers who made the trip and prepared the report. According to the pictures, the line-ups for both the outpatient and maternity wards are substantial. Babies are pictured being weighed and held by their mothers, smiling pictures of staff abound, but not one name accompanies the pictures, except that of Major Joan Gibson, who served at Howard since the early 1980s. As a nursing teacher who headed the program, Major Gibson contributed greatly to the lives of thousands of people, but it is her length of service that drew the most attention from the rank and file within the Salvation Army.

Major Gibson's long history at Howard directly refutes one of the reasons offered for the Thistles' transfer, namely statements made by Canadian Salvation Army officials, that officers are regularly transferred and that it is rare to stay in an appointment for more than five years.

The article focuses heavily on Howard's many programs and accomplishments, but glosses over its current failures or fails to mention them at all. Although the article mentions the fact that the nurses training centre at Howard has received a "high pass rate" from the province's Medical Director, there is no mention of Pedrinah Thistle, who helped to train the nurses and taught them midwifery.

According to the article, 1,000 babies are delivered each year. The hospital attended to 60 patients in the first half of 2013, which still leaves more than half of the 144 beds unfilled. On a daily basis, as reported, the hospital now sees 150 patients, down from the average 200 to 300 per day during Dr. Thistle's tenure.

There is no mention of the achievements of Paul Thistle or any of the previous Chief Medical Officers who provided exceptional care and helped to establish Howard Hospital as the "go-to" facility in Zimbabwe. Nor is there any credit given for the continually-expanding programs that these doctors brought on board. In fact, the Tariro Clinic was devised, developed and funded by Paul Thistle. Not only does the Army fail to mention his contribution, it takes full credit for all the achievements over the past 85 years.

After 17 years in the Army's service Paul Thistle is mentioned only briefly in passing:

"Following the departure of the previous Chief Medical Office in July 2012, the hospital is in a state of transition as the number of patients and surgical procedures are reduced as complicated cases are referred to Harare and Bindura – an accepted practice for a rural district hospital."

This tag is added for one purpose only: to support the Army's agenda to reduce Howard Hospital from a full-scale surgical facility to a down-graded rural district hospital.

Less is More

The article states that *"the hospital no longer has a specialist gynecologist, but it is now the same as other district hospitals."* Except that this particular hospital did have one, but no longer does. It is hard to understand how this can be promoted as a positive outcome.

The article goes on to say that *"district hospitals do not necessarily offer specialist obstetrics services"* and that *"Howard Hospital maintained surgical capacity throughout 2012 and 2013 since two Zimbabwean doctors are trained to perform a number of surgical procedures including C-sections."*

Here again, these statements circumvent the truth by failing to mention that in the first half of 2012, the hospital's surgery was indeed above and beyond capacity under the direction of Dr. Thistle and a variety of volunteer surgeons. And in the second half of 2013, the hospital was in a state of near collapse, with very few in-patients to fill the beds and only the most basic services being offered.

> *"Historically, it has not always had a trained surgeon on site. The fact that Howard Hospital had a doctor with these skills was beneficial, but it is certainly not a requirement."*

The Army's contention that the hospital has not always had a trained surgeon on site is inaccurate. Since the early 1960s, Howard Hospital has had a continual supply of surgeons with varying qualifications. All of the previous Chief Medical Officers had, in fact, surgical training and were able to handle any emergency presented to them. In 1972, Major Watt was joined by Dr. Pat Hill, who holds a Diploma in Obstetrics and Gynecology. During her six years at Howard Hospital, she performed about 50 Caesarean sections a year. Dr. Hill also introduced some excellent maternal health initiatives, and since 1995, when Paul Thistle joined Dr. Watt, there has been a full-time obstetrician/gynecologist on board. Ironically, August 2012 to the present is the only time in 50 years the hospital has been without a physician capable of handling advanced surgery.

The Army's statement that an obstetrician/gynecologist is not a necessity is another blatant attempt to ignore the role of Paul Thistle, the only fully-qualified ob/gyn working among the poor in Zimbabwe in bringing quality medical and surgical care to the poorest third-world patient—a milestone in social justice.

Men who have given the better part of their lives to save other lives are barely recognized or acknowledged by their own church, but to the people of Africa, these same doctors were their lifeline.

According to the Army, Thistle's skills were not a requirement, but try telling that to a mother who is suffering with prolonged seizures from eclampsia or whose uterus has ruptured; or a woman with cervical cancer that only surgery can cure. Patients requiring emergency surgery can barely afford the cost of transportation to government-run hospitals, let alone the cost of such surgery in these hospitals. Many cannot afford the cost of lab tests or medication.

Without surgery, many patients who could otherwise be saved are doomed to a slow, agonizing death. And even death presents a problem for the families trying to retrieve and transport their deceased loved ones back home for burial.

Instead of celebrating the fact that Howard Hospital was able to attract skilled surgeons and maintain an exceptional level of service, the Army refuses to recognize their contribution. Surgical services are now treated like an aberration when, in fact, they are more cost efficient and sustainable than "primary care." This argument supports the widely-held misconception amongst African officers—that mission doctors worked for a higher salary to theirs. They could not imagine that doctors would do it for the love of God. But officers' salaries are commensurate on years of service. Moreover, mission hospitals do not operate on the same scale as hospitals with large influxes of public and private donations.

When Dr. Watt was assigned to Howard Hospital, his stipend started at $2.00 per day. The government grant for the doctor was divided amongst lesser staff and helped run the hospital. The main cost of "complex surgery" in conventional hospitals is the cost of the surgeon, not electricity, blood or drugs. Doctors who are assigned to work in mission hospitals are essentially volunteers. As Paul Thistle did not charge for his skills, any profits went into the running of the hospital.

Only another physician can appreciate the dire consequences of such a trade-off in service. Unfortunately, the decisions surrounding

Howard Hospital are no longer being made by people with medical expertise. Instead, the fate of 270,000 people is being decided by a group of bureaucrats with no direct knowledge of the exceptional challenges facing doctors in the bush. A soldier who has never been on a battlefield has little knowledge of actual war, up close and personal.

The Provincial Medical Director is quoted as saying that the decline in patients at Howard was due to misinformation and the local people's misconception about the presence, or lack of a doctor, at Howard. This statement smacks of superiority and is refuted by local residents, who contend that they initially avoided Howard Hospital due to the presence of the Zimbabwe secret police, who were there at the request of Commissioner Chigariro to stifle further protests over Dr. Thistle's dismissal.

People from within the community who have formed relationships with individuals who served at Howard Hospital over the years, in various capacities, have shared their eye-witness accounts of what is actually occurring at Howard. According to local citizens, people avoid going to Howard because they don't want to be referred to the provincial hospitals, which are not up to the standards that were available at Howard prior to August 2012. Much is made of the maternity services currently in place at Howard where mothers remain in the hospital for three days following the birth of their babies. Prior to September 2012, new mothers were released after one day, due to the lack of available beds resulting from the popularity of Howard Hospital's maternity program. This statement implies that the three-day stay is superior. Actually, the extended time is not due to extra care or compassion for mother and child, but can be directly attributed to a decrease in services and a lack of trust on the part of mothers. Take away the hospital's Chief Medical Officer, who also happens to specialize in maternal and child medicine, transfer all but basic surgery to other hospitals and make the most basic services unaffordable and you have a prescription for disaster. The people who suffer, though, are not the administrators, but the local citizenry.

Is There a Doctor in the House?

The Army has spent considerable time searching for a replacement doctor for Paul Thistle. The Army's plan was to replace him with a Zimbabwe national, but one could not be found because many young doctors, after completing their residencies, seek employment in other countries. As mentioned in the article, the Army approached another Salvationist who served as Chief Medical Officer in another Army facility, Chikenkata Hospital in Zambia. Dr. Pachuau was not approached until October 2012, more than two months after Dr. Thistle's departure and wasn't officially on staff until a full year later, at the end of August 2013.

The young doctor and his family were from India, but his expertise leaned more towards administration than medicine. Under his administration, the numbers improved. However, reports from the local community indicate that he was not as skilled as the two Zimbabwe doctors, who received additional training from none other than Dr. Thistle. They held out hope for Thistle's return, fearing that without him, Howard would be just another clinic.

A retired Swedish surgeon, Dr. Per-Göte Lindgren, was also appointed to join the team at Howard to train the existing medical team in more advanced surgical procedures and to strengthen the health system at the new hospital. According to the Army, The Medical and Dental Council had assured them that it could register him for this work. They stated that Dr. Lindgren would not work as a general medical officer; his focus would be providing advanced surgical training. He would also oversee the move into the new building and the development of management and clinical systems to improve the quality of care and services. Once again, this flies in the face of the Army's own statement: *"The period of 2004-2012 saw the development of an extensive surgical program at the hospital which stretched the hospital's capacity. Before 2003, the hospital operated at the level of a rural district hospital with some additional services depending on the capacity of the staff at the time. The intention is to return to this sustainable level of working."*

With new money in their hands, the Army promoted this new initiative as neat and orderly and proceeding nicely according to plan. During Dr. Thistle's tenure, there was no plan to upgrade either the old hospital or complete the abandoned "new" hospital, with little help or money provided from their end. And the money raised by outside donors to keep the hospital running was either depleted or went missing by the former administrator with no accounting for where it went.

This statement also begs the question: if Howard Hospital is strictly a rural district hospital—a primary clinic offering basic services without the need for an extensive surgical program—why hire another physician to focus on "advanced surgical training?"

Whether the Army is prepared to admit it or not, the fact remains that the Salvation Army was not the drawing card. It was not the Army's reputation that drew patients to Howard's door or brought in thousands of dollars, goods and supplies to keep the hospital operating, but the reputation of its doctors—Paul Thistle and others before him who established its reputation for quality service at an affordable price. It is the Army's own actions that have reduced it to a skeleton of what it was.

Our Way or the Highway

Better planning, including a period of transition, could have averted many of the problems caused by Dr. Thistle's abrupt forced removal, but the Army failed to act or listen to suggestions to improve the situation. When news of Paul Thistle's departure first surfaced, Dr. Watt suggested that instead of referring patients to provincial hospitals, they be offered transportation to Karanda Hospital. With three surgeons and three staff doctors available at affordable rates, Karanda offered a viable solution, but Dr. Watt received no response to his suggestion. Nor was the local community consulted on what their needs were or the Army's plans to address those needs.

The local population is expected to buy into the notion that less is better, that diminished medical services will better serve the community, but no one in the community feels better off as a result of the Army's decision to reduce services at Howard. In fact, local citizens reported that patient transfers to Parirenyatwa hospital in the capital were not working out well—many go there, but few return alive.

In February 2013, Dr. Watt expressed his concern about maternal deaths in Chiweshe to both Major Gillian Brown in Toronto and Major Dean Pallant in London, asking them to check on the reports. He again suggested that difficult cases be transferred to Karanda, and once again he was ignored. But Karanda is more remote than Howard. Transporting patients to a more remote mission hospital provides no incentives for the local administrators, whereas a trip to Harare, just an ambulance ride away, can easily be combined with shopping and a visit to relatives.

A Shaky Foundation

The 2013 article is keen to shift focus away from the awkward facts to the completion of the new hospital with the injection of funding provided by the Salvation Army's Eastern Territory in the U.S. They make a particular point of noting that "Funding is donated by USA Eastern Territory and is being held at IHQ," but it is hard to fathom why anyone would need to know where the funding is held. This statement appears to be a thin attempt to display transparency and accountability, the inference being that as long as IHQ holds the funds, everything is open and above-board.

The Army presents the construction of the new hospital as one long project that was completed in various phases. In fact, the original building *was* completed, but deemed unfit for use by the Zimbabwean government. Cost overruns hyper-inflated the original price to twice the estimated cost. Because the original construction was poorly supervised, poorly constructed and never used, it had deteriorated. This second phase, rather than being the final phase of completion, is more about correcting past mistakes. Here again, there were problems getting the job finished. The $3 million from the US Eastern Territory was donated in 2011. There were problems with the contractors and engineers assigned to the project who jacked the price up to $9 million. In 2012, the Salvation Army relieved the old engineering firm and hired a new one to work within the budget.

The article makes no mention of other building projects at Howard, particularly the project to construct a duplex residence to house visiting medical professionals. This building could have been completed by now if the $18,000 worth of building materials donated by supporters in Peterborough, Ontario had not suddenly disappeared from the grounds on the heels of Dr. Thistle's departure. If, in fact, the materials are not missing, as the Army reported following their internal investigation, this building should be part and parcel of the entire building program for Howard.

The article talks about bringing the Howard in line with "an agreed sustainability plan," which is to be supervised by the Canada and Bermuda territory, but fails to give details as to who developed the plan or whether or not the local community was consulted.

Help not Wanted

Another point of contention is the hospital volunteer program, which, according to the article, "was sadly halted in 2012 due to a disruption in the latter half of the year." The truth is that the volunteer program had nothing to do with the public protest over Dr. Thistle's removal which the Army coyly refers to as a "disruption." The program, in fact, was cancelled months before. A letter dated May 16, 2012 announced that the volunteer program was suspended "to develop a program that will be more manageable." Once again, it was all about the need to control.

As recently as the date that the article appears, the school's educational program was also terminated and donors who had previously handed over school fees directly to the Salvation Army-run schools, have been forbidden to do so.

———

The Salvation Army's response to their responsibility and involvement regarding employment issues in the Howard Hospital situation is duplicitous at best. On the one hand, Paul Thistle's legal proceedings are labelled ecclesiastic, while the nurses' case is seen as civil, and, therefore, since it's not church business, they can distance themselves. But they had no qualms about getting involved in legal matters when they demanded that nurses and visitors be arrested by the police, nor any problem with showing up in court as witnesses against them.

Their response to transparency and accountability in respect to missing funds also varies widely between different countries.

The Salvation Army's response to recent scandals in Ontario compared to those in Zimbabwe has been more confusing. In November 2012, when an anonymous whistleblower alerted the Army that two million dollars' worth of donated toys had gone missing from the Army's Toronto Warehouse, police were called in to investigate, an internal audit was conducted and the Executive Director of the warehouse was fired.

Similarly, when it was discovered that $250,000 had gone missing from the Salvation Army's Booth Centre in Ottawa, Ontario over an 8-year period, the Army's National Office swung into action, calling on Toronto Police to investigate, putting their insurers on notice and hiring external forensic auditors. They also hired auditing firm KPMG to conduct a separate procedure and security audit to prevent future fiscal abuses.

According to Major John Murray, the spokesman for the Salvation Army's Ontario Central East Division, "When you're defrauding the Army, you're defrauding the most vulnerable in the community. The Salvation Army will do due diligence to ensure that we get every nickel back and that every stone is unturned throughout these investigations." Noble words indeed. In these cases, the Army stepped up and did the right thing, admitting faults in the system and taking steps to correct them.

The Army's response to a humanitarian crisis in rural Zimbabwe was nary a murmur for the plight of the 270,000 citizens of Chiweshe District who were left to fend for themselves following Dr. Thistle's removal. Their plight was far more serious than missing goods or stolen money. This action by senior officers was tantamount to criminal negligence that led to death, and the people involved in this decision are directly responsible for those deaths. To let it happen in the first place is a crime; to let it continue is beyond criminal.

CHAPTER 20

The Sally Ann – Then and Now

*The greatness of a man's power is the
measure of his surrender ...*

WILLIAM BOOTH

GO TO ANY SALVATION ARMY citadel and you will find more people in uniform than you see at an officer's ball. But what does it mean? Does the wearing of a uniform make you a better Christian? Is its original purpose still being served or has it outlived its usefulness?

In William Booth's day, there were few social agencies available to help the poor, but today there are many. But no matter how many agencies exist, there are never enough funds or people to cover the needs of the millions of lives who depend on their help and the Salvation Army has a long track record of exemplary service throughout the world. Still, there are old practices that need to be examined and perhaps discarded or changed to adapt to modern times.

With so many charitable organizations appealing for donations to combat social problems, fundraising is a constant challenge. Governments, desperate for money, have come to recognize the duplication and have begun to slash grants to many social agencies, the

Salvation Army included. The public, bombarded by appeals for donations from so many sources, have also become more prudent about what their donations are used for and how much administrative fees eat up. Christmas Kettle donations, the Army's largest fundraising campaign, are down in numbers from previous years. Indeed, if it were not for the large injection of funds from corporations, the numbers would be significantly lower.

Military Style and Structure

Branding—instant recognition through the use of symbols—has become synonymous with big business, but branding is nothing new. In the 1880s William Booth recognized its significance and put it to good use. Booth realized that in order to distinguish his church from others and establish legitimacy, he would have to first devise a method; and nothing spells authority than the wearing of a uniform. Gone were the trappings of the old black robes and collar and in came the new official garb—an ersatz uniform, replete with epaulets and badges. The church's Red Shield, more than any other symbol, became a beacon of hope for millions of people in need.

This Christian Army wasn't just working for God, they were marching to glory in the service of mankind. Booth's concept worked. Once the symbols of the Salvation Army were adopted, they became instantly recognizable, and have continued to command respect throughout the world.

The wearing of uniforms—this symbol of authority and respect—is well entrenched throughout Africa. This is evident in the swollen ranks within the Salvation Army in Zimbabwe and similar countries in the developing world. How reliable these figures are is questionable. During a visit to Kenya in July 2002, Allan Bacon, former Director of Overseas Development for the Salvation Army Canada, was informed by an Australian officer that he had just completed a review, resulting in the removal of 42,000 non-existent Senior Soldiers from the rolls and 46 officers who did not exist, but whose salaries had been paid regularly to their divisional leaders.

African leaders, especially those who belong to despotic governments, are unusually fond of uniforms, regardless of their origin or whether or not they have actually earned the right to wear them. Who can forget the image of Idi Amin or Muammar Gaddafi parading around in uniforms festooned with multiple rows of medals and ribbons? And, in Zimbabwe, Vice-President Joice Mujuru is not averse to donning her Salvation Army uniform when she attends political rallies, the better to bolster her image by representing herself as a woman of faith.

Perhaps, too, the wearing of the uniform has more to do with honoring the wearer than the people the Army aims to serve; because the higher the rank, the more insignias on their shoulders, the more removed they appear to be from its founder's vision.

TIN SOLDIERS

National Post columnist Christie Blatchford wrote an interesting article about her surprise encounter with men in uniform. When Ms. Blatchford was freshly returned from Kandahar as an embedded reporter travelling with Canadian troops, she was invited to speak to a Canadian army reserve regiment—or so she thought. In her zeal for an opportunity to commiserate with soldiers and address them, she readily accepted. She then set about to learn more about the unit. As she reports, reserve army units are sometimes hard to track because they tend to be scattered around the country between small town and big-city armories. What she discovered was that this unit was not reserve, but a group of re-enactors who dress up in period costume to keep old rituals alive. She felt only slightly less stupid than a friend who had made the same mistake, but it was too late to back out. As it turned out, she and her friend had a lovely time. But it is still a curious sight to see people dressing up in uniforms, pretending to be soldiers. For them, it is no doubt preferable to joining the actual military and getting a taste of life in the trenches or spending months aboard an aircraft carrier or down in the depths of a submarine.

This begs the question: Are some Salvation Army soldiers truly in love with God or are they just in love with the chance to don a uniform to declare to the world some type of authority or respect? And what happens when power goes to their heads; when control trumps compassion and fairness? When God's Army is run by people desperate to get their share of the donor pie? When some will stop at nothing to protect and preserve their image?

The previous General, Linda Bond, surrounded herself with handlers who cushioned her from having to deal with difficult questions. She had bodyguards at airports, people in London who acted as brokers between herself and Dr. Thistle and only one letter from his supporters was answered directly by her, with a dismissive response that "there are two sides to this story," with no indication what the other side was. All other letters in support of Dr. Thistle and regarding the controversy at Howard were diverted to Salvation Army headquarters in Canada. It was not her style to lower herself to talk directly to mere commoners or officers of lower rank. Open discussion, transparency, and compassion for the people in Chiweshe were totally absent from the picture and this omission filtered down through the various ranks beneath her.

Spiritual Authority
The road to glory for those who choose to become officers starts with training college, a two-year program that prepares young cadets for a

life of commitment to God; but more often than not a commitment to a life of obedience to those in charge—their "spiritual authority." Once they are commissioned as officers, they are financially trapped and prone to frequent moves within the Army's vast network of territories. Refusal is rarely an option and those who buck against the system are likely to end up like Paul and Pedrinah Thistle, battling a bureaucracy absent of common sense and compassion.

Those who adhere to the Army's rules and regulations, their tightly-controlled public persona and rise to lofty heights within their ranks are, in fact, well rewarded. But Christianity began with one humble man, Jesus, whose goal was to spread the word of God and help the poor and needy, not to accumulate wealth and status. Today, the Catholic Church is one of the biggest financial powers on earth, but its leader, Pope Francis, publicly decries priests living in mansions and driving top-end cars. Many clergy have taken note, forced to give in to higher pressure to relinquish their fancy trappings.

When Paul Thistle became an officer, he had no doubts as to who he was. Officership was an enhancement of everything he had done before. His faith and love of the church and commitment to its principles remained the same or stronger. The words power and glory were not in his vocabulary, except as they applied to God. But as time went on, he certainly had many reasons to doubt or question the motives of the officers involved in making decisions about the hospital. The Army was well aware of the fact that, as a physician, his mandate was to heal. His faith was manifested through his work. Every time a new healthy baby was brought into the world, every time a child's broken arm was mended, each time he brought a smile to a patient who had only known pain before his hands touched them, he was rewarded and his faith strengthened. Most of what he accomplished was despite rather than because of the help of local leadership.

AN ARMY DIVIDED

What happened at Howard Hospital is an aberration, not the norm. Inside every Salvation Army citadel are a raft of people in uniform, but inside those uniforms are hearts of gold—people proud to wear their uniform—whose lives revolve around the helping of others. Here you will find infinite warmth and friendship—a welcoming atmosphere and outstretched hands extended to all who enter. This is the real Salvation Army.

The Howard Hospital debacle has caused a deep divide amongst the rank and file of the church, with members questioning the very foundations of their faith.

An article entitled *"Identity Crisis - As officers, knowing who we are is vital to The Salvation Army's Mission"* by Major Ray Harris appeared in the December 28, 2013 issue of The Salvationist, the Salvation Army's magazine.

The article delves into the very heart of what it means to be ordained and commissioned. *"Officers are commissioned in an act that is most public and most sacred. It is an identity conferred, not self-made or chosen."*

It talks about the notion of authority: *"An officer's ordination and commissioning is an expression of authority"* and the dangers of misusing it. *"Those dangers are very real, sometimes tragically so."*

It also addresses the issue of accountability. *"The notion of accountability carries with it the sense of being answerable to someone and (sic) for something. Officers are entrusted with much—with appointments, with a heritage, with a doctrinal tradition, with important symbols, with finances, with living accommodation. What officers* do with this trust matters. Thus, in the undertakings signed by officers, it is stated that 'I will undertake to account for all monies and other assets entrusted to me…' This accountability is two-sided. On one hand, officers are accountable to their supervising leaders; on the other hand, their leaders 'have a duty to encourage me, enlarging my vision of all I can be in Christ'."

The Salvation Army, however, appears to be strengthening their stand on "spiritual authority." In introducing General Cox at the 2015 Canadian Congress, then Commissioner Brian Peddle read a very carefully-worded pledge designed to endorse this notion of what it takes "to have men and women able to lead the Salvation Army in 127 countries around the world."

"We will do so by being attentive to the messaging that comes out of THQ on occasions where we are called to support particular thinking and actions points. We will do that by respecting them as our spiritual authority here on earth. They are God-ordained people established to lead us in the days in which we face many challenges and more importantly this Territory will support our international leaders with our prayers."

Apparently this declaration didn't hurt Peddle's chances for promotion to Chief of Staff, a position secondary only to the General's, a few short days following this gathering in London, England.

―――

Harris talks about the early Christian church and the emergence of Bishops who were appointed to oversee other clergy, but by the Third or Fourth Century, he found, "the church's organization structure became an end unto itself."

In this 21st century, the Salvation Army appears to be moving in the same direction, where the importance of structure often supersedes its core beliefs. As Harris concedes, the Christian church no longer has a privileged voice. "We live in an extraordinary moment of history when the integrity of the church's life is essential for our culture to hear the gospel." Harris could have added, but did not, that perception is everything in this media-crazed technology-savvy world and every story that carries even a hint of moral corruption or financial irregularity taints the church as a whole. The public has grown wary of false piety, of people who pretend to belong to the Kingdom of God, whose actions bely their words; and wary of church leaders who dictate principles to their congregations which they themselves don't follow.

No one expects those serving in the ministry to be perfect. Churches are led by human beings with all their flaws and the public is willing to accept that fact. What they expect in return, though, is truth and accountability from those in authority; and for a church especially, nothing less will do.

Marching to a Different Drummer

Is it time for The Salvation Army to abandon the military structure that has been in force for some 130 years? Is the uniform that was designed to represent goodness and humility serving a different purpose today? Is it leading to corruption of authority and power-brokering amongst its ranks? These are questions now being raised and openly discussed by church members, current and former officers, and with the spate of recent scandals, the general public as well. Some would even say that the modern Salvation Army has morphed from a church to cult.

Today, the dear old Sally Ann has a perception problem. Their red shield has developed a few cracks over the years, but since August 2012, with the forced removal of Dr. Paul Thistle from Howard Hospital, those cracks are wide enough for people to see through and question what they find behind it. Between lost toys and missing money, the Army appears to have lost its rudder. The old way is not working and the new wave of officers, educated though they may be, leave much to be desired. The people at the top, the people in charge who can make a real difference continue to issue sweeping and ambitious statements about their commitment, while failing to deliver on those promises.

One of the Army's new initiatives is the International Social Justice Commission that partners with the United Nations and other global forums. The Commission's mandate is to "pursue justice in today's world…to raise strategic voices to advocate with the world's poor and oppressed, be a recognized centre of research and critical thinking on issues of global justice… represent the world's poor and oppressed."

Unfortunately, this pursuit of justice and critical thinking was not applied to the poor and oppressed people of Chiweshe. When questioned by a member of the church about these particular ethics as they apply to Howard Hospital, Lt.-Colonel Dean Pallant, who heads the International Social Justice Commission, replied that he and the member hold different views on what justice and accountability look like at Howard Hospital. His message ended with the pithy comment, "I suspect we are not going to agree this side of Heaven." What the Director of this ambitious project fails to recognize is that a difference of opinion is no excuse for failing the poor.

———

According to its website as of January 2014, The Salvation Army world-wide has over 108,000 employees, and over 26,000 officers. As Allan Bacon observed, there are many instances where lay people who are experts in their field report to officers who have little or no training in practical matters, but the decisions of those officers, right or wrong, carry the day. More often than not, rank supersedes common sense or compassion and, sadly, sometimes both.

After what happened to Dr. Thistle at Howard Hospital, new candidates are fearful of their future and more difficult to recruit. While recruitment numbers in developing countries appear to be increasing, other countries have experienced lower levels overall. Whether they like it or not, the Salvation Army has been forced to make changes or stagnate.

In 2008, the United Kingdom territory relaxed the rules to allow officers to marry people who are not members of the Salvation Army and/or people who practice other faiths or have no faith at all.

In 2012, the Salvation Army placed its Positional Statement on Homosexuality under review after receiving adverse publicity about its content. Prior to 2012, practicing homosexuals were ineligible for full membership or appointment as ministers, but the Army's latest official position has softened and states:

"We do not believe that same sex attraction is blameworthy and we oppose the vilification and mistreatment of gays and lesbians."

This also applies to its position on women. Salvation Army officers were previously allowed to marry only other officers (a rule that varies in different countries); but this rule has been relaxed in recent years. Husbands and wives usually share the same rank and have the same or similar assignments. The major exception to this is the General's spouse, who is given the rank of Commissioner.

Increasing recruitment, then, appears to be the driving force behind the changes.

Army Culture – Practical Training and Education

In any army, it's the foot soldiers—the grunts on the ground—who get the job done. In the Salvation Army, its corps officers and those assigned to social services who fight the real battles—down in the trenches with the alcoholics, the drug-addicted, with people suffering from mental illness and life's hardest knocks. It takes strength and compassion in equal measure to bear witness to the ravages of poverty, hopelessness and disease and to put into action the tools to fix these broken lives.

The Army's missionary doctors have the hardest grind of all. While the foot soldiers like Dr. Thistle and those before him fight fatigue—working impossible hours, on call seven days a week—the top brass of this Army enjoy comfy desk jobs, plotting strategy and damage control far removed from the fray.

Today's Army has officers who are ill-equipped to perform the jobs they are assigned—people charged with handling funds who have no knowledge of fiscal responsibility, and senior officers and non-professionals, with no medical expertise or appreciation of what it takes to run a hospital, in charge of hospital administration. Many officers are sent out into the field with inadequate training or knowledge of the risks and sacrifices involved in missionary work and little to no support from their superiors. But the bigger question involves the training and qualifications required to lead and manage a worldwide organization operating in 127 countries.

Both the former General, Linda Bond and her under-secretary hold degrees. General Bond has a Bachelor's Degree in religious education and a Master's Degree in theological studies. Twice she was involved in training cadets at officer training colleges in Toronto, Ontario and St. John's, Newfoundland. Her degrees in theology are perfectly suited to religious training, but hardly qualify as useful prerequisites for practical tools needed to survive in foreign and dangerous locales.

Major Dean Pallant, the under-secretary charged with handling plans for the completion of the new Howard Hospital holds a Doctorate in Theology from King's College London. He grew up in Zimbabwe, with first-hand knowledge about the lands and its people. This knowledge should have armed him with enough insight to make qualified decisions about the needs of Zimbabwe's rural population, but he appears to share the neo-colonial perception about rural African poor—that you can't be too kind to them; that you must force them to stand on their own two feet; otherwise they develop a "culture of dependency." Although he appears to be much liked by African Commissioners, he is neither liked nor respected by the local Salvationists who see him as more of a hindrance than a help. They distrust his support of local administration they consider to be corrupt and believe that he was instrumental in Dr. Thistle's removal.

Pallant's wife is a qualified physician, whose specialty is treating addictions, which would serve well in an inner-city setting such as London, where she resides, but is not particularly useful in a rural hospital where drugs are in short supply.

The new general, Andre Cox, was also born and raised in Zimbabwe. In an interview conducted shortly after he was elected, General Cox had this to say:

> *"First and foremost, I would like to say that the poor should not be looked at as a subject of pity. The poor are extremely resilient and often have ideas about how they can improve their situation. We should come alongside them and seek to understand what their situation is and to try and help them to identify how they can help themselves. They need to have a sense of ownership in finding solutions to their problems."*

General Cox's lofty vision, though, seems to have little relationship to what is happening on the ground. It is significant that Chiweshe's citizens were never consulted about their needs or invited to meetings regarding plans for the new hospital. Yet, without consultation, this same group of people in London were making decisions that directly impact the lives of 270,000 people in a foreign country 5,000 miles away. Instead of consulting the very people who need affordable access to health care, the Salvation Army decided what is good for them. Contrast that to the Stephen Lewis Foundation, a Canadian NGO whose goal is to eradicate AIDS in Africa. All the projects of the Lewis foundation are designed and run by local community members. By doing so, the Stephen Lewis Foundation gives dignity to the people being helped; not by forcing Western ideas of development on their communities.

Almost in the same breath, General Cox adds:

"I also think we should use the influence we have within the political sphere. We need to work with politicians and policymakers on policy issues that have a direct impact on this problem."

In Zimbabwe, however, the Army has learned how to bend to the will of politicians while the local people are left wanting and without answers to their vital and most pressing questions: Why was Dr. Thistle, who deeply cared about their overall needs, removed and how do they afford health care in the future?

In both cases involving Howard Hospital, the old and the new, the focus was squarely on control—control of money and control over the people the hospital is intended to serve.

Howard Hospital is a prime example of Army—authority and control—taking precedence over Salvation. The hospital that was formerly a welcoming haven of healing and reassurance quickly morphed into a fortress surrounded by uniforms of one kind or another—either civil or secular. Visitors are no longer welcome.

We Feel your Pain

Who is this new Army? Is it a church, a charity, a pseudo-Army of military posers, or is it, as some Salvationist have come to believe, more akin to a cult? When current and former officers are silenced, when people are expected to toe the line and not break rank by questioning or speaking out, when every statement uses the same benign language and people who do express a differing opinion are ostracized and shunned, it is easy to draw that conclusion. The removal of position is one thing—shunning is another. Former friends avoid talking to you, for fear of appearing "disloyal" and being contaminated. It brings to mind a compliant and repressed society that follows protocol, like a group of lemmings, marching to the same happy-clappy tune.

Most people's perception of the Sally Ann is of an old-fashioned institution, full of bible-thumpers, cloaked in tradition, who also happen to do a lot of good in the world. The modern church has many more tools of communication at their disposal, but even though they make ample use of social media, they often fall short of their targets.

A recent article that appeared in The Salvationist, the Army's on-line magazine, features Commissioner Brian Peddle, Territorial Commander of the Canadian and Bermuda Territory. Prior to the Peddle's appointment, he and his wife served in the U.K. In the spring of 2011, according to the article, they chose to "Live below the line" on £1 per day for five days in order to "raise awareness of the nearly 1.4 billion people around the world who are forced to survive on less than £1 a day."

Exactly how this particular gesture was supposed to help the 1.4 million people who are forced to exist in the direst circumstances is questionable. No doubt it reached the 1.5 million members of the Salvation Army who are abundantly aware that poverty exists throughout the world and consistently contribute to world-wide humanitarian causes.

But people outside the organization are no strangers to widespread poverty and the dire conditions that a huge percentage of the world population live in. The same message could have been posted without the need to highlight the 5-day self-imposed sacrifice that appears to serve the Commissioner and his wife far more than the people it is designed to help. Had the Commissioner and his wife forfeited their symbolic gesture and, instead, ventured into the cold cruel world and lived amongst those people to deliver hands-on help, that, indeed, would be a story worth crowing about.

To quote the irrepressible Canadian pundit, Rex Murphy: *"What is being done no longer matters: what matters is being seen doing… anything."*

CHAPTER 21

A New Beginning

The roads diverged in a wood, and I .... I took the one less travelled by and that has made all the difference ...

ROBERT FROST

AFTER MONTHS OF DEALING WITH the Salvation Army and their intractable position concerning the fate of Howard Hospital and its disintegrating service to the people of Chiweshe, it was time for Paul Thistle and his family to concentrate on their own future. Although there were certain legal considerations still to be worked out with the Salvation Army, it was obvious that all communication had come to a halt. But his commitment to serve had never wavered and giving up was not an option. Although socio-economic conditions in Zimbabwe had improved overall, there was always more work to be done:

- Average life expectancy – 52, a huge improvement over the 2006 figures of 34 years for women and 37 for men
- 83,000 deaths of men, women and children from AIDS – down from 200,000 eight years previously
- US$307 – the average annual income

- Over 60% of people were unemployed according to 2012 World Food Program figures, Other agencies put the figure at close to 95%
- 78% of the population considered to be "absolutely poor" reported by the United Nations Children's Fund in 2010.

The only thing he could do was move forward and find a job that suited both his beliefs and his dedication to the people of Zimbabwe. Several job offers had appeared on the horizon. But the one that Paul and Pedrinah decided on was to work at Karanda Hospital.

Karanda sits on the edge of the lush Zambezi River valley about 50 kilometres from the nearest town, Mount Darwin, some 200 kilometres north of Harare. For eight months of the year, the region is hot. In mid-November to mid-April it is not only hot, with temperatures ranging between 30 to 40C, but wet. This is the rainy season. From mid-April to mid-August, the days are typically cold and dry, then back to hot and dry from mid-August to mid-November.

The hospital is run by TEAM, The Evangelical Alliance Mission, a Christian agency that sends missionaries to work in areas pertinent to their expertise. Volunteers have many areas to choose from: evangelism, community development, healthcare, education, social justice, business as mission. Today there are 575 TEAM missionaries and staff serving in 35 countries on almost every continent—Africa, Asia, Australia, Europe, North and South America.

At Karanda, Paul and Pedrinah are part of a team that consists of six physicians—three Americans and three Canadians plus an American physician's assistant—who run the 134-bed facility that is typically 90% full. They perform 3,500 to 4,000 surgeries per year and attend to 2,000 deliveries.

Like Howard Hospital, Karanda is a teaching facility that works with the University of Zimbabwe to train surgical residents on a

3-month rotation. It also operates a Nursing and Midwifery school, as well as a primary school from Grades 1-7 for children of hospital staff to attend.

On an average day, the hospital's six doctors will perform 10-20 surgeries and tend to 200-300 outpatients. At Karanda, Paul is involved with overseeing obstetrics and attending to the female ward, that includes a mixture of medical and surgical patients with HIV/AIDS complications, to the care of ovarian cancer. Pedrinah teaches at the nursing school, while preparing for and writing her exams in public health. Karanda offers similar challenges to Howard: communication challenges and electricity cuts, plus the proliferation of snakes and scorpions following the heavy rains. Its location is more remote than Howard's and the temperature is more humid. The work is equally rewarding, but not as difficult to maintain. Here there are as many jobs, but more hands to accomplish them.

Since leaving Howard, Paul and Pedrinah have had to make tough choices and personal sacrifices. Although working for TEAM at Karanda fulfills their need for service, it does have its drawbacks. The first is monetary. Because they are volunteers, their only means of income comes from donations. Luckily, donors who previously supported Dr. Thistle's work at Howard, have continued with their commitment to his work at Karanda with sufficient donations to cover his salary. Anything that is left over after living expenses, goes to running of the hospital.

Thankfully, Paul has maintained connections with a number of individuals and organizations. The Rotary Club provides medicines and equipment to support the Maternal Health program at Karanda, as well as bicycles for the Home-Based Care volunteers. The Thistle children continue at school in Harare, staying with their uncle, aunt and cousins during the week, but now the trip takes longer. Often the roads are awash in water due to flooding, making transportation more difficult.

As with all mission hospitals, Karanda relies on basic support from the Ministry of Health and patient fees, supplemented by donations from supporters at home and abroad. Here as at Howard, Karanda is a little outpost of heaven. Rural Zimbabweans, who make up the majority of the population, flock to Karanda from across the country. On any given day, half of the inpatient ward may be filled with patients from Howard Hospital's catchment. Some of the patients Dr. Thistle treated at Howard are willing to make the trek across country to Karanda. Wyson, a 42-year-old man with metastatic cancer in his abdominal wall offers a smile out of his pain. As Paul says, "this kind of character you will not find in a normal world." They are able to alleviate his suffering with surgery.

Another patient to arrive at Karanda is Miriam, who previously lost both her left leg and her baby in a crocodile attack near Howard Hospital. She has little means of support and her children were expelled from school because she had no money to cover the fees. Paul has no idea how she made the 100 kilometre trip to Karanda on one leg and no bus fare, but she did. Paul says he has stopped asking those questions. As for Miriam, she was grateful for the little doctors could offer through the support of a friend in Canada.

On February 14, 2013, soon after taking up their posts at Karanda, the Thistles learned that Milton Zindoga, the Howard Hospital nurse charged with "public mischief," which included overturning the Salvation Army vehicle, was sentenced to two years in jail. He was subsequently released on bail March 26, 2013.

―――

In early August 2013, when the Thistle family arrived back in Zimbabwe after their annual summer break in Canada, things were eerily quiet following the elections held on July 31. September provided a respite for Paul to spend some time with colleagues from TEAM at a men's retreat in the eastern highlands, while Pedrinah was selected to facilitate a Ministry of Health workshop on Prevention of Mother to Child Transmission of HIV. Although it remains to be seen if the new Minister of Finance will provide an infusion of medicine into the country's beleaguered health care sector, the good news is that Zimbabwe is moving towards the provision of full antiretroviral (ARV) therapy to all pregnant women who are HIV positive. For Paul and his supporters, it was gratifying to know that the ARV program for breastfeeding mothers that began eight years ago at Howard Hospital with the help of Ve'ahavta, the Canadian Jewish Humanitarian and Relief Committee, was being expanded to all mothers infected with HIV.

In late September, Paul and Pedrinah were invited to facilitate the Canadian emergency obstetrics course in Bulawayo, teaching a group of mission doctors and midwives in drought-stricken Matabeleland, whose hospitals are struggling.

Slowly but surely, the Thistle family adjusted to their new surroundings with the same commitment and dedication they had devoted to Howard.

When asked to describe a typical workday at Karanda, Paul offers this formula:

0600:	Dogs stop barking; roosters start crowing
0601:	Wake-up time
0700-0715:	Morning devotions with staff and students
0800-900:	Inpatient ward rounds
900-1800:	Outpatient consultation and surgery
1800:	Dogs start barking; roosters stop crowing
1800-0600:	On call

One thing that hasn't changed are the Sunday night field hockey games with local children, a tradition begun at Howard that has been received with equal enthusiasm by the youngsters at Karanda.

CHAPTER 22

Consequences

A man's vanity tells him what is honor, a man's conscience what is justice. Delay in justice is injustice …

WALTER SAVAGE LANDER

ALTHOUGH PAUL AND PEDRINAH HAD physically left Howard Hospital behind, their thoughts and prayers were still with the people of Chiweshe and the good Samaritans in Canada continued to fight for justice for the people he had left behind. But every attempt by former volunteers to visit the hospital were quickly thwarted or dismissed out of hand.

In April 2013, two Norwegian theatre nurses trained in anesthesia asked permission to return to Howard for a three-day stay in order to continue their project to help 600 children and young people to attend school as the schools they were helping were all in that area. Their request was denied.

In October 2013, three women from Canada decided to visit Zimbabwe and reconnect with friends at Howard Hospital. Shirley Watkinson and Jan Corley are lay Salvationists who had previously volunteered at Howard Hospital. Lorraine Irvine is a retired doctor who has spent many months volunteering at Howard and has raised thousands of dollars for its programs. None of these women are young. Dr. Irvine, in fact, was 84, but still sharp of mind and fit for travel.

The three women made their way to the hospital with the help of their hired driver, making stops along the way to familiar places. At the local primary school, they were greeted by community leaders who had gathered to meet them and express their concerns about the decreased level of medical care in their catchment. Several village leaders offered to accompany the ladies to the hospital, with others suggesting a police escort, but the ladies declined and continued on their way to Howard. It was hard to ignore the obvious changes. At the front gates, usually packed with people and cars, there were few vehicles or people. The male ward had few patients, the female and children's wards were half full and there were no patients at all in the outpatients department.

Outside the operating theatre, they met the new chief medical officer from India, Dr. Pachuau, who told the women they were always welcome at Howard Hospital. Shirley Watkinson, an operating theatre nurse from Winnipeg, was pleased to see many of the staff she had worked with in the theatre. While friends hugged and greeted each other, she took pictures with her small digital camera.

As they made their way back to the outpatients department to leave, two Salvation Army officers approached them. Although the men didn't introduce themselves, Shirley was able to recognize their rank. One was a captain and the other a major. The women introduced themselves, explaining that they were at Howard Hospital to see their friends. The officers insisted that the ladies accompany them to the Administrator's office to discuss why they were there, but since the women had already stated their purpose, they felt that this was redundant. The officers continued to demand that the women "go to the office to discuss." Since the ladies didn't want to make a scene, they walked out of the hospital and through the front gate without incident.

As they continued along the main road, past the hospital, approaching the primary school, a policeman on a bicycle came up behind Watkinson, demanding that she stop and hand over her camera. Shirley refused and continued to walk. The policeman climbed off his bicycle and grabbed her left wrist. He continued to demand her camera and again she refused. He then grabbed her wrist with both hands and held her. Shirley hollered at him to let her go.

By this time, a Salvation Army vehicle had pulled up with two Salvation Army officers on board. The hospital's administrator was in the passenger seat and an unknown officer, a Major, was driving. Shirley was pushed and shoved into the back seat of the van. She remembers a lot of shouting from people gathered around the van—men, women, and school children. Her two friends were also forced into the van and all three women were driven back to the police building on the grounds of Howard Hospital, where the two officers continued to insist that the women go to a room to discuss the situation. Since the two officers had not identified themselves, and judging by the way she had been treated and the lack of information provided as to why they had been detained, Shirley refused their request. Once again, they were piled into the Salvation Army vehicle and taken to the local Glendale Police Station. The unidentified Major drove, with the young policeman accompanying him in the passenger seat. The three women sat in the back seat, along with a friend and her two children who had greeted them along the road. This lady told them that the policeman had assured her that they only wanted to remove the pictures from her camera and that she would get it back safely. Shirley gave it to her and she handed it to the policeman who proceeded to remove the pictures on the instructions of the Salvation Army Major, before handing it back to her. Subsequently, her friend and her children were released.

The women were detained for four to five hours, but report that at all times, the police were kind and friendly. After taking the women's personal information, the police asked them to continue on to the police station in Bindura. It was dark outside and they were accompanied by their driver and another policeman. At Bindura police station, they were received with courtesy and kindness, as is the Shona way. The desk sergeant called in his superior for support. After being assured that the pictures had been erased from the camera, the women were wished a safe trip back to Karanda Mission Hospital in Mt. Darwin.

What the women were unaware of at the time was later revealed by their driver who had acted as their advocate throughout the long day. He told them that the crowd who had gathered on the main road and witnessed the women's confrontation with police had wanted to fight with the Salvation Army officers, but he had intervened telling them not to do this, as it would only make the situation worse. He said that the Salvation Army officers kept telling the police to restrain the women and put them in the vehicle. He also mentioned that at the Glendale Police, the Salvation Army Major kept insisting that the police lock them up in the cells. The police saw no need, because no charges had been laid. The driver also said that the people on the road and in the police station were praying for their safety. What the police and Salvation Army officers were unaware of was that Jan Corley had also managed to take photos of the empty wards, which were hidden safely away on her camera.

If this encounter was meant to discourage former supporters of Howard Hospital, it didn't work. The Thistles' supporters remained solidly behind their new mission. Donors who had supported their efforts at Howard Hospital now switched their allegiance to Karanda Hospital. In December 2013, three men from the Peterborough area,

Larry Gillman, Brian Nichols and David Abramsky travelled to Karanda Mission Hospital to distribute food and clothing. They were greeted by 400 orphaned children who were just as glad to see them as Paul and Pedrinah. As Larry Gillman reported, "You can see Paul and Pedrinah starting to get their tentacles out into the community."

Months after the new Chief Medical Officer at Howard Hospital took over, a photo appeared on his Facebook page announcing work on a new project.

The entry was noted by Jan Corley, the Salvation Army member from Peterborough and one of the three women who had travelled to Howard Hospital in the fall of 2013 and were detained and questioned by police for several hours afterwards. The picture shows three men assembling a wooden structure, and behind them stands a single story newly-constructed brick building. The caption accompanying the picture reads: "Our Projects Department has brought the Donwood Housing Project up to this level, already an encouraging sight indeed!"

When Corley wrote to the Canadian Territorial Command to question them about the Facebook posting, and whether or not this project is related to Donwood United Church in Peterborough, she received a reply from Major Gillian Brown, Canadian and Bermuda Territorial Command, cloaked in the same flowery but innocuous language prevalent in all Salvation Army communiques.

> *"I have noticed that you have found Dr. Zaia, the CMO for Howard Hospital, Facebook page, and through this are receiving news of the activities at the hospital as well as the prayer concerns. Thank you for your prayers for the staff, patients and community surrounding the hospital. God continues to work amazing miracles through the ministry of Howard Hospital."*

As this triplex staff house was not the duplex volunteer house of the Donwood project, and the visible materials were new and not those of the original donation, it was clear that a misappropriation of funds and materials had indeed taken place, which was approved by the leadership and made worse by a request, without apology, for more money.

When Brian Nichols of Donwood United Church was alerted to the posting, he expressed his surprise and displeasure in an e-mail to Major Brown on February 17, 2014. His comments were finally acknowledged in a reply from Commissioner Brian Peddle on March 27, 2014 addressed to both Nichols and Donwood's minister. The e-mail refers to Peddle's first-hand experience regarding his recent extended visit to Howard Hospital and, specifically, to the progress of the "Donwood Project" that, he says, will provide staff housing for three families. He goes on to mention his participation in the dedication ceremony on March 14 and the excellent quality of construction. Included with his message is a financial statement "which accounts for your support", followed by an outright appeal for a further $12,000 to $14,000 needed to complete the project, adding that "I am sure you would understand that The Salvation Army would be happy to facilitate any further support from Donwood United Church."

———

While supporters continue to keep pressure on the Howard Hospital situation, Salvation Army leaders insist on maintaining the party line of denial and deflection. Major Brown, Director of World Missions appears to be the designated spokesperson with the unenviable task of having to answer or refute the continuing controversy over the Army's handling of the Howard Hospital affair.

When a member of The Salvation Army in Canada subsequently attempted to post a comment on the Army's official website, the editor received instructions not to approve it because the administration did not want to reopen the debate on the Howard Hospital. Their main objective was to put to rest the controversy and move on. The website's editor suggested that the comment would likely be approved if references to Howard Hospital were removed. This was followed by a call from Major Brown, who responded to the correspondent's concerns. However, the exchange not only failed to put concerns to rest, but raised further alarms, because it appeared that Dr. Thistle was being held responsible to a large extent for his dismissal as CMO of the Howard and transfer as an officer. Once again, each response deflected any responsibility from the Army. Their initial statement that Dr. Thistle's dismissal was a "routine transfer" had now morphed into the blame game.

———

On March 16, 2014, Thistle met with Canadian Commissioner Brian Peddle over dinner in Harare. As before, Peddle shied away from any responsibility in the loss of life after August 2012. Instead, he shifted the blame to the people of Chiweshe "who die from malaria every day in Chiweshe by not using mosquito nets at home." As for those who have been denied affordable surgery, Peddle's solution was that "people who need operations can get them elsewhere."

Dr. Thistle's push for a "Truth and Reconciliation" committee for Howard Hospital within the community was met with equal disinterest, with Peddle telling Paul that it was unlikely to happen. He blamed the negative publicity on Howard to a few troublemakers in Zimbabwe and Canada, who, he said, would be "dealt with." Paul left the meeting with an increased concern for workers at Howard, who were likely to be further victimized, when he learned that, once again, there was a move afoot to dismiss more staff who had dared to speak out.

But on the home front, the Thistles' summer brought joy and a reason to celebrate. On August 29, 2014, shortly after returning home from Canada, they welcomed their third son, Andrew Jacob, into the world. His birth was a double blessing, as he arrived on his parents' sixteenth wedding anniversary.

The New Old Howard Hospital

At Howard Hospital, a succession of doctors came and went following Paul Thistle's dismissal. Immediately following his departure, Dr. Aaron Musaka was appointed Chief Medical Officer and served until August 2013, with the arrival of Dr. Zairemthiama Pachuau, who had previously served as Chief Medical Officer at another Salvation Army hospital in Zambia. Shortly after, in December 2013, Dr. Per-Gote Lindgren, a retired surgeon was brought in to instruct medical personnel at Howard, though he would not be performing surgery himself. In July 2014, Salvation Army officer, Dr. James Miller, a general practitioner with extensive experience in both Iraq and Afghanistan, arrived at Howard.

According to the new Chief Medical Officer, everything was moving along like clockwork. The new Chief's Facebook page began to fill with pictures of daily activities at Howard, including pictures of smiling mothers and children waiting patiently in line and the doctor himself smiling above his surgical mask. Also included were pictures of patients' surgeries, replete with graphic pictures of what he had just removed. No pictures of smiling patients here—the patients in question were silent, still heavily sedated, but they certainly debunk the myth of the Army's version of a Primary Care Facility.

The Brand New Howard Hospital

Finally, with the influx of new money from the Salvation Army's Southern Territory in the United States, the completion of the new hospital forged ahead, requiring multiple visits from senior officers from International Headquarters to get the job done. On November 17, 2014, the new hospital was officially opened and dedicated by the Army's Chief of Staff, Commissioner William Roberts and attended by a flock of other senior officers and local dignitaries. Notably missing from both the invitation list and the ceremony were the two former Chief Medical Officers, Doctors Paul Thistle and James Watt, who had both been involved in the initial planning. Indeed, this was the second such opening and dedication. The first took place 11 years prior, on November 1, 2003, marked with a plaque dedicated to "The Glory and Service of God."

The new hospital turned out to be three times the size of the old hospital, but almost immediately after opening, rumours of proposed staff cuts surfaced, with staff being encouraged to resign with compensation. Patient attendance and staff morale were low, with nurses reporting that daily life at the new hospital "resembled a Sunday."

Patients also experienced problems. As they reported, drugs were in short supply and many times prescriptions had to be filled in Harare. In the summer of 2015, the community reported concern over the number of patients dying—some from lack of medication and others from possible errors in diagnosis, such as a mother who was diagnosed as being past her due date and was mistakenly induced. The baby was actually premature and died.

Other patients, referred to government-run hospitals in Harare, end up not being treated if they can't afford to pay the high fees. Some simply give up and go home to die; others travel to Karanda by bus, and the few who can afford it, make their way to private clinics.

All of these facts were laid out by Dr. Watt in a six-page letter to Commissioner Susan McMillan at Canadian territorial headquarters in Toronto on February 3, 2015.

Despite numerous attempts to obtain answers and understand the Army's reasoning and insistence in designating the new hospital as a Primary Care site, he was no further ahead. But that didn't deter Watt from trying again. He refuted the claim that Dr. Thistle was putting the hospital in debt and neglecting primary care with a program of complex surgery. Volunteer witnesses and statistics from annual reports proved otherwise. Records from 1994 through to 2011 show a four-fold increase in the number of outpatients treated at Howard. This was due to deterioration of medical services elsewhere in Zimbabwe, the increased need for AIDS prevention and treatment, in addition to increasing political violence, the victims of which other facilities refused to treat. Nevertheless, as Watt pointed out, Howard Hospital stood alone as a place of care and refuge in the community, providing for their needs at affordable costs.

Recorded statistics on operations and deliveries also dispute the Army's version of "primary care." These procedures increased at the same rate as primary care and for the same reasons. There was no disproportionate increase in operations. The complicated major cases that brought in the most fees were minor in number; therefore, as Dr. Watt assured the Commissioner, the Army's claim of an extensive surgical program was false.

But the Army that had so much trouble separating fact from fiction, continued to devise new ways of shifting responsibility for deteriorating conditions at either the old or new hospital squarely onto the shoulders of Paul Thistle. Dr. Watt referred back to the former General's public statement at Toronto airport that the Army had to remove Dr. Thistle from Howard because his "complex" surgical program had put the hospital into debt with a $30,000 electrical bill. But as Dr. Watt pointed out, even the most complex surgery does not require vast amounts of electricity. In fact, Dr. Thistle can attest to the fact that the actual bill owed to ZESA, the Zimbabwe Electricity Supply Authority, was in excess of $200,000. As Paul Thistle states, "The General probably had not been informed about the free electricity in officer's quarters and subsequent private chicken runs and commercial bakeries. Electricity was the one major debt hanging over expenditure boards. For some reason, Howard Hospital administrators had not paid or had underpaid ZESA for years, resulting in a six figure bill in US dollars. In reality, when the country adopted the U.S. dollar, ZESA re-valued the hospital's electricity bill using industrial rates. They also respected the work that the hospital was doing and never cut off the power. Blackouts occurred daily on their own."

The Army also focused on the "high salaries" of the skilled surgeon and theatre nurses, completely ignoring the fact that highly skilled staff work for pittance—officers' salaries—and their expertise attracts other sources of revenues, both in government grants and patient fees. Well-run mission hospitals ensure that patients no longer need to be transported to central hospitals, thus reducing costs in transportation.

If anyone involved in the Army's internal investigation process had bothered to ask Dr. Thistle how much it costs to operate a mission hospital, he could have provided the answers. He could tell them where the money came from and how it was delivered. What he could not tell them was where the money went or how it was spent. That was a question only a certified auditor could answer.

Howard Hospital needed $50,000 per month of income to cover operations. Patient fees generated $20,000 to $25,000 monthly, leaving the remainder to be sourced elsewhere. With government funding at $5,000 to-$10,000 per annum, the combined input at its most generous failed to meet almost half the monthly figure required.

The gap was filled with:

- Administrative funds from community projects, e.g. the Children First orphan project or the Stephen Lewis Foundation – generally 15% of the total budget

- Direct project support, e.g. laboratory, anti-retroviral drugs and fuel supplied by Rotary Club International and others as formal donations
- Unspecified donations from international donors as direct deposit to Howard Hospital's Reliance Bank account and later to the hospital's Barclay's Bank account in Harare when Zimbabwe adopted the US dollar.
- Out of pocket donations of cash and drugs by volunteers, who risked customs clearance with full suitcases worth thousands of dollars.

When the roof of the Maternity wing collapsed in January 2011, it was a volunteer who pitched in with finances and labour. As Paul Thistle noted, the fact that the volunteer was a professional carpenter also helped.

As usual the Army, insisting that all was well at the new facility, provided no answers as to where the drugs had gone, no accounting for mis-diagnoses, no concern for staff cut-backs or low morale, nor the patients who suffered as a result. But the collective body of senior officers who had so much trouble separating fact from fiction, continued to devise new shape-shifting ways of deflecting responsibility for deteriorating conditions at either the old or new hospital away from themselves and onto the shoulders of Paul Thistle. As Dr. Watt informed Commissioner McMillan, many officers in Canada were led to believe that he had resigned his officership voluntarily and many expressed shock when they learned how his own church had treated him.

———

In September 2016, the Salvation Army sent out an appeal for donations accompanied by an article entitled "Hope for the World" that features a glowing report on the new and expanded Howard Hospital, calling it "the go-to- facility for conditions that can't be treated at rural clinics." The article highlights a mother and her high risk pregnancy, and boasts about "a medical team second to none," also quoting a nurse at one of those clinics corroborating that statement. However, local people who actually live in Chiweshe, who have access to the hospital, tell a different story.

In May 2016, Thomas Kavhai, headmaster of Nyachuru Secondary School in Chiweshe, met with local citizens to share their collective concerns about the ongoing problems at Howard Hospital since the departure of Dr. Thistle. This was a chance for the community to air their concerns and relate their experiences. The result was 52 pages of testimony collected from 26 people that refutes the Army's message that the new Howard Hospital is "a place where people are cared for." This is raw data, as expressed by the people of Chiweshe, many of whom are or were Salvationists. They have put themselves at considerable risk for speaking out, but all they ask is that their concerns be heard, investigated and remedied.

Witness Gutsa describes the day that Dr. Thistle was removed from the hospital as "a day of war with people saying 'no' to the chasing of Dr. Thistle from Howard Hospital Mission." Chipo Handara reports that on August 15, 2012, Dr. Thistle "was told to leave everything he was doing in theatre. He had to plead to them to finish the patient who was on theatre who was already given medication to sleep." Nineteen people confirmed that Dr. Thistle was ordered to stop operating while in the middle of surgery. The patient, Mrs. Mware, was left with her intestines exposed, which were wrapped in a plastic bag and taken to the Governor in Bindura, causing the patient's death two days later. This incident refers to the first reported death following Dr. Thistle's departure from Howard, when doctors at Bindura Hospital attempted to repair and reconnect the woman's bowel.

According to nine others, "Pharoh Ngandu was discharged during the confusion and later died at home."

Eric Choto and Tariro Kumadiro confirm the chaos that changed their lives forever: "we shall never forget that day as people. It was and still remains a dark day to us."

Stella Chandavengerwa and Livingstone Ngunda report that hospital statistics give a clear record of unwarranted deaths that have occurred since the day that Dr. Thistle was forced to abandon his patients—some caused by negligence and others by a shortage of drugs. This fact is confirmed by fifteen locals. Augustine Mufuka recalls a cancer patient who died "after being opened twice and closed twice in an operation that was done as an experiment" and others who "receive no meaningful treatment." They died after paying $400 US per patient. Another female patient was operated on twice in two days and died of perforated intestines. Eleven people testified about the woman with dislocation of the shoulder who died instantly after being injected and her shoulder socket forced back in.

Other concerns address the hospital's cavalier approach to drugs:

- The administration fails to purchase ordinary drugs for blood pressure and diabetes, saying they are not important at all.
- No pain killers
- Intravenous drugs are hard to come by
- Patients being told to buy drugs from pharmacies. If drugs are there, they are very expensive to buy
- Non-medical personnel are in charge of drug buying

And how the level of care has deteriorated:

- Outpatients are left unattended. It could be 3-4 days before they are seen by a doctor.

- Older people and children under 5 years of age who used to receive free treatment are now being charged $10 for a consulting fee, with no drugs available to treat them
- Patient numbers continue to dwindle due to lack of trust in the new doctor(s).

The community is also shocked by the attitude of medical staff, especially the doctor whose "utterances are frightening":

" 'I can do as I please with patients in an African country because Africans do not know their rights. I will experiment to the fullest in the theatre room.' "

The group also expressed solutions to address their concerns. They all agreed that the administrator must be a medical practitioner, that a qualified surgeon and better qualified nurses should be appointed and that night duties should not be delegated to nurses with no doctor present. But the most resounding solution was the return of Dr. Paul Thistle: "It would be in the best interest of the patients, as well as the community at large, if Dr. Thistle is allowed to come back to Howard Hospital and be given the sole responsibility to administer the hospital."

The likelihood of that occurring is very slim to non-existent. The only thing that could make it happen is a seismic shift in attitude, directed by the present General or one of his successors, to admit their mistakes and do the right thing for the people of Chiweshe, in place of preserving the Army's "brand." Removing Dr. Thistle, leaving patients without adequate care in his absence, was a deliberate act sanctioned by people who had the power to stop it. People's suffering cannot be so easily dismissed by tepid talk of "mosquito nets" and "people dying all over Africa." Such statements are a mere band-aid for a gaping wound. They are an insult to the local people's intelligence; they may be poor, but they are well-educated. Their loved ones did not die because they failed to buy mosquito nets. They died because the Salvation Army abruptly cut off their medical care when they were most vulnerable. Their loved ones were not mere statistics—anonymous, fictional Africans, but patients with names and hospital records and children who loved them. There is no "moving on" from this worst of crimes—manslaughter. For the people of Chiweshe especially, there is no moving on. All they have lost can never be forgotten or replaced, and those who defend what was done are culpable in the loss of those lives. In the summer of 2012, the Army decided what was good for the local citizens and they have been forced to deal with the consequences of that decision ever since.

The Army's great experiment, the "new, re-purposed" Howard Hospital is an abject failure. The two doctors brought in to serve the community have since left. Dr. Lindgren has gone to supervise clinics in Uganda. Dr. Pachauu has left Howard Hospital to return to India. The official reason given by the Salvation Army is that his contract is up. His reputation as a womanizer, however, followed him from his former post at Chikankata Hospital to Howard Hospital, where patients' testimonies support these accusations.

The huge new Howard Hospital, which was supposed to be such a boon to the Chiweshe people, has become a multi-million dollar boondoggle—with only one doctor, few patients (except on Maternity) and almost no medicines—a mere shadow of its former self. No replacements are anticipated, as patient numbers are too low. Sadly, for the people of Chiweshe, a long chain of loss has wrapped itself around their community and squeezed the life from the hub that held it together.

———

For the Thistles, who have also paid a high price for decisions not of their making, they had no choice but to move on. Life continues

100 kilometres away in Karanda, complete with annual flooding of nearby rivers, followed by water shortages when they subside, as well as loss of electricity, and deflated tires on bumpy roads. But these are mere interruptions to the Thistles' broader mission to improve the lives of those they serve, wherever that may be.

As for the future? Paul compares life to the road at Karanda— "a washed-out road of twists and turns, with unexpected pot holes. You cannot see what's around the bend."

Just like the surrounding area, there are plenty of hills to climb. In Zimbabwe the struggle will go on. For Paul and Pedrinah Thistle life will go on. Their sons will continue to thrive. He will always be a doctor, and despite his struggles with the church, he will always be a Salvationist. No one can take away his God-given talent and no one can take away his faith or commitment to serve the people of the land that he loves. Asked what keeps him grounded and committed, he replies: "Commitment to and perseverance in the task at hand, using the resources of the Holy Spirit to sustain me during the darker days. Goodness can spring out of the most desperate situation. Joy will find a way."

Epilogue – The Accountability Movement – Where to From Here?

―――

Your most unhappy customers are your greatest source of learning…

BILL GATES

FOR THE SALVATION ARMY, THE year 2017 began with a new vision. Their latest initiative is an invitation from Commissioner Brian Peddle, Chief of Staff, for all officers to join General Cox in "calling, covenant and service compelling them to be good stewards of all that we have and are."

The article begins with the word "Trustworthy" and continues "It is the essence of our declaration that, in all circumstances and at all times, we behave ethically and responsibly. The claim to be trustworthy has to pass the test and bear up under scrutiny."

The rest of the new vision covers four main points, but the wording is obscure and invites more questions than it answers:

1. Child Protection – is described as an effort "to build an international team, create a strategy and enable a lift in capacity building." It adds: "No one should criticise our commitment

or the resources being allocated." *Capacity building*? What does it mean in the context of child protection? More children? A driving force towards greater enrolment? No one knows for sure, but it sounds like more money being thrown against good intentions, and "if it doesn't work, you can't blame us for trying."
2. Finance – This is a pledge towards a newly agreed financial standard. However, it fails to address the real issue: that there was nothing wrong with the old standards, except that, in many cases, they weren't followed. It ends with "Imagine if, by pursuing diligence in this area and by honouring God, our resources become such that growing and expanding the Army has no limits." Again, this directive appears to be more about money and recruitment than honouring God.
3. Governance – is described as "a desire to move from good to better in our governance and align ourselves through excellence in leadership and management. Our aim and our hope are to realize maximum efficiency for the Kingdom's sake. You can trust us. Our ethos, our systems, our infrastructure with built-in accountability and our governance must declare, and stand the test of others, that we are who we say we are."

The word "Trustworthy" means just what it says: *you can trust us*, but those words do not convey the trail of broken promises to the people of Chiweshe, or to Paul and Pedrinah Thistle, nor the broken trust with donors and volunteers. Trust is based on truth, but there was little truth forthcoming from the Army's glowing public press releases that all was well at Howard Hospital. Where is trust to be found in resistance to truth and false statements that deny bad decisions and mismanagement? Or misinformation to cover up unethical or illegal activity? In nurses being falsely accused, arrested and

tortured? In deaths due to hasty decisions and withdrawal of services? When every Christian venture that has succeeded has started with prayer, repentance and turning away from sins of the past—why not this one?
4. Impact Measurement – talks about "a new focus on input leading to Kingdom-based outcomes."

For the *Kingdom's sake* and *Kingdom-based*? Noble words, but whose kingdom exactly—the Kingdom of God or The Salvation Army's?

Finally, the new vision talks about viewing the Army's relationship with governments, business partners and other like-minded organizations, donors, the public and volunteers with due respect. But what does any of this mean? And why is it framed in the same obscure language as every other pronouncement coming out of The Army's International Headquarters?

In a recent sermon during daily Mass, Pope Francis raised the issue of hypocrisy amongst Christians—those who say one thing and do another. In simple and direct language, he addressed the very essence of Christianity. "To be a Christian," he said, "means to do: to do the will of God. On the day of judgement," he added, "the Lord will not ask what was said about Him, but about the things we did."

Where To From Here

The title of The Accountability Movement asks "Where to From Here?" But patently absent from the message are words like *repentance, compassion, truth and humility.* Any trace of apology appears to be overshadowed by ambiguous ambition. The movement accounts for money, but not for human lives entrusted to the Army's care.

If The Salvation Army aims to move in a new direction, the people at the top need to adopt a new vocabulary:

Authority needs to be replaced with *Trust*.
Humility should replace *Ambition*.

In many cases words like "*Spiritual Authority*" (another term the Army is fond of using) are sadly lacking in spirit.

If The Salvation Army wants to improve its brand and image, it would be wise to take a page from corporate management.

Axioms that good companies live by have become clichés, but for good reason—because they work.

- You can't fix what you don't acknowledge
- Learn to listen *and* Learn to Communicate
- Trust is earned, not given
- Finally, a nod to the physician's handbook—the Hippocratic Oath—Do No Harm. Be part of the solution, not part of the problem.

For this new initiative to work, every Territorial Commander needs to be an advocate for those in his or her charge—those who report to him, employees, donors and volunteers and most importantly, the poor and needy people in the local community who will benefit from the Army's help. *Truth* and l*oyalty* are both virtues, but when they collide, *truth* must triumph.

Despite the inscrutable wording, there is hope that the Accountability Movement was born out of past mistakes, even an inkling that the General has been paying close attention to the Howard Hospital crisis and is taking steps to fix it. His choice of those appointed to implement the new initiative, though, is curious, given that Commissioner Peddle, who will manage the movement, and Lt.-Col. Dean Pallant who will co-ordinate it, have both been directly involved in events at Howard Hospital. In an interview conducted by Major John Murray that appeared in the Salvation Army on-line publication *Southern Spirit*, Pallant stated: "The Salvation Army will not have any credibility in calling for justice and reconciliation in the world unless we exemplify justice and reconciliation internally."

If the Army wants to move forward, their focus should be directed outward, not inward. Money spent on mass congresses and pomp and ceremony may promote and satisfy a feel-good moment, but does nothing to help the people most in need. For a start, what they need is communication—talking to the local people, finding out what they need, not what you decide is best for them.

It remains to be seen what results will emerge from the various consultations going forth within the Army's vast network, but regardless of the outcome of new developments, what happened at Howard Hospital should be used as a teaching tool throughout the organization—a fundamental lesson for all in "what not to do." Although Pallant refers to reconciliation, there has been little reconciliation with the people of Chiweshe.

In implementing its new initiative, the Army's first priority should be directed towards Zimbabwe to do whatever is necessary to alleviate the human suffering.

Give Help Today!

The year 2017 does not bode well for Zimbabwe. The situation in the country is dire. Food prices continue to rise, medicines are unavailable, even in hospitals, and surgery is limited to emergencies due to lack of anesthetics. Deaths and suicides are up and people have taken to stealing to survive.

In the case of the new Howard Hospital, "build it and they will come" did not work, as evidenced by the lack of patients. The situation at Howard continues to deteriorate. Two doctors have left and the one doctor remaining is unable to cope with the workload and profound shortage of supplies. The hospital pharmacy is bare. The doctor has to write prescriptions for patients to take to Harare, as there are no medicines available. Fracture patients are sent there as well, because the doctor has no plaster bandages. He is forced to send obstetric emergencies to Harare, as there is a shortage of anesthetics and intravenous fluids. Although he has tried to buy medicines, he's forbidden to do so—all money must go through Territorial Headquarters in Harare.

Staff at Howard Hospital are not receiving their pay because of the shortage of cash in the banks. After going into town and waiting in line all day, they come back with $20 to $50, if they're lucky. If they come back with nothing, they go hungry. Patients continue to try to reach Karanda Mission Hospital where Dr. Thistle is able to take care of them. But, with this imploding situation, Karanda will be under considerable stress. They face the same challenges as other hospitals and the general public. Locally made medicines are in short supply because pharmaceutical companies cannot get sufficient foreign exchange to buy raw materials. They have to bank their earnings, but cannot exchange enough American dollars for new imports.

It is hard to believe that an organization well practiced in disaster relief has not responded to the deteriorating situation in Zimbabwe. Since General Cox's election in July 2013, there has been little improvement in the situation at Howard Hospital, only continuous deterioration to the point of collapse. If these problems are to be solved, the hospital needs better management. It needs to be run by and financed through trusted medically-trained personnel. What it does not need is more untrained THQ staff with their own agendas and priorities and private discussions amongst themselves.

Above all else, any discussion on the way forward needs to be opened up to the people of Chiweshe. No decisions should be made without transparent and open consultation with the very people who use the hospital. Threats and penalties against informants and people with different opinions must stop immediately. Not only are they against Salvation Army policy, but this practice prevents progress.

If The Salvation Army can't find a way to address patient needs as opposed to their own needs, perhaps it's time to get out of the hospital business altogether and turn it over to professionals with a clear and proper vision.

- The End -

ACKNOWLEDGEMENTS

As with all worthwhile pursuits, this book would not have been possible without the efforts and co-operation of a village of people—volunteers and witnesses to the great tragedy surrounding Howard Hospital, its doctors and patients and the legion of supporters who helped keep Howard Hospital afloat throughout Dr. Thistle's seventeen remarkable years.

My sincere thanks to the following: Dr. Michael Silverman for his great efforts in the fight for justice on behalf of his friend and colleague, Dr. Paul Thistle, and for providing permission and access to his files; to all of Paul's supporters: The IFFHH—Inter-faith Friends of Hospital—Larry Gillman, Jennifer Reid, Sarah Zelcer and Brian Nichols for their contribution to this book.

Special thanks to Allan Bacon for providing access to his files, during his service, to bring funding to much needed regions throughout the world; to Dr. John Sullivan and Sarah and Chris LeBouthillier for providing access to their diaries and notes during their visits to Zimbabwe. Thanks also to the innumerable friends and colleagues who supported Dr. Thistle and pleaded with the Salvation Army to reverse their decision. Sven Ljungholm for bringing the story of Howard Hospital to light through his blog. To Jolinda Cooper for summarizing the events at Howard, as they unfolded, in her Special Report.

To my fine editors:

A huge debt of gratitude to Dr. (Major) James Watt for his wise counsel and contribution to the history and accuracy of the contents. Special thanks for providing his original drawing of the Chiweshe village that graces the cover.

Sincere thanks to Harold Hill for his sage advice and suggestions for improvement to historical facts and to Stan Watt for his keen observations and for providing the inspiration for the subtitle. And to Cynthia Green, fellow writer and dear friend who held my hand throughout this project, providing editing and encouragement every step of the way.

Finally, to Dr. Paul Thistle who, through knowing him, has taught us all how to live a better life.

REFERENCES

Barger, Scott. "Standing up to Mugabe." *The National Post* 30 March 2013. <www.nationalpost.com>.

BBC News Africa. 9 November 2014. <www.bbc.co.uk/news/world-africa-1411261 BBC News-Zimbabwe country profile - Overview>.

Bell, Alex. "Howard Hospital facing bleak future as funding runs dry." *All Africa Stories SW Radio Africa* (2013). http://allafrica.com.

"Howard Hospital violence case postponed again." *All Africa Stories SW Radio Africa* (2012). http://allafrica.com/stories.

Break, Barry. "Zimbabwe declares cholera emergency." *The New York Times* 4 December 2008. Newspaper. <http://www.nytimes.com/2008/12/05/world/africa/05zimbabwe.html>.

CBC News. "www.cbc.ca/news/world/2012/08/20/zimbabwe-toronto-doctor-salvation-army.html." 20 August 2012. *www.cbc.ca.* Television website.

Cooper, Major Jolinda. "FSAOF Special Report on Howard Hospital." August 2013.

Dugger, Celia W. "Cholera epidemic sweeping across crumbling Zimbabwe." *The New York Times* 11 December 2008. Newspaper. <http://www.nytimes.com/2008/12/12/world/africa/12cholera.html>.

Eagle, Galen. "Surviving in Zimbabwe." *Peterborough Examiner* 11 February 2011: 8. Newspaper Article.

Embassy of Zimbabwe. n.d. www.zimbabwe-embassy.us.

Epstein, Edward Jay. *The Rise and Fall of Diamonds - The Shattering of a Brilliant Illusion.* New York: Simon and Shuster, 1982.

Foss, Krista. "U of T Magazine." Summer Edition 2005. http://magazine.utoronto.ca/summer-2005/sick-kids-hospital-separating-conjoined-twins-tinashe-tinotenda-mufuka/.

Hellbrunn Timeline of Art History. n.d. <www.metmuseum.org>.

Hill, Captain Harold. "Howard: The Years That Have Gone." Article. 1973. The Salvation Army News Publication.

Kachare, Phyllis. "Chiweshe community fights for Howard doctor." *The Sunday Mail* 18 August 2012. Newspaper. <www.sundaymail.co.zw>.

Karimakwenda, Tererai. "Trial of Nurses suspended as Howard Hospital saga." *SW Radio Africa* (2012). http://www.swradioafrica.com/2012/09/05.

Kellner, Mark A. "Questions Swirl as Salvation Army Leader Steps Down." *The Washington Tmes* 20 June 2013. Newspaper. <http://www.washingtontimes.com/news/2013/jun/20/kellner-questions-swirl-as-salvation-army-leader-s/#disqus_thread>.

PBS Archives on Nova. *The Mystery of Great Zimbabwe.* Prod. Peter Tyson. New York, 22 February 2000. Television program.

Report, PHR Special. *Health in Ruins - A man-made disaster in Zimbabwe*. Human Rights Report. Washington, D.C.,U.S.A.: Physicians for Human Rights, n.d. 2009. <http://physiciansforhumanrights.org>.

Scallon, Niahm. "Marching Orders." *Toronto Star* 14 July 2013. Newspaper.

Silverman, Dr. Michael. Howard Hospital Special Report. with Alex Bell. SW Radio Africa. London. 26 September 2012. SW Radio Africa (London).

The National Trust for Scotland: David Livingstone Centre. n.d. Website. <http://www.nts.org.uk/Property/David-Livingstone-Centre/>.

The Star. "Star find Herbie Quinones Jr. health at 30." 18 April 2009. *www.thestar.com*. Newspaper.

Till, Brian. "God's Surgeons in Africa." 28 December 2012. *The Atlantic*. Website www.thatlantic.com/health/archive 266635.

Trotter, Marleen. "Separate Lives." *CTV News - W5*. Bell Globe Media. Toronto, April 2016. Television Program. 12 November 2016. <http://www.ctvnews.ca/w5/a-reunion-with-conjoined-twins-successfully-separated-a-decade-ago-1.3156750>.

Watt, Major James. "Howard Beginnings 188l-1970." August 1998.

Why Mugabe dumped Bishop Kunonga. 6 December 2012. <http://nehandaradio.com/2012/12/06/why-mugabe-dumped-bishop-kunonga/>.

Wikipedia. *Cecil Rhodes*. n.d. Website. <wikipedia.org/wiki/Cecil Rhodes_Africa>.

History of Zimbabwe. n.d. Website. <en.wikipedia.org/wiki/History of Zimbabwe>.

ABOUT THE AUTHOR

TINA IVANY WAS BORN IN Edinburgh, Scotland and grew up in Toronto, Canada. Before turning to writing and editing, she worked in education, advertising, manufacturing and for professional and retail organizations. Since then her work has appeared in *Today's Home*, the *National Post*, *The Toronto Sun* and *The Toronto Star*. Her articles have earned First Prize for column-writing and a Merit Award for technical writing. She is also a contributor to *Artsforum* Magazine. She and her husband David live in Whitby, Ontario.

CPSIA information can be obtained
at www.ICGtesting.com
Printed in the USA
LVHW111009080919
630304LV00001B/73/P